ABOVE THE FALLS

Second Edition

Joe Schapers' homestead on Upper Glenn Creek, 1913

ABOVE THE FALLS
Second Edition

An Oral and Folk History of Upper Glenn Creek,
Coos County, Oregon

by

Lionel Youst

Including tape-recorded interviews, narratives, and other material by Alice Wilkinson Allen, Warren Browning, Belle Leaton Clarke, Hattie Leaton Cotter, Helen Cummings, Lillian Austin Edgehill, Wilma Leaton Hoellig, Allen Lively, Charles Middleton, Robert Milton, Erma Ott, Harold Ott, Jerry Phillips, Elwin Saling, Franklyn E. Smith, Marvin Stemmerman, Patricia Wilkinson, and George Youst.

Written at Allegany, Oregon, September 1991 to September 1992, with revisions based on material received between 1992 and 2003.

Golden Falls Publishing   Allegany, Oregon

Golden Falls Publishing, Allegany, Oregon
© 2003 by Lionel Youst
All rights reserved. First edition 1992
Second edition 2003
Second impression 2003
Printed in the United States of America
ISBN 0-9726226-1-6 (pbk.)

Library of Congress cataloging data: F882.C7
Dewey Decimal cataloging data: 979.523

      Youst, Lionel D., 1934 -
          Above The Falls, Second Edition
          Includes index, maps, bibliography, & photographs

          Frontier and Pioneer Life – Oregon – Coos County
          Logging – Oregon – Coos County – History
          Lumber Trade – Oregon – Coos County – History
          Coos County, Oregon – History

Quotations at the beginning of each of the major parts of this book are from *Rethinking Home: A Case for Writing Local History*, by Joseph A. Amato, University of California Press (2002). They are used here with permission from the Regents of the University of California.

Passages from *A Century of Coos and Curry*, by Peterson and Powers (1952), and *Glancing Back* (1972) are used with permission from the Coos County Historical Society.

Passages from *Coos River Echoes,* by Charlotte Mahaffy (1965), are used with permission from the author.

Photographs were obtained from many sources and every effort was made to obtain permissions and to give credit as appropriate in each case. A listing of all photographic credits appear on pages 266–7.

To contact the publisher:

Lionel Youst
12445 Hwy 241
Coos Bay, OR 97420
(541) 267-3762

Acid free paper.

Contents

Maps

Charts and Tables

CHRONOLOGY OF UPPER GLENN CREEK

Pre 1440's: Indian settlement at Marlow Creek, probably over 1000 years old.

1440: Forest fire on Upper Glenn Creek.

1770: Another forest fire.

1840: A smaller forest fire.

1840's: Fur trade established between Coos Indians and Hudson's Bay Company at Elkton. Indian trail, Allegany to Scottsburg in use.

1868: Coos Bay fire burns 92,000 acres. Did not come into Glenn Creek.

1870's: First whites settle East Fork of Millicoma; Frank Ross "discovers" Golden Falls.

1877: First log drives on the East Fork. William Glenn settles at mouth of Glenn Creek.

1880: First tourists visit Golden Falls; named in honor of one of them.

188?: Someone named Harris settles above the falls; dies and leaves a widow.

1889: Government survey of west boundary of T24S R10 WWM.

1891: Joseph Schapers buys Harris' improvements; moves above the falls; his sister Elizabeth Ott moves in May; Joseph in July.

1894: Joe Larson moves above the falls.

1894: George Schapers claims the falls; John Hendrikson below the falls.

1896: Government subdivision survey of T24S R10 WWM.

1898: Final proof on Joseph Schapers and Elizabeth Ott homesteads. Entries made for Joseph Larson and George Schapers.

1899: Oregon & California RR receives patent on 14,082 acres in Coos County.

1900: Road survey, Glenn Creek to Douglas County line.

1901: Trail blasted across top of falls.

1902: Northern Pacific RR obtains 61,860 acres; sells to Weyerhaeuser.

1903: Elizabeth Ott marries Alfred Tyberg.

1904: Final proof for Joe Larson, John Hendrikson, and George Schapers homesteads.

1906: Pack trail widened at falls. Forest Homestead Act opens Lake Creek to speculators.

1908: Joe Schapers marries Laura Wilkinson, with her four children.

1909: Glenn Creek to Douglas County road opened to vehicular traffic.

1910: Joe Larson and George Schapers sell their homesteads to a Minnesota timber company.

1911–1916: One-auto stage line, Allegany to Scottsburg.

1915: O&C lands revested to the U.S. Government.

1916: Stage line discontinued. School opened at Tyberg house above the falls.

ca. 1918: Golden Falls school built.

1920's: Weyerhaeuser obtains title to former O&C lands in T24S R10 WWM

1925: Glenn Junction school closed.

1933–1941: Civilian Conservation Corp (CCC) above the falls.

1935: Golden Falls and Silver Falls State Parks established, merged.

1939: Joseph Schapers and sister Elizabeth both die.

1940–5: George Youst sawmill on old Joe Schapers place.

1941: Golden Falls School closed.

1943–8: Vic Dimmick sawmill on old Elizabeth Ott Tyberg place.

1945: Army C-46D aircraft crashed near Lake Creek; large search party.

1948–9: Morrison-Knutson builds Weyerhaeuser logging road, Allegany to top of Matson Creek.

1949: December, last scheduled mail boat trip on Coos River.

1950: Weyerhaeuser logging begins on Matson Creek.

1953: Last splash dam log drive on East Fork.

1958: Golden Falls road closed to traffic. Cleland Wilkinson, last resident above the falls sells place to Weyerhaeuser.

1960's: Earl (Curly) Barker purchases Tyberg place; land trade with Weyerhaeuser.

1970's and '80's: Glenn Creek drainage logging completed; replanted.

1989, January 4: The last log raft goes down the Millicoma River.

1992: Weyerhaeuser logging ends at the Allegany side. Big mill in North Bend closed.

Site of the former Hanis Coos Indian settlement at Marlow Creek. The mound is about twelve feet high, the largest of its kind on the Coos watershed.

Introduction to the Second Edition

The first edition of *Above the Falls* was meant for the people who lived or worked up there, but I was surprised to find that other folks were also interested in it. The 1500 copies that I had printed in 1992 were all sold within a couple years. Almost every month since, I've received a plea from someone who absolutely has to have a copy.

I made revisions because I know more now than I did in 1992. Publication of the first edition brought me a large number of letters and visits from people who had lots to say, and hoping that it makes the story even better, I'm including their information in this second edition, and I'm changing a few other things around, and correcting a few mistakes that were brought to my attention. In doing this, I had to change every page, and scan in the photographs, and experiment to see whether they would come out well enough. Some of the pictures that were in the first edition wouldn't come out well enough in this new, digital process and as a result I've eliminated some of them, rearranged others, and included a few new ones.

Two fine histories of the surrounding forest have been published since 1992: Jerry Phillips' *Calked Boots and Cheese Sandwiches: A Foresters History of Oregon's First State Forest 'The Elliott'* (1997) and former Weyerhaeuser forester Arthur V. Smyth's *Millicoma: Biography of a Pacific Northwestern Forest* (2000). These books provide significant new information, especially for the post-WWII era, and I have drawn on them quite freely in updating this second edition. There have been a few other helpful new books, which I have included in the bibliography.

The end of the twentieth century brought an end to a cycle when Weyerhaeuser finished the first logging of its lands in Coos County and closed its sawmill in North Bend. A symbolic beginning of the new cycle came with the second logging of the old Joe Schapers Homestead in 2001. Industrial logging during the last quarter of the twentieth century was not without its public criticism. A history of the land above the falls would not be complete without an account of the altered relationship between the public and the new, global timber industry. The days of Frederick Weyerhaeuser's paternalistic regard for the economic stability of the communities near his timberlands is as much a thing of the past as the subsistence homesteads above the falls. I have added a section near the end which gives a community view of at least some aspects of those changed relationships.

Lionel Youst, May, 2003

P. S. While I was revising this second edition, a real inspiration for local historians was published by the University of California Press. Joseph A. Amato's *Rethinking Home: A Case for Writing Local History* says many things that I would have said myself, if I had thought of it, and so I inserted a quote from that book as an epigram for each major section of this book. I thank the Regents of the University of California for giving me permission to do so.

Acknowledgments to the first edition

It is customary to thank the people who made it possible to put together a project like this. I obviously am indebted to all of the folks I interviewed; all of the folks who let me make copies of pictures from their family albums; all of the folks who heard I was doing this and came to me with stories and information that I hadn't dreamed existed. I hope I've included all their names at the appropriate places throughout the book. Photo credits are on the captions of some of the photos, but not all. There is a complete list of photo credits on pages 266–7. Most of the rest of the sources I used are in the text, the footnotes, the bibliography, or some combination of the three. I haven't been consistent.

I will single out a few who contributed exceptionally to this history. Pat Wilkinson and her sister Alice Allen were probably my original inspiration for undertaking it. If Pat hadn't called me back in 1989 to find out if I was the same Lionel Youst she had known when she was in the third grade, I wouldn't have gotten the idea. Before she called, I had assumed that the history of Upper Glenn Creek was lost and irretrievable. How wrong I was.

Jerry Phillips, former manager of the Elliott State Forest and current president of the board of the Coos County Historical Association, showed intense interest in the project from the moment he first heard about it. He located maps, photos, and informants for me and gave me more help than it is possible to acknowledge. Several major parts of the book owe their accuracy to help that Jerry gave to me. Errors are not his, however. They are mine.

My wife Hilda gets credit for my having completed the project as soon as I did. She just kept on me, reminding me that the people who want to see it completed aren't getting any younger, and some are dying. If I don't hurry up, she reminded me, it will be too late. So I hurried.

My daughter Alice lettered in the legends of the maps. My other daughter, Julia, proofread the entire manuscript. She corrected my idiosyncratic use of capitals and commas, and made the manuscript comply with standard English usage! My son Oliver and my friend Dave Lyons, with infinite patience, taught me how to use the computer. From there on the whole thing was between me and it.

Lionel Youst, November, 1992

In the eleven years since that first reunion above the falls, most of the old-timers I interviewed at that time have passed on. Their names are listed here:

In Memoriam, 1992–2002

Cleone Stemmerman Melton, d. 1992
Joyce Ott Gault, d. 1993
Doris Browning, d. 1993
Robert W. Wilkinson III, d. 1994
Harold Ott, d. 1994
Erma Ott, d. 1994
Grace Gray, d. 1994
Bud Weltzheimer, d. 1996
Adeline Larson, d. 1996
Benson Judy, d. 2000
Hattie Leaton, d. 2002
Charles Middleton
Lillian Austin Edgehill

GLOSSARY of selected terms

Land measure: Land is divided into **townships** that are six miles on each side, thus containing 36 square miles. Each square mile, called a **section**, contains 640 acres. Each section is divided into four **quarter-sections** of 160 acres each – the size of a **homestead** under the Homestead Act of 1864. Each quarter-section is further subdivided into four "**forties**" (40 acres). A 160-acre homestead normally consisted of four contiguous forties, arranged in one of five possible configurations, to take advantage of the lay of the land and the flow of the creeks (see map on page 52). To obtain title to a "free" 160 acre homestead, there were certain residency and **improvement** requirements. **Proof** that these requirements had been met was presented to a federal land office, upon the completion of which it was said that the homesteader had "**proved up**" on his claim. A **patent** to the land was then issued, which gave the homesteader exclusive possession and control as the first owner of what from then on was private property.

Timber: Timberland is usually sold in 40-acre lots (forties), and the volume of wood is measured or estimated in thousands of board feet. One **board foot** is twelve inches square and one inch thick. **One thousand board feet (designated 1M)** would theoretically be a unit of lumber one inch thick, one foot wide, and 1,000 feet long. The "**thousand**" is the basic unit for buying and selling logs, standing timber, or sawed lumber.

Logging terms: A "**bull team**" is a yoke, or several yoke, of oxen formerly used in logging; "**hand logging**" used only hand operated jackscrews to roll logs downhill to the river. A "**yarder**" (also known as a "**donkey**") is a hoisting engine used to move logs by use of cables. Originally, the cables pulled the logs along the ground (**ground lead**). By 1915 or thereabouts, most logging was done with cables which ran through huge pulleys hung high in a tree supported with **guy lines**. That type of logging, still in use today (with steel towers rather than trees), is called **high-lead logging**. Originally, yarders (donkeys) were steam powered, hence "**steam donkey**." The operator of a donkey is called a "**donkey puncher**." By the 1930's most donkeys were powered by gasoline or diesel engines. The men who fell the trees are called "**fallers**;" those who cut the trees into logs are called "**buckers**;" those who connect the cable (the choker) around the log are called "**choker setters**."

Minor forest products: The homesteaders obtained some of their cash from sale of minor forest products such as **sword ferns** (for floral arrangements) and **chittam** (cascara bark used in laxative preparations), thus "**fern pickers**" and "**chittam peelers**." Some of them also trapped fur bearing animals, especially mink and martin. Others collected bounties for killing predatory animals such as cougars, lynx, and bobcats.

PART ONE

AN INTRODUCTION AND A REUNION

Silver Falls with ice and snow, winter, 1942

*How can one measure the privilege of being joined in a unique
conversation with passing generations?*

--Joseph A. Amato, *Rethinking Home*

COOS RIVER DRAINAGE

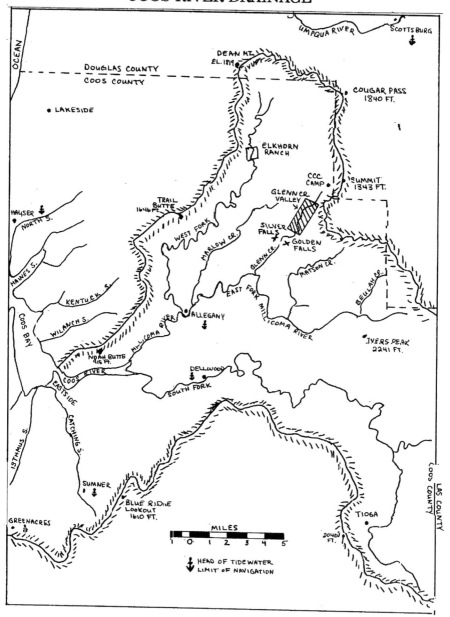

Chapter One

An Introduction

During the summer of 1942 the eccentric and brilliant Smithsonian anthropologist, John Peabody Harrington, was in Coos County and interviewed nearly all of the older Coos Indians who were alive at the time. Lottie Evanoff, who once lived above the falls, told him more than all the rest together, and much of what she told him was not known to anyone else. She was the daughter of Chief Daloose Jackson, who was an old man when Lottie was born. In fact, he was so old that he already had a family by the time the whites arrived to settle the area in the early 1850's. He died in 1907, about 80 years old.

The old Indians in 1942 were telling Harrington what they could, and he wrote it all down in a scribbling longhand on hundreds of pages of notepaper. At one point they were talking about a huge redwood stump from California that had drifted onto the beach a little south of Waldport hundreds of years earlier. As they discussed this stump, Lottie interjected the following story.

The Stump[1]

Hummingbird and Bumblebee were the surveyors.
    That was when they put that stump there,
        at the center of the world.

The Coos Bay Indians also had a stump.
The trail went right by there, up Allegany way.
    You had to give him something
        to go through there.

Once a youth went by there and they told that youth,
    "You've got to throw something in there
        every time you pass."
They throw beads,
everything in there.
And that young fellow:

---

[1] Transcribed and arranged from John Peabody Harrington "Alsea/Siuslaw/Coos Field Notes" (Microfilm edition: Reel 24, Frames 572-3).

"Yes, I'll give him something–"
and he got a big heavy limb
and he just clubbed that stump around,
and he went on
and in the morning
           he was dead.
And they looked at him
           and he was as if clubbed all over.
He was dead.

Father used to tell about this story.
Lots of young fellows don't believe
all about these things.

The trail went right by there, on the way to Scottsburg.
It was beside the trail.
           It is still there, unmolested.
           It was a great big stump, and hollow
           and stood there many hundred years
           and never got rotten.

They give it clothes,
and they always camped there.

There was a big spring near there.

This stump is the other side of Coos River,
           but way this side of Scottsburg.
It is up by the tip of the mountain where they
would camp overnight when out hunting
           on the way to Scottsburg.

That stump may easily have a name,
           but I never heard it.

My father used to tell about it.

But you know how children are:

Never find out fully
           about anything.

Lottie Evanoff and her father, Coos Chief
Daloose Jackson. Lottie lived above the
falls, on the Douglas County side of the
line, around 1900. She was the last of the
full-blood Coos at the time of her death in
1944.

Lottie was right. Children never find out fully about anything! That's the reason history, very often, is bunk. Sometimes it's lost altogether. If John Peabody Harrington in 1942 hadn't recorded the little bit that Lottie remembered about the story of the stump, we wouldn't have a single tradition of what the land Above the Falls had meant to the Indians. Not one.

And that is the reason I have gone to the trouble of collecting the material for this book. I don't want lost what the land Above the Falls had meant to those who came after the Indians. I think it is worth preserving for the same reason histories have been assembled since the beginning of the human race. "The hope of preserving from decay the remembrance of what men have done" is the reason Herodotus gave for publishing his *History* in 450 BC. That reason hasn't changed.

The Land

The two forks of Coos River drain more than a half million acres of timberland in northern Coos County, Oregon. This land was almost entirely virgin Douglas fir at the time of the first settlement in 1853. By 1900, only two major changes had occurred. First, in 1868 there was a catastrophic forest fire which destroyed 300,000 acres of old growth. This was mostly on drainages into the West Fork of the Millicoma, Tenmile Lakes, and the Lower Umpqua. Much of this burn is what we now know as the Elliott State Forest. The second change was that logging and land clearing, as well as several smaller forest fires, had occurred on much of the land adjacent to tidewater around Coos Bay and its several inlets.

Above tidewater not much had changed at all. On the East Fork of the Millicoma and the South Fork of Coos River in 1900 it was pretty much as it had been when the whites first arrived. Ninety-nine percent of the timber was still standing. It had barely been penetrated, and was virtually impenetrable. Hand and bull-team logging had been done on the East Fork, with logs driven downstream by natural freshets and splash dams, but this logging hadn't made a serious dent in the "inexhaustible" stands of Douglas fir. There hadn't been a serious dent in it even by 1951, when Weyerhaeuser Timber Company finally began logging this forest. By 1990, however, it was nearly all gone.

This virgin forest was a wonder to behold. It defied the descriptive abilities of all but the most articulate observers. To several generations of the less articulate, it has provided the basis for a mental image of what Longfellow meant when he said, "This is the forest primeval." It has been, for generations who lived around its fringes, an almost mythic location, infinite in the depth of its mystery. For those few who were fortunate enough to have spent part of their life inside it, it was a most formative influence.

The Golden Falls of Glenn Creek plunge and cascade for 375 feet over a massive siltstone cliff. These falls impress by size, power, ruggedness. The nearby Silver Falls of Silver Creek, only a few hundred yards away, are softly curved and symmetrical. One might say that the two waterfalls represent the masculine and the feminine of nature. It is very special place indeed.

It was the falls themselves, and the 200-foot cliff that impressed upon people the mystery, the inaccessibility, and the romance of that great forest. It was only at the falls that people could see a part of that massive siltstone formation, said by geologists to be more than a mile thick, the formation known as "Tyee." Tyee: from the Chinook Jargon, meaning "Chief." Only at the falls was it clear that another land lay above, a land that ordinary people could only imagine.

Golden Falls from the air

Above the falls there is, surprisingly, a lovely valley which runs about three miles along Glenn Creek. It was in this little valley, isolated and serene, that there was human habitation for about fifty years. No one had lived there before or since, but from a little prior to 1900 until a little after 1950, a few families blended their lives into that little valley. Their story is of a life and a land gone forever.

The People

Someone named Harris, it is said, was the first to settle up there. Following closely were the Schapers brothers – George, Jerd, Joe, John, Charlie, and their indomitable sister Elizabeth. They were of German descent, frontiersmen from Missouri. Their frontier attitude is reflected in the name given Elizabeth's second son, born in Drain, Oregon, in 1886 from her first husband, James Pasteur Ott. They named the boy Jesse James. Known through life as Jess Ott, he was a riverboat captain on Coos River during most of the years riverboats ran on that stream. He passed on in 1989 at the venerable age of 103, a legend in his own time.

All of the land on tidewater had long been taken up by settlers by the time the Schapers arrived in the 1890's. The tidal lands had been improved a little, sold to others, improved some more, and either held or sold again. The tidewater part of the Coos River drainage had the look of old world respectability, with farmers of German, Scandinavian, and English descent making up most of the population. Above tidewater, however, the scattered acreages flat enough for a house and a small field were taken by "stump ranchers." These were people who lived off the woods. They were, in season: loggers, hunters, trappers, chittam peelers, fern pickers, subsistence farmers, or casual laborers. The country was rough and wild and so were the people who lived there.

It was sometime in the 1860's or 70's that Frank Ross went as far as he could go and "discovered" the Golden Falls. In 1880 the first "tourists" arrived, three prominent men from Marshfield. One of them was Dr. Charles Golden. His companions named the falls in his honor. About that time an old shipwright from the state of Maine settled where the creek from the falls enters the East Fork. His name was William W. R. Glenn and the creek became Glenn Creek. Glenn died in 1901 and is buried at the

Allegany cemetery, one of the two Civil War veterans there. Jesse Ott, who knew him, told me that Glenn was a tinker by trade and could fix anything, especially clocks. Clocks, it seems, were becoming more important further down river. Time, as measured by clocks, wasn't used very much up Glenn Creek.

The next creek up the East Fork was Matson Creek, named for Dan Mattson. He was a Swede from Finland who homesteaded there in 1893. Jerd and Charlie Schapers had claims near Matson Creek. When Jerd was quite old, he told my dad how he had put 500 logs in the river there, by hand, one season. They took only the butt and second cut of the old growth in those days, rolling and sliding them downhill to the river with jackscrews. Jerd said he did it "with nobody to help me but this kid here," gesturing toward his brother Charlie, who was by then in his 70's. Charlie was always a "kid" to Jerd.

Jerd was convinced that the area contained platinum. He mined hundreds of tons of sandstone, sinking shafts, sluicing and panning out the trace minerals, and saving them in jars. His brother John came down with appendicitis in 1911 while they were working the claim near Matson Creek. His appendix burst, and he died there, with Jerd helpless to aid him. After John's death, Jerd abandoned his claim and moved to the place of his sister and brother-in-law above the falls on Glenn Creek. As late as 1940, he was still there, sluicing trace minerals out of the Tyee sandstone, convinced that the zircon and garnet he saved was platinum.

There were a lot of Swedes among the loggers and stump ranchers on the East Fork of the Millicoma. Around the turn of the century most of them were working at one of the two big logging camps – one at Hodges Creek five miles above Allegany, or the one at Matson Creek, six miles further up. Among those Swedes were Alfred Tyberg, Joe Larson, John Hendrickson, Alfred Stora, Abraham and Andrew Mattson, and many others. Along with the Schapers brothers, these Swedes filed homestead claims on the land along Glenn and Matson Creeks, and along the upper East Fork. By 1901 there were homesteads, claims, and squatters the full length of Glenn Creek. By that time William W. R. Glenn had sold his homestead at "Glenn Junction" to James R. Bunch. Charles Crane had the next place up, then John Hendrickson. The Golden Falls themselves were claimed by George Schapers.

First above the falls was the homestead of Elizabeth Schapers Ott, soon to be married to Alfred Tyberg. Her older brother, Joe Schapers, soon to be married to Laura Wilkinson, had the next homestead. Above him was Joe Larson, on the place known later as the Leaton's, and later still as the Middleton's. Newell Price lived a mile and a half further up on a small place later occupied by Charles Howell. Just over the Umpcoos ridge, on the way to Ash Valley, was the Russian-Aleut, Alex Evanoff and his wife the Princess Lottie, daughter of the Coos Indian chief, Daloose Jackson.

The Women and Other Survivors

These first settlers left few descendants. On this frontier, as on other frontiers throughout the world, women were scarce. The women that did happen to be in this world Above the Falls, however, were most remarkable. They were living not far from the tip of the mountain between the Umpqua and the Coos drainages. It was, as they say, as far into the woods as you could go because if you went any further, you'd be coming out the other side.

At the beginning, and only dimly remembered, would be the widow of a man whose name may have been Harris. He is said to have been the first settler above the falls. It is said he died, leaving his wife with a few improvements to the property, but no title. Joe Schapers is said to have bought the improvements from her when he filed for the homestead rights. After that, she disappears from all memory. We don't know who she was and what she might have gone through, the first and only woman up there, and her husband dead.

Next there was Elizabeth, sister to the Schapers brothers. She had cooked in the logging camps on the East Fork, raising her two boys, Jesse and Sam Ott. With her brothers she homesteaded above the falls, and later married the Swede logger, Alfred Tyberg. The stories about her, told to this day, place her in the realm of legend.

Only one of her brothers found a wife. Joe Schapers must have had more of a literary flair than the others, and was able to engage in correspondence with a widow in the East. The widow was the mild mannered Laura Wilkinson. She was on her own and in poverty with four young children.

The options were very limited for a woman in her straights at the turn of the century, and so she took a chance on this logger-homesteader out in Oregon. Joe bought her the tickets, and Laura with her four small children rode the train from Pennsylvania to Portland, then on the steamship *Breakwater* from Portland to Coos Bay. There, Joe Schapers married her on the dock and took her above the falls where she lived the rest of her life. After raising her own children she raised two of her grandchildren.

During the 20's the two Wilkinson girls, Agnes and Jane, came of age. Agnes married Al Leaton, who also had grown up there, and they lived a wilderness life for many years; Bernice Howell married Al's brother Bill and they raised three children there during the 20's and 30's. During the depression years of the 30's there were newcomers. For example, there was Frieda Middleton and Reta Milton, who ruled over a large clan of Middletons and Miltons. Then there was Molly Stokes, a Canadian nurse during World War I. She nursed Elizabeth Tyberg in her last illness and stayed on several more years with her Texas-born husband, Al.

World War II brought a new generation. My own mother, Doris Youst, drove truck, hauling lumber down over the Golden Falls road through much of the war. Blanche Mast ran the cut-off saw in the mill. Alfreda Leaton and Alice Wilkinson were among the first women in these mountains to man the remote fire lookouts during the 1940's. All of them, from grandmothers to granddaughters, were the finest models and inspiration for both their own and for later generations.

Chapter Two

The First Reunion

I n July 1990, an unusual school reunion was held on Glenn Creek, above the Golden Falls. It was the forty-ninth year since the Golden Falls School had closed, and all four members of that last class, the class of 1941, showed up: Carol Youst, eighth grade; Pat Wilkinson, third grade; Al Lively, second grade; and Lionel Youst, first grade. As we visited and talked, it dawned on all of us that there were quite a few other alumni who were still alive and kicking, and it might be fun to have a full-scale reunion of all the survivors of all the classes the following year, and in fact of anybody we could find who had been connected. And so it was that on September 14, 1991, some middle-aged to elderly individuals who had lived or worked above the falls met for a picnic on the grounds of the old Joe Schapers homestead and talked and visited and reminisced. In addition to the four former students who met the previous year, there were three more: Pat's sister Alice Wilkinson Allen, and her cousins Wilma Leaton Hoellig and Hattie Leaton Cotter.

I had a pleasant time tape-recording remembrances of several of those present, and what I found whetted my appetite for more. There were obviously some good stories to be told, and some fascinating history to be preserved. Following are excerpts from those interviews, and the beginning of a quest for the lost history of the land above the falls.

Continuity

Six generations: Hattie, standing left, her daughter right, her granddaughter seated with her great-granddaughter. Her mother Bernice Howell Leaton far right, and her grandmother Georgia Jeffers Howell, far left. Georgia was descended from Chinook Indian parents and was the oldest member of her tribe when she died at 102 years. It was the women who preserved the photos, the letters, and the memories of the past. Without them, I wouldn't have had much to put into this book!

School reunion, left to right: Lionel Youst, Carol Youst Baughman, Al Lively, Helen Cummings, Wilma Leaton Hoellig, Hattie Leaton Cotter, Pat Wilkinson, Alice Wilkinson Allen.

The Interviews

CHUCK MIDDLETON: I will begin. I graduated from Marshfield High School in 1933 and moved immediately to the Middleton place up here on Glenn Creek. Everyone knows that those were depression years. Very tough times. I know.

I lived with my brother and his wife in Eastside and they sent me through high school. I don't know how, but they did. I remember now that they even bought me a suit to graduate in. It cost eight dollars and eighty-eight cents at J. C. Penny's.

Slim and Frieda Middleton were the people that lived up here on this ranch. Slim was my brother. Frieda was my sister-in-law, of course, and Fred Middleton was their son. That was Freddie Middleton who went to the school here. Freddie died of a heart attack while he was driving an over-the-highway truck somewhere in Arizona in about 1962 or somewhere around there. Of course, Slim died in 1946 of cancer, and Frieda also died shortly after they left here.

Bill Leaton, the one-armed man, lived on this place before we did, and he made a living selling deer and elk meat. He had a horse, and he had several dogs. How in the world he got around to kill that game and butcher it with one arm, I don't know. But he did. There was a trail there, right at the place, that went over the hill to Gould's Lake, we called it at that time. I guess it's known as Elk Lake now. He went up that trail, and he went up other places around there and killed deer and elk.

He wanted to sell us those dogs when he left, but we wouldn't have them. He left them anyway. We shot all of them, because you couldn't even find a chipmunk within a mile of the place with those damned wild dogs running loose around there all the time. The horse was a hundred-year-old black horse, more or less. He left that with us. We may have bought him, I don't know. He got down in the barn one day – but I'm getting ahead of the story. I used to use him to plow and harrow with around,

10

but he wouldn't work worth a damn by himself. But if I'd take hold of the bridle and walk alongside of him, he thought I was helping him and he could pull the harrow and everything all right. But he got down in the barn one day, and he wasn't going to get up, I could see that. And that's where I first found the devastating damage of a 12-gauge shotgun at point-blank range. I bored a hole in that horse's head two inches in diameter with that 12-gauge gun. I've thought to this day that if I had ever been attacked by a lion or a bear or anything else I'd rather have a shotgun than any other type of gun at close range.

Now, we peeled chittam bark, we picked ferns, we trapped mink, we trapped martin, we caught fish out of the creek, and we raised a garden, and we raised hay. But the best way that we made a living was that a 3-C camp moved in two miles on up the road from our house. Now, John Milton, a brother to Slim's wife, was a wheeler-dealer. He and my brother got together and they immediately ran in a bunch of cattle up there and we started milking cows and selling milk to that 3-C camp. We used to sell them about twenty gallons of milk every day. We drove up there with it and delivered it; then we picked up their garbage and came back and fed it to our hogs and we raised hogs. Frankly, we lived high on the hog, as the saying goes, for depression years. We were really well fed and well housed.

It was raw milk that we sold them. Of course we had no means of pasteurizing it on the place. There was a little creek that ran through the barnyard, by the barn, and sometimes if I was a half gallon or so short of milk I'd pour a half gallon of water in the milk can. But those guys didn't know any better. That was raw milk!

Charles Middleton

These kids was all from Saint Louis. They'd walk down the road here, looking up at these tall fir trees like I would if I went to Saint Louis and looked at the skyscrapers, I suppose. They were amazed that *that* much cream would raise on a gallon of milk. When they'd dip into a milk can, it was a foot down through it before they got to the milk. They were absolutely amazed at we "pioneers" or whatever they wanted to call us out here.

I can tell you a story about those 3-C camps up there that might interest you backwoodsmen around here. When we delivered the milk up there every morning, which we did, there quite often was a crew around the yard there. One morning there was a crew of seven or eight men standing around a buckskin. You guys know what a buckskin is – about five feet in diameter. With a cross-cut saw, three men on each end of the saw, pulling on the doggone thing, trying to cut off a block to make wood out of. I observed the situation, and bigshot expert woodsman that I was, I went over and told them, "If you just get a little kerosine and pour in that cut, one of you on each end can pull that saw all right." They didn't know that. They was from Saint

11

Louis and they didn't know what the hell was going on. They were clear out of their element.

I logged on Fox Creek, shortly after that. . . . I logged for Jim Rookard, who apparently was a relative of Jim Lyons. And, this Golden and Silver Falls State Park down here, I was an ax-man on the crew that laid out that park. Couple of county surveyors came up here, I don't know when, maybe '35 or '36. Here I was a rugged, big hillbilly and they hired me to clear the brush and chop blazes out of the trees. So I was on the survey team that laid out that park.

I can elaborate on the cattle rustling mentioned in this letter here. The Wilkinson's had three prime steers in a pasture right up next to our property up at the north end of Glenn Creek pasture, and they disappeared one night. Cle Wilkinson didn't like that, of course, and he came up looking at me and my brother and the rest of us up there, and was inquiring about that. We didn't know anything about it, of course, but my brother, who had been out picking ferns was way up the trail towards Gould's Lake. It was three miles by trail through there to Gould's Lake, then you could go on down Elk Creek a ways and then you go up over the hump and down onto the West Fork. Well, he noticed cow droppings clear up there on the ridge, way up that trail. He alerted Cle Wilkinson to that. So, he and Cle, and they got the sheriff and everybody else, and they followed that line of cow droppings. And that's where it went. Clear up over the top, down the other side, and down the creek and beyond Gould's Lake and ended up another trail up over the hill and went into Elkhorn Ranch, over there on the West Fork. And that's where they found what was left of those cattle, with their hides on the fence and their meat in smokehouses and everything like that. How the hell they ever got those cattle turned from the road up that trail past our place we'll never know. Didn't even alert our dogs that we had around there.

About this school up there. It was a branch of the Allegany School District in Allegany. It only had two or three or never more than ten students that I know of. So one year the school board decided that they ought to close the school up here. Well, Cle Wilkinson, Pat's father, was on the school board. There were only three members of the school board. When Cle got word of that, why he came up and talked to my brother, and he said, "You better run for the school board." And he did, and won the position. So then we had two of the three members of the school board from up here above the falls! The politics of those years, let me tell ya! (laughter)

Aside from that, I'm not unused to public speaking, but I know this: If you've got anything to say, well say it. If you don't, shut up! (more laughter).

BOB MILTON: I'm a nephew. Frieda was my father's sister. She was the oldest of the girls. There was a younger brother named Joe. He was crippled. He had no use of his legs from the waist down. He lived with Slim and Frieda up here. He drove a Model-A up and down this road. The way he'd shift gears would be to lift up his leg and put it on the pedal and take his hand and push on his knee to press the pedal [driving over the Golden and Silver Falls road]. He was the one who went to town, to market. My brother and I would get to ride in the back seat. We'd spend a week or maybe two weeks up here in the summertime, during vacation. . . .

Bob Milton

Polio. He had shoulders like a Jersey bull. And legs like wet noodles. He just crawled. He drug his legs everywhere he went. There was a short period of time when they bought a set of braces for him, to try to make him so he could walk. It just didn't work for him. It didn't last long, and he threw them away. He's the one who wrapped the ferns, fifty-two in a bunch, and tie them, and cut the ends off square.

AL LIVELY: I remember him. They'd pick the ferns and bring 'em in, and he'd sit down at the trail where it left the road, and straighten ferns.

BOB MILTON: I don't know if any of the rest of you remember, but what we called army worms [millipedes]? I remember one time we drove up here and they were so thick on the road, you could feel the car move from them. And when you crushed them they had a terrible odor.

AL LIVELY: Remember when they got in the school water? Don't you remember that? The water started tasting funny at school. It was getting really putrid. And we went – Mr. Smith took us, and we went up where the pipe was and dug all those army worms out. Remember? Man, that was awful!

What brought me up here was through my grandma and grandpa, Molly and Allen Stokes. She came up to nurse Mrs. Tyberg toward the end of her life. She was up here I suppose maybe three or four months, then finally my grandad came. I think that was in 1939. They came up and stayed on the Tyberg place. We came in the spring of 1940 and rented the Middleton place. It runs in my mind that Mr. Howell had control of that, but I don't remember the in's and out's. But anyway, they rented it for a year.

At any rate, they were building the mill. George Youst was putting the mill in down here in its first setting. My dad worked for him. Ran the edger, and we stayed here through the summer of 1940 and through the winter. The reason I couldn't finish school is that I got strep throat real bad. That was a serious thing in 1940 and '41.

13

They had me in the hospital and the doctor wouldn't let me continue school. That was in March. Then the truck went through the Silver Creek bridge and shut the mill down and we moved out. When we left we went through Loon Lake to Grants Pass, and from there we moved to California. I came up in the summer, though, and visit with my grandma and grandpa. They moved off the Tyberg place, I think, in '43, and moved back onto the West Fork.

Al Lively

WARREN BROWNING: In the fall of 1939 I just came up and went to work for

Warren Browning, 1945

[George Youst]. I boarded at the old Tyberg place with Al Lively's grandparents [Al and Molly Stokes]. When Stokes first came up here, Mrs. Tyberg was still alive. Molly Stokes nursed her. She died shortly before I came up, so I stayed with Stokes and worked for George. I worked in the mill some, but mostly logging that hillside right over there [pointing] on the other side. I worked here about a year and a half. I was here when my "Friends and Neighbors" drafted me, selected me, you might say. That's the way it used to read, you know. After that, I left and went into the army.

HELEN LIVELY CUMMUNGS (Al Lively's mother): That's right. Well, my dad lived up here, and so I came up here to visit him. When my boys grew up a little, they came all the time. They like the hunting and fishing and all of that. Eventually, they married Oregon girls. I stayed down south, mostly in Southern California at that time. But I went to school and grew up in Texas. When I first came here, it seemed to me like that I was at the end of the world, and the largest, biggest forest I'd ever been in. I couldn't see very far. I had to look straight up, and I'd been used to looking way out! . . . I thought it was nice here, too, and I like it here. I liked the streams of water and the green trees and all of that. Anyway, we moved up the road here, and my son started school here. We lived here awhile and then we left, and moved back to California. And I'm amazed that fifty years later I'm up here again! I can't believe it. It was out of my mind. I cannot imagine – not in my wildest imagination think that I would ever be back up here at this little place where I lived up the road from here.

But when I got up there today, as last year when we were here, there was something about it. I felt it again. And also, those plants that I planted up there: the roses and the honeysuckle I planted when I was there. There was nothing there so I went to town one day and I got that, and some flower seed. I remember doing that. And they're still growing. The roses

Hellen Cummings

14

still wild, all over, growing. And the honeysuckle, they found it today. Some of it, in a tree. Can you imagine it being there this long? [The apple trees] were not nearly that big when I lived there. But I find this whole thing just fantastic. Just being here today; seeing all these people. Everybody has something to say, something to tell. And I also remember you, as a little boy, and your brother and Carol. I remember her. She was a young girl around twelve or thirteen years of age. I suppose right then and there that I was probably next to the youngest thing around here for her to talk to. She used to come to the house once in a while and talk to me and visit with me. And I knew her mother. I went to town with them a couple times from up here, which was a big deal then!

HAROLD OTT: I used to enjoy visiting with Grandma Tyberg. I started coming up when I was pretty small. She had a lot of intestinal fortitude. She'd try anything, and she could think pretty well, too. They had a bunch of Jersey cows. The milk was pretty rich and they separated for cream, so they got quite a bit of cream for the amount of milk. But Jerseys are very nervous.

Whenever I went out to the barn to watch them milk, she'd take me before the cows came in and hide me off in a corner someplace. She'd say, "Don't you make any noise." Then she'd have the cows come in, and when they left it'd be all right because those cows knew if there was a stranger around. If there was a stranger, they'd start kick'n and snort'n and jump'n around there and you couldn't do anything with 'em.

She decided one day she needed an automobile. In those days – that was a long time ago – it was Model-T Fords was about all you could get, I mean in the low-price range. And that was before they had self starters on 'em. So, by golly, my uncle, my dad's brother and him, they got this Ford one day. I think they picked it up on a Saturday. On Sunday my dad drove his car and Sam drove the Ford and they brought this car up to Grandma. They showed her how to start it and stop it. It had those three pedals in there and one was to go ahead and one was to back up and one was the brake, and all that kind of stuff; the handles under the steering wheel for the spark and gas. So they said, "You practice with that, out in the field. We'll come up next Sunday and show you how to drive on the road."

Now that was up above the Golden Falls. . . . [The road] was terrible. So, anyway, that was on a Sunday, I think it was. Along about Wednesday, in the middle of the day, she come driving up to the store at Allegany with that Ford. That was the first time she had ever driven a car on the road. Within a mile from her place she had to drive down over that falls! I don't know how she ever made it, but she did. Dad got after her. She said, "No use to waste the gasoline. When I could stay on the ruts and the cow paths and get through the gates without knocking a post down, why can't I drive on the road?" So she did it.

Her brother, Charlie, he had lots of nerve. Just plain nerve, that's all. Plain guts, if you want to say it. He had to go with her because he'd crank that car. She couldn't crank it. So he had to go with her everywhere she went. She had an accident, I think, on every turn on that road. She'd run off the road or run into somebody, or something like that. But she seemed to get by all right. She had a philosophy: she says you have to drive fast to get around the turn before the other guy gets to it. She really believed that, too. They all knew that, and if they seen she was coming, they got out of the way. So she got by all right.

I know one time she and Alfred [Tyberg] and Charlie [Schapers] were going down to Allegany in the old "T" and they drove off the road just at the George Stemmerman place, which is just above the Allegany store. She drove off and it turned over once or twice and lit on its wheels down in the field. Whoever was at the Stemmerman house saw that happen and went running over. They figured they would have all been killed, but pretty soon they saw the cloth top wriggle a little bit, a head came up and looked, a head come up on the other side, and they laughed and thought that was awful funny. They pushed it on the road, cranked it up, and went on.

But they traveled all over. They even went back to Yellowstone Park in it. She drove. I say, she had nerve enough to try anything. Jerd wouldn't try [to drive], and Charlie had to go to crank it. I say, he had guts! But she could try most anything she wanted to put her mind to, and she could just about do it. She was the boss. Alfred didn't have too much to say about things. She had him cranking the separator, because he was awful good at that. He was awful crippled up. He had to walk with two canes. I don't know if any of you knew him or not, but he was a heck of a nice guy. He taught me how to fish. I'd go up there and he'd give me a fish pole and hook and worms and stuff and I'd catch a few trout once in awhile. Also, both Grandma's place and Joe's place, and all the places up there didn't have too much way of having an income. So Grandma, she would board people. Any of the fellows that liked to fish, they would board at her place, she would allow them to fish on her property. So, therefore, it was kind of a popular fishing place. They had quite a few trout.

Well, Charlie [Schapers], you wouldn't think he'd do very much, but he was pretty good helping around the place. The main thing was his mustache! You guys have all seen it, I think. It was long enough, he could put it over his ears if he wanted to. Called a *schnurrbart*. By golly, all my life I'd never seen him without that mustache. One day there was a stranger down at the store. He was down there and he'd cut that mustache off and there wasn't a soul – his family or anybody – who knew who he was. But his talk, he had a very different voice, if you know what I mean. He didn't mumble or talk loud, but his voice had a sound to it that you'd always know it.

As far as Jerd was concerned, I wasn't around him too much. He and George [Schapers] were out prospecting a lot. I don't know what they prospected for, but they had jars of some of the heaviest material I ever saw. You'd take it up and pretty

16

near drop it. I don't know what it was. Heavy as lead. And he built a waterwheel, which I have seen. It was a homemade waterwheel but they used it to run something so they could grind up that stuff. I was pretty small, and didn't pay too much attention to that, whether they had rollers, or what. I don't think they found anything that was worth anything, but they sure worked years at it.

I can think of a little joke they had one time on these old prospectors. This prospector was going through there, and it was getting along about mealtime. He stopped to visit for awhile. They got talking and the guy wanted to know if he wanted to eat with them. The guy looked, and everything looked awful clean, and he said "all right." He gave him something, and it wasn't bad eating. He got through, and he says, "Man, these dishes are clean." "Yeah," the other guy says, "they're just as clean as soap and water can make them." He took the dish and put it on the floor and said, "Here Soap, here Water!" Here come the two dogs!

Now, the Cranes were down there, and Los Angeles, Lossy, was going to school. . . They had a Baltimore Crane, and a Los Angeles Crane. They had the names of the various cities where the kids were born. The newspapers had a lot of fun with a girl's name that was Los Angeles. At one time — any Cranes present? They had a lot of fun because they were a fairly numerous family, and Lossy was the girl. Of course, Baltimore, he was older and he was over in World War I. Anyway, Lossy, one of her relatives was a school teacher, and her mother was on the school board, and I forget, but every one of that family was connected with the school.

One year . . . we had one student here [Pat Wilkinson]. It was kind of hard to get teachers and all of that, and transportation and one thing and another. I was on that school board, a long time ago. It's a little fuzzy. So we got talking with them, and made a proposition that if we would take that student and pay their tuition at Marshfield, we would rent a house for them to live in and pay her grandmother to stay down there and take care of her. Everybody seemed to be happy about it.

Erma and Harold Ott

17

ERMA OTT: When I came up to visit school, Alice [Wilkinson] was in the first grade and Hattie and Wilma and Clifford, and I think Alfreda [Leaton]. I can't remember that one. Anyway, I had told Florence [Ott] how we had enjoyed Grandma Tyberg's. She always made us feel so welcome and at home. So we decided that maybe Lillian [Austin] would let us come visit school. We asked her, and she said that would be fine, but come on a weekend so that she could come back down with us. So, one morning we got up at four o'clock and ate breakfast. Harold brought us up to under the falls. Florence and I started walking and we were reminiscing about our own school days. How that we had all started school together, all three of us. When we got there, Grandma Tyberg was having breakfast. Nothing would do but we eat again. She had those delicious sourdough pancakes, she had biscuits, ham that she had smoked herself, bacon and eggs and applesauce and everything imaginable. We went on to visit school. Lillian told us about some hunters that had broken in when she had come up there that morning. They had cooked meat and smoked it, and had hides hanging on the fence.

We were so interested in Alice and the children telling cute stories. The children all looked so nice and clean. So, we visited school that day, then went back to Grandma Tyberg's where she had apple pie and coffee again, and told us many stories about up here that Florence hadn't heard. She went down with us, and we met Harold under the falls again, and we went back home.

Alice Wilkinson Allen

Sometimes Lillian stayed with my mother. We had a wonderful time. I'll always remember it.

ALICE WILKINSON ALLEN: I believe it was my sixth-grade teacher, Miss Reames. I don't know her first name or anything else, but she boarded down at Tyberg's. No one in the valley cared very much for her. Her personality was different from the people up here. But she boarded down at Grandma Tyberg's, and they had an altercation in Miss Reames' room. I don't know what the altercation was about, but Miss Reames had a violin. She had it in her hand, and finally she said to Mrs. Tyberg, "Old lady, you get out of my room, or I'm going to hit you over the head with this violin." And Mrs. Tyberg says, "Hee, hee, hee. What you t'ink I be doing?"

[Grandmother Laura Schapers] was a widow in Pennsylvania, left with four children. Her husband died shortly after my father was born. She worked for awhile in West Virginia, keeping house for people. I remember her telling about my uncle Bob walking along the railroad tracks and picking up the coal that would fall off the cars so they could warm their house for the winter.

18

I don't know how she got in contact with Joseph Schapers. . . . It was probably through a matrimonial association. . . . She was a mail-order bride, but she and Joseph Schapers corresponded and he sent money to bring her and her four children out here to marry him. Of course, she had never seen the man, or anything like that. She came across country by train and from Portland by steamboat, and met him in what was then Marshfield. She married him, and came up here to live and raise her family. After she had raised her own four children, she had to raise my sister and I after my mother passed away when my sister was born. She didn't have a very easy life.

She had never seen large trees in her life, and Joseph Schapers had sent her some postcards that showed some of the California redwoods. I don't know what she would have thought of them, but she thought these trees here were huge! Compared to today's trees, they were. She lived here until, what, 1946 or something like that? We had to move Grandma to town because of failing health. She passed away there in Coquille.

. . . I needed money to go to college and it was also during the war. They had never tried women for lookouts. They always thought it was a job for men. But most of the men were going into the army and so forth, so they decided to try women. They found that they made better lookouts because they could stand the loneliness better than the men could. You know, the sameness, and the being there. In my case, I didn't have a vehicle. Most of the other women didn't either, so you couldn't leave. My sister was also a lookout. In fact, she got broke in on Cougar Pass, where I was.

I had sixteen lightning strikes, I think it was, in one night, up above Loon Lake. The fire crews used the lookouts as relay stations with the two-way radios. I had to relay the messages from the fire crews to the headquarters in Coos Bay. I had been up for probably forty-eight hours straight when Pat came up to see me. I asked them if she

could relieve me. [She] stayed about a week. She'd take one shift and I'd take the other until the fires calmed down. I believe it was during that time that Japan surrendered. I relayed the message to the fire crews that the Japanese had surrendered, and all the guys wanted to walk off and go to town and celebrate! Ivan Young was in control of the fire crews out there and he used some language on the radio that should have not gone on it, because the crews wanted to walk out on it and go to town and celebrate! He finally held them in line and they got the fires out.

Cougar Pass Lookout

It was a great life up on the lookouts. I used to look forward to it every year. It was kind of like coming home again to go up on the forest fire lookout. I worked on Cougar Pass, Trail Butte, Deans Mountain, and Vaughn's Point. Actually, I guess my cousin, Alfreda Leaton, was a lookout a year before I was. She was on Blue Ridge. I went up and stayed with her for a few weeks that summer. The next summer I decided that was a good job for me, too.

PAT WILKINSON: There was a lot of work, but there was a lot of play and a lot of fun. Just a good place to live. I remember living on what you'd call a "real farm," with pigs and chickens and cows and all of them had to be taken care of and fed and cared for.

Pat Wilkinson

Some years that was real hard because of heavy snows. Oh, there were a lot of good times. During haying season we would have what to us were picnics. All of the neighbors would gather at each place to put up the hay. Everyone would gather and have a good meal, and more or less a picnic. It was one of the few times during the year that the few kids in the valley would get together to go to the swimming holes and play part of the time and work part of the time. Everyone worked — the kids, the old people.

My dad trapped every winter, and that's where a lot of our cash came from. He trapped up on Lake Creek, and later over on Matson Creek. He built cabins in two or three different places. All in all, it was a good life. We were a quite self-sufficient little valley where neighbor helped neighbor, and if someone was going to town everyone sent their mail in and got their mail, or ran errands for each other. Sometimes during the winter

Golden Falls School, 1918–1941

there would be a couple of months that the roads were closed. Occasionally someone would have to go to Allegany just with a packsack to get a few needed supplies.

WILMA LEATON HOELLIG: We started school here in first grade. We moved

Wilma Leaton Hoellig

away, and then we moved back when I was in fourth and fifth grade. Then I left when I was twelve years old. It was fun to go to school up here. It was fun to live up here, and to know these people. First place we lived on the Middleton place when we was real little there. We came back here three different times, folks did, three or four. When we was ten we moved back to my grandpa's house [Charlie Howell], up by the CCC camp. Then we went from there to Middleton's chicken house, after we had lived in the big house first. Then we moved to Wilkinson's little cabin, across the creek on this place here. I left here when I was twelve years old.

HATTIE LEATON COTTER: I'd like to inject something now. Grandma Schapers tithed, being a Seventh Day Adventist. Do you remember the year that she took her tithes and bought all of us in the valley a Bible? I still have mine, and to this day if I have something I want kept, it goes in that Bible. Every time I put something in there, I think of Grandma Schapers, and being up here. I wouldn't take a farm in Texas for that Bible. That's where all my important stuff goes. That's where my report card was at! That's "hands off" if it's in my Bible!

Hattie Leaton Cotter

"Reunion recalls tales of Oregon backwoods"

John Griffith, a correspondent to the *Oregonian* newspaper, was with us on that picnic. Before he became a journalist, he fell timber for Weyerhaeuser right there on Glenn Creek. His falling partner was killed, and John quit the woods for a quieter life as a sportswriter for the big daily in Portland. He waxed poetic in his by-lined article: "Douglas fir and berry vines have reclaimed the site of the Golden Falls School and abandoned homesteads in a serene Coast Range valley," he wrote. "But on a recent sunny afternoon, a double handful of people gathered to commemorate the closing of the tiny school in 1941." He listened to all the tales. "Their stories brought back to life the years when their families lived off the land by hunting, trapping, logging and farming," he said. And indeed they did, but those stories were just the beginning and within a short time after the picnic I was inundated with letters, phone calls, and visits correcting on one point and elaborating on another. Eventually, I had to go to the archives at the Coos County Courthouse to get some of the dates and names correct. It was a year-long quest.

The author, left, tape recording remembrances of Warren Browning, center, and Harold Ott, right.

21

Cattle Rustling and Other Perils of Oral History

Oral History is fraught with dangers. I found that out soon after the picnic. Traditional historians know nothing of those perils, because they are working with documents that cover events long past. No one remembers those things, the documents speak for themselves, and historians can fill in the blanks however they want to.

The oral historian, on the other hand, works with material that people remember, or think they remember, or almost remember, or remember hearing about. Much of the fun of oral history is not in finding out what really happened, but in finding out what people *remembered* about what really happened.

This project has been a lot of fun for that reason. By interviewing more than one person we get several impressions of a given event or character. As a result, we get a much fuller picture than would be possible with documents alone, or with only one informant. But there are sometimes problems, and the cattle rustling incident turned out to be one of them.

In the innocence of relating a good story about a brazen case of cattle rustling, one of the participants remembered Bill Leaton as having been the "one in charge." It seemed to be one more example of the legendary status of this one-armed woodsman. Unfortunately, there was the impression that this person thought Bill Leaton was a cattle thief, a characterization that no one who knew Bill would countenance. A few days after the picnic, I was informed from several quarters that the accusation was in error, and that feelings were hurt.

Well, this was an event that happened almost sixty years ago. Memories become faulty in that time. And, it seems that Bill's brother, Al Leaton, was more or less in charge of tracking down the thieves, and therein lies the possibility of confusing one Leaton brother for another, and of being mixed up on what he was in charge of: the rustling or the catching of the rustlers! In sixty years these things start to run together in the memory.

No one could remember the names of the actual culprits. No one could remember even the year in which the alleged cattle rustling occurred. Everyone who was old enough, however, remembered that it did occur.

In the Upper Glenn Creek Valley there were no locks on the doors. Loss from theft had never happened before. It was a one-time, unique event. And the audacity of driving the cattle over the mountain and through the brush all the way to Elkhorn Ranch had fired the imagination and had been the subject of conversation for years. It had fallen into the realm of folklore.

I decided that this was one incident that needed documents to settle the matter. I went to the Coos County Courthouse with this odd request: I wanted to find the court records of a cattle theft case which had allegedly occurred in the early thirties. The theft had been against Cleland Wilkinson. I didn't know anything else.

I was given access to the trial registers, and started on page one, 1930. By the time I got to 1932 I had figured out the numbering system so that I didn't have to read everything! I worked my way up to 1934 and stopped. This took two or three hours. I had taken notes on all of the cattle theft cases that had come to trial during that period.

The records are in the basement of the courthouse and the lady in charge of the court archives made three trips to the basement for me before I gave up. None of the records I had sent for were the right ones. It seemed futile. It may never have even come to trial, for all I knew.

A few weeks later, I received a letter from Cliff Leaton, who lives in Arizona. He was thanking me for sending him the transcript of our interviews at the picnic, and he said that the "cattle rustler bit" had brought back some memories. He said, "I don't remember if it was Alexander and his two boys, or what , but I do know that Alexander was the culprit."

That was the clue I needed. The very last cattle thief case that I had noted was dated early 1934 and the name was Alexander. I went back to the county courthouse and asked for that record. It was the right one.

In the indictment for Larceny of Livestock, Frank Alexander was accused of stealing on the 11th day of December, 1933, one two-year-old Jersey heifer, one black yearling bull calf, one yearling bull calf, and one yearling Jersey bull calf, the personal property of one Cleland Wilkinson. It added that this was contrary to the statutes in such cases, and against the peace and dignity of the State of Oregon.

District attorney was Ben Flaxel and the defense attorney was James McKeown. Mr. Alexander pleaded not guilty. The trial was on March 15, 1934, and the jury returned a verdict of guilty. B. L. Biddy was the judge, and he sentenced Mr. Alexander "to be confined in the Penitentiary of the State a prisoner and there kept a prisoner for the maximum period of two years."

When I told this to Pat Wilkinson and her sister Alice Allen, they both immediately remembered that indeed it had been a man named Alexander. They also remembered that there were some under-aged youths, sons of an Allegany resident, who were involved but not prosecuted. They couldn't remember the names of the youths. Thank goodness for the frailties of memory! We are sometimes lucky that we don't remember everything.

When I relayed the information to the daughters of Bill Leaton that we had found their father not guilty of having been in on the great cattle rustling caper, there was general rejoicing.

The Elkhorn Ranch on the Upper West Fork. It is about eight miles and across two ridges from the Wilkinson place.

23

A Letter from Charles Middleton

Keizer, Oregon
Nov. 11, 1991

Dear Lionel:

I want you to know that I thoroughly enjoyed the opportunity to visit the Glenn Creek Valley after 50 years and meet other folks who resided there – all of which was made possible mostly thru your generosity and interest including the cost of printing and mailing your "Above the Falls."

Bob Milton and I are the only surviving members of the "Middleton Commune" who actually resided there. Slim (my brother) and Frieda Middleton were often havens of last hope for many Middletons and some Miltons during the depression when they lived at Eastside and then above the falls. They always seemed to have something to eat and a place to rest when there was no place else to go.

Scotty and Wilma Sneddon lived by us for awhile. Scotty is dead and Wilma remarried long ago and lives in Lowell, OR. Wilma was mayor of Lowell several years. She is one of six Vineyard girls who never seem to age. My sister-in-law Edna is a Vinyard girl (87) but two sisters are older. Stella (oldest) is the widow of Jim Hill who operated Jim's Tavern on Broadway for years (Big Jim).

I regret your inability of locate Lem and Grace Gray. Grace was the school teacher and Lem was a rabid hunter and deer killer as well as logger.

Other school teachers are Marjorie Baird who was in my graduating class at Marshfield High, and Bernice Reames from Grants Pass whom I sparked not very seriously.

Frieda Middleton's father, old Fred, and her brother Joe (crippled) were permanent residents of our commune.

My brother Wayne and his wife were frequent visitors as well as a host of other persons whose names I don't recall. It's hell to get old.

Frieda and Reta cooked for the whole mob. I find it hard to believe we ate as much as we did. For each man (always six or seven) we ate a whole 12-inch skillet of steak plus mashed potatoes and gravy and a vegetable. In addition, I drank an average of 3 pints of milk per meal.

In retrospect, I have considered the five years I lived in the Glenn Creek Valley some of the best years of my life.

Thank you again for the wonderful outing you afforded us last September.

Chuck Middleton

Another letter from Charles Middleton

Keizer, Oregon
Jan. 3, 1992

Dear Lionel:

I didn't know until your picnic that Charlie Howell was related to the Leatons. He lived two miles on up the road from our place. He didn't have a car. He rode a saddle horse. He set cougar traps around his home area. I don't know that he ever caught a cougar but he caught black bears. He brought the feet tied to the saddle horn to show us. He had a .30 Remington pump rifle which he thought was a 30.30. He bought 30.30 ammunition for it. When he came to our place to complain about his malfunctioning gun we immediately recognized his problem because we had both types. We traded him .30 Remington shells for his 30.30 shells and sent him away happy. He rode into my camp years later when no one lived at the old place and I was camped there with 3 other men for hunting deer. While he was there other hunters stopped in for a visit. After they left I uncovered a venison carcass that we had for camp meat and gave Howell a hind quarter.

Coos County didn't maintain roads above the Silver Creek bridge. When necessary we natives performed maintenance and sent bills to the County. They were always paid promptly and never questioned.

I remember Jerd and Charlie Schapers, brothers of Mrs. Tyberg. We sent someone to town every week to deliver cream to the Coos Bay Creamery. Of course we stopped at the neighbors to see what they needed from town. Invariably Jerd wanted a gallon of whiskey. I was only 19 or 20 but never was I challenged at the state liquor store when buying booze for anyone including myself.

So much for Glenn Creek in memoriam. It spawned a lot of character in a lot of people for one small valley.

Did you hear of the moth at the birthday party for the two year old? He was burning his end at both candles.

Chuck Middleton

25

A Letter from Clifford Leaton

Dolan Springs, AZ
Oct. 14, 1991

Hi Lionel:

I got the transcripts of the picnic you guys had up at Glenn Creek and I really thoroughly enjoyed it.

It brought back a lot of memories. One in particular was of the cattle rustler bit. I remember Cle telling me years later that they – the cattle rustlers – I don't remember if it was Alexander and his two boys, or just who else, but I do know that Alexander was the main culprit and that they had taken a branch and swept the trail clear of cattle tracks and even scooped the cow crap up off the trail and throwed it away till you got almost to the top of the hill and Cle said he was almost ready to turn back when old Al Leaton – my dad – who had been walking along parallel to the trail but about 20 feet off found tracks of one cow or steer and of course then they knew the cattle had come that way. Before that they had been kidding Al about wandering along in the brush, and he said there is always one critter in every herd that will not follow the trail when you come to a big rock or a stump next to the trail it will always go around the back side of the rock or stump and that's what he was looking for and he found it just when Cle was ready to turn back. So after they determined that the cattle had come that way there was only one logical conclusion as to where they were taking them and that was the Elkhorn Ranch. You might ask Alice Allen about that cause I'm sure Uncle Cle – her dad, must have mentioned that fact to her that it was old Al that spotted the tracks just when they were about to turn back as they had swept the trail clean of tracks but my dad was one of the best trackers and woodsmen in the country and they didn't fool him.

He, my dad, used to run moonshine and hunt for a living. In one year alone he killed 103 deer and never wasted one speck of meat. He jerked it and sold it to Doctors and Lawyers to pay our hospital bills and food and stuff and he sold the hides to the Marshfield Bargain House. Old Cle was pretty self-sufficient, even put in a water turbine and generated his power to run a radio, washing machine and all the lights for the 2-story ranch house and separator house.

Your friend,

Cliff Leaton

The Middleton "Commune"

Picture taken at Arthur and Frieda's place above Golden & Silver Falls about 1939; courtesy Audrey and Bob Milton.

Front row seated: Joe Milton holding Robert Milton, Donald Nelson, Patrick McHale.
Front row standing: Gerald Nelson, Marybelle Nelson, Joseph Milton.
Second row standing: John R. Milton, Charles Nelson, Hazel Nelson, Frederich Charles Milton (Old Fred), Reta Lane Milton, Evangeline McHale, Joe McHale.
Back Row: Raymond (Fred) Middleton, Freida Middleton, Arthur Slim Middleton, Fred Nelson.

W ith the fascinating but confusing information gleaned from the interviews and visits at the picnic, and the preliminary documentary research I had started, it was plain that my work was cut out for me if I wanted to put the whole story together. First, I would have to compile a history of Glenn Creek, from available sources, and that is the subject of Part Two.

Glenn Creek looking upstream from Joe Schapers' house. Barely visible in lower center are people driving home the cows, past a huge windfall.

PART TWO

GLENN CREEK AND THE EAST FORK

A History Based upon the Census, Deed Records,
and
Other Published and Unpublished Material

Forest Service mile sign (1952)

All History is local. Every place is a universe unto itself.
--Joseph A. Amato, *Rethinking Home*

The Glenn Creek Homesteads

There were seven homesteads strung along Glenn Creek, four below the falls and three above. Each contained four forties (160 acres) and extended for about one mile along the creek. The map shows the relative position of the houses of the Glenn, Crane, Hendrickson, George Schapers, Elizabeth Ott, Joe Schapers, and Joe Larson homesteads.

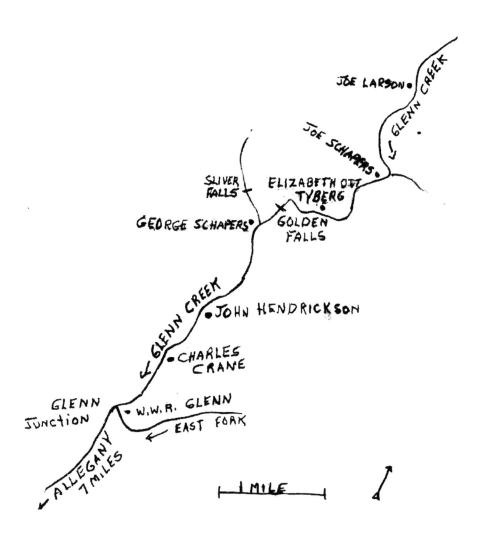

Chapter Three

A History of Glenn Creek and the East Fork

Harold Ott lived at Allegany for over 80 years and knew more about it than everyone else put together. He told me that he had tried a couple times to write a history but that it just can't be done. He heard once that history is "about something you don't remember, written by someone who wasn't there." And, he complained, if you include one family and don't write it up the way they would like it, you're in trouble. On the other hand, if you leave them out, you're still in trouble.

In this book I'm trying to mention as many as I can of the families that had something to do with Upper Glenn Creek. I am trying to let the voices of those who were there speak of what they *do* remember. That is the essence of oral and folk history.

The problem is that no one remembers anything about some of these families. In some cases, even the names have been forgotten. And so, our little history needs some help from documents. Documents, of course, are what traditional historians rely on almost exclusively. They believe that if there is no document, there is no history. I don't believe that, but I do know that a document here and there can surely help!

The documents I am relying on to supplement faulty memories include the Government Survey Field Notes, Homestead Patents, Records of Deeds at the office of the Coos County Clerk, and the U. S. Census of 1900 and 1910 for the North Fork of Coos River. Those kinds of documents can be pretty dry and boring, but it is possible to "flesh them out." Even these statistical and legal materials can be made interesting with the aid of a little memory and imagination.

Everyone who arrives in a new place considers himself as a "pioneer," of sorts. Surely the loggers in these camps, hiking as they did for five or ten miles from tidewater with their bedrolls on their backs, considered these conditions primitive even by the standards of 1910. The surveyors before them must have thought that they were the first humans to set foot in these hills.

Things were happening above the falls before the time of the first surveyors, however, but we don't know much about it. For example, Frank Ross is said to have "discovered" Golden Falls, but no one knows when. It would probably have been sometime in the 1870's. There may have been lone hunters or trappers in and out of Upper Glenn Creek a generation before that. Around 1950 Clyde Allen found a .44 caliber rim-fire Henry repeating rifle lying in Upper Glenn Creek, near the line fence between the Tyberg and Wilkinson places. The stock had rotted off and the barrel was worn away, but the brass parts were intact. It had a full magazine of rim fire cartridges in it. According to the serial number (28958), it came out of the factory in 1866, and it may have been lying in Glenn Creek since it was new! As with so much of what happened, we'll never know the full story.

The Coos Indians

Prior to the early backwoodsmen there was another people familiar with the area. These were the Indians. The site of Allegany itself had no doubt been an Indian settlement at one time. There was another Indian settlement about one mile upstream from Allegany, where Marlow Creek flows into the East Fork. That is the head of tidewater and as far upstream as canoe travel is possible. From there on, you walked.

There had also been a settlement at the junction of Glenn Creek and the East Fork. Wilma Lund told me that her father Walter Devoe had found a number of items while plowing his field there. She showed me one — a large pestle— but the rest had been taken by others over the years. It seems that the Indians had lived at one time or another almost everywhere that whites later built their homesites.

I don't know for how long the Coos Indians had traveled through this area on their way to and from the Umpqua River, but there is no doubt that they did. I think the big stump, which I quoted Lottie Evanoff as telling about at the beginning of this book, was located near the ridge at the upper end of Glenn Creek Valley. Lottie told of her father, Daloose, as a young man (probably in the 1840's) walking from Allegany to Scottsburg packing a load of beaver hides.[1] Jean Baptiste Gagnier of the Hudson's Bay Company was buying the furs, and with the pay for the hides Daloose bought some clothes. He said those were the first clothes he ever put on.

The trail wouldn't have gone on up the river because of brush and sheer cliffs. The early trails usually followed the ridges, and there was a trail that took off from the settlement at the mouth of Marlow Creek. It went up the ridge dividing Marlow Creek from the East Fork. Following that ridge would bring the traveler to the Upper Glenn Creek Valley, and at the upper end of that valley there were some enormous trees, snags, and stumps. There were some that were over 500 years old in 1950. One of them might have been the stump that Lottie had talked about.

There is no doubt that the Indians used the Upper Glenn Creek Valley, because arrowheads and projectile points have been found in the creek. They were not abundant. In a lifetime, Cle Wilkinson had found only three or four of them, but that is certainly enough to prove beyond a doubt that the valley had been used by people long before the whites got there. Cle's daughter, Alice, remembers that the points were of flint, and that one of them had a reddish tint. The one with the reddish tint was probably of jasper. Neither flint, chert, nor jasper was found naturally in the Coos River drainage, but were traded from the Coquille, the Umpqua, or further afield.

---

[1]Harrington, op cit. Reel 24, frame 936.

The trails along the ridges were kept open by the elk, and there were enormous herds of elk in these woods at the time of the first white settlement. A herd of 60 or 100 elk can make quite a highway through the brush. The old timers would say that the roads were crooked and steep because they just "followed an old elk trail." The first white followed elk trails, and most certainly the Indians before them had done the same.

On that ridge between Marlow Creek and the East Fork a neighbor of mine, who walks those woods a lot, recently found an obsidian projectile point. Somebody, before history began to be recorded in this area, had lost that obsidian point. There is no doubt that the old elk trails were used by people.

The Indian concept of "ownership" of land probably didn't include land away from the village or settlement. Most of the settlements were permanent and belonged communally to the men, whose wives came from other villages. These sites were often very old, going back hundreds, perhaps thousands of years. That could have been the case with the site at Marlow Creek.

Certain rights extended beyond the village. For example, the exclusive right of the men to fish or hunt in certain places, or the right of the women to gather berries and roots for food and fiber, are examples. But probably open to anyone was the right to travel an elk trail from one major tribal area to another, such as from the Coos to the Umpqua through the upper Glenn Creek Valley. Those people did quite a bit of trading with each other. Transportation and communication routes had to be free and open or trade would suffer.

A blade from the Coos River Hanis village of Willanch. 6 ½ inches long, reddish color (chert or jasper), 1,500 to 3,000 years old. From the collection of Rachel Swenson.

The Whites

The whites had their own problems and weren't very interested in what the Indians had done before. I don't think they knew that these trails had been used prehistorically. They knew about the Marlow Creek site, and talked about it a bit. They dug around it, out of curiosity. In the early 1930's somebody dug up quite a few items, including some skeletons, and who knows what became of them.

When the whites showed up they brought with them concepts of land ownership that had developed in Europe and the Mediterranean over a period of several thousand years. Land surveys, with the establishment of boundaries and corners and the recording of title deeds goes back to ancient Egypt. The idea, however, of owning land one didn't use, and the expropriation of common lands to private ownership was a comparatively new development. By the time the land above the falls was surveyed the concept was well developed. There were people in places of power who knew very well how to turn it to their advantage.

The descendants of the English and other Europeans who came to America were a legalistic lot. They recognized that the ownership of land was actually the ownership of the source and scene of all property, and of all life. As a result, they went to great pains to ensure that legal title to land would be solid and unassailable, at least for those who understood the system and were in positions to take advantage of it. Those who didn't understand the system, or were not in a position to take advantage of the laws, were out of luck.

Among those who were out of luck were the Indians. Their title was quickly extinguished, all quite legal and for the most part without their knowledge or consent. It was done by the Congress and the President of the United States a long ways away and in the most legalistic terms imaginable. For the land in Coos County, this all happened in the 1850's.

About 40 years later, in the 1890's, the land above the falls changed title again. By and large it hadn't been used by anyone during the intervening period. There were some trees that had been growing since the 1400's and they just kept on growing, many of them until they died of old age. Other trees that had sprouted after a big forest fire in 1750 grew to maturity. There were several new fires, the largest of which was the great Coos Bay fires of 1868. This fire didn't get over the ridge into Glenn Creek and so when the last great land grab occurred at the turn of the century, the Glenn Creek Valley stood in the middle of one of the finest stands of old-growth Douglas fir in the world.

During this last great transfer of ownership of the land above the falls the overwhelming bulk of it was transferred directly to the Northern Pacific and the Southern Pacific Railroads. Through them, directly and indirectly, it went ultimately to the Weyerhaeuser Timber Company. The Congress, the President, and the courts facilitated this transfer, as they had at the time that Indian title was extinguished. A few hundred acres went to actual settlers. Those few hundred acres and those settlers are what most of this book is about.

On the Names of Places

One of the first things newcomers have to do is settle on the names of things. There is a magic in names, and deep in the human psyche there seems to be the assumption that if one has the name of something, one has control over it. Thus, an immediate problem was: What should they call all these rivers, creeks, and other features, so that they could actually have control over them? The names that the Indians had used were either unknown or unpronounceable to the whites. The Penutian Indian languages contained sounds that very few whites could handle. Many of the words contained long series of consonants with very few vowels. As an example of the result, there are at least ten inlets to Coos Bay and only one of them, Wilanch, still has its original Indian name. The rest have names like Ross, Catching, Larsen, Haynes, North, South, etc.

By the time settlers were coming into the East Fork and Glenn Creek during the 1870's, nearly all of the Indians were gone anyway. There was no one to ask. The Indians had been removed to a reservation at Yachats fifteen years earlier, where they remained until their reservation was opened to timber speculators in 1875. Many of the surviving Coos Indians returned, but by then the whites had placed their own names on almost everything.

Starting from scratch on the naming of a vast new piece of geography inevitably leads to confusion. Some of that confusion still exists. For the most part, the original settlers named the creeks and other features after themselves. This was one of the last places on earth where descendants of European peasants could give their own name to a creek, river or town. Sometimes the names of creeks changed each time a new settler moved in. Sometimes the mapmakers who came later couldn't tell what the local name of a creek might have been. Following are my comments on some of the more confusing aspects of names relative to the East Fork and Glenn Creek.

Coos

"Coos," it is fairly well documented, is derived from a local Indian word meaning "south" or "southerner." The Coos Indians were the southernmost of what anthropologists call the Oregon Coast Penutian and were thought of as southerners by the Indians further north. South of here the Indians were unrelated to the Coos and were comparative newcomers, speaking Athabaskan languages. Thus, the bay with its surrounding region came to be known as Coos Bay, Coos River, and when political subdivisions were established, Coos County.

Coos River has two forks, usually called the North Fork and the South Fork. Coincidentally, there were also two branches of the Coos Indian peoples: the Miluk and the Hanis. The Miluk lived near the mouth of the bay, South Slough and the ocean beaches, as well as the mouth of the Coquille River. The Hanis lived on Tenmile Lakes and Coos Bay from about the present site of Empire up all the sloughs (except South Slough) and up Coos River to the head of tidewater.

Millicoma

Tradition has it that during the summers the Miluk would migrate up one of the forks of the Coos River, and the Hanis would use the other fork. They would presumably catch eels, pick berries, bask in the sun, swim, and generally live it up in the warm, inland climate near the head of tidewater. It was thought that the Miluk used the North Fork, and on current maps it is known as the Millicoma River. The Hanis, it was thought, used the South Fork, which on current maps is called Coos River.

Lottie Evanoff, when talking to the anthropologist John Peabody Harrington in 1942 said that she thought the river of the Miluk was actually the South Fork. She said she was sure that was the way her father referred to it. Harrington, who specialized in the field of "ethnogeography," agreed that Lottie's suggestion made sense. The great sweep of country between the South Fork and the ocean would thus be Miluk, whereas that immense area between Tenmile Lakes and the North Fork would have been Hanis.[2] Who knows?

If what Lottie said is correct, then we have the rivers named backwards! The South Fork would be the Miluk river (Millicoma) and the North Fork, now called the Millicoma, would be the Hanis, or Coos River. It is more than possible, but at this late date it doesn't make any difference.

Some maps show the two forks of the Coos River as being the North and the South Forks, and that is generally what the people living there call them. The North Fork of the Coos has as its tributaries the East and West Forks of the Millicoma River. Modern mapmakers have decreed that you cannot have an east and a west fork of a river without having the main river itself, and that is the reason the North Fork of the Coos is now called the Millicoma River on most maps.

Golden Falls from top

It has always been a bit confusing. I have a township map dated 1905 in which the North Fork of the Coos is called the Millicoma, as it is on modern maps, but the East Fork of the Millicoma is called the "South Fork of the North Fork." Oh well!

Glenn Creek

One creek on which there is no confusion of names is Glenn Creek itself. It was named for William W. R. Glenn, a State-of-Mainer, Civil War veteran, shipwright, homesteader, and tinker. Glenn settled at the junction of Glenn Creek and the East Fork of the Millicoma in 1877 or earlier. His homestead patent is dated 1882.

In August, 1880, three businessmen from Marshfield visited the Glenn Creek falls and decided to name them after themselves. Dr. Charles B. Golden got the honor

---

[2] Harrington, op cit. Reel 24, Frame 553.

of having the falls named after him. The trio elected to name the creek Anderson Creek, after Edmund A. Anderson. The third member of the trio, Thomas Hirst, would give his name to the cascade midway between Glenn's place and the falls. Fortunately, only the name "Golden Falls" stuck. The cascades are known only as "the Cascades," and the creek is definitely "Glenn Creek."

The Glenn Creek tributaries

All of the tributaries to Glenn Creek except one come in from the northwest. About a mile upstream from the mouth of Glenn Creek, Darius Creek comes in from the northwest. Three quarters of a mile further Silver Creek comes in, after running over Silver Falls. The first creek to come into Glenn Creek above the falls is Frog Creek, at the extreme west end of the Elizabeth Ott homestead. It's two more miles before another creek comes in, and that is Woodruff Creek, the only named creek that enters Glenn Creek from the west. It enters Glenn Creek at about in the middle of the old Joe Schapers homestead. (It is not be confused with the Woodruff Creek that empties into the Millicoma River a quarter mile below the confluence of the East and West Forks, at Allegany.) A quarter mile up Glenn Creek from Woodruff Creek is a small spring near the site of the Golden Falls School. Locally, it was known as "Schoolhouse Creek," but it remains unnamed on maps. Next above it is the creek which is shown on maps as Schoolhouse Creek. This creek had been known to the old-timers as "Bill Leaton Creek." It enters Glenn Creek near the lower boundary of the old Joe Larson place, which is where old William Leaton and his family lived from about 1910 until the 1930's.

Next is the creek shown on the maps as Creighton Creek. It was never known by that name, and there was never anyone in the Glenn Creek Valley by that name. According to Alice Allen, the people who lived in the Glenn Creek Valley didn't call it by any name.

The next creek up was known as Slideout Gulch, from a big slide that occurred there sometime in the nineteenth century. It is shown on maps as Slideout Creek. A half mile further up, we come to the West Fork of Glenn Creek, and a half mile beyond that is Howell Creek. Charlie Howell, father of Bernice Leaton, lived there as a bachelor for many years. The original settlers there were Newell Price and his family.

The last of the Glenn Creek tributaries is Cedar Creek. It comes in at the State Forest Camp. Another mile by road will bring you to the summit of Umpcoos Ridge, the divide between the Umpqua and Coos drainages.

Allegany

To conclude this section on names, the name of Allegany is worth an explanation. William Vincamp, Allegany's first postmaster, is credited with choosing the name in 1893, at the time the post office was being established at "The Forks," as the location was known up to that time. It is said that he was from Allegheny County, Pennsylvania, but didn't know how to spell it. An alternative story has it that the Post Office Department had advised him to spell it "Allegany" so that it wouldn't become confused with the one in

Pennsylvania. Who knows the truth of the matter, but in actual fact there are three recognized spellings of the name.

"Allegany" is the spelling of the Seneca Indian Reservation on the New York–Pennsylvania border. The reservation was established in 1797 and the spelling goes back at least to that time. There is an Allegany County in New York, and another one in Maryland.

The "Allegheny" River runs through the Allegany Reservation, however, and the county and National Forest in Pennsylvania have that spelling. The mountain that separates Virginia and West Virginia is also spelled "Allegheny."

The third spelling is "Alleghany." There is a community in Virginia and another in California that spell it that way. Both Virginia and North Carolina have counties spelled "Alleghany."

However it is spelled, the word is said to have meant "beautiful river" in the Seneca Indian language. I suspect that William Vincamp knew exactly what he was doing when he named it. "Allegany" is the simplest of the three spellings, and I wouldn't have it any other way.

Allegany store, about 1935.

A Firsthand Account of the Naming of Golden Falls

T he following is a newspaper communication of August 1880, written in the flowery language of the period. It describes the trip of the first tourists to the Golden Falls and the way in which the falls were named. The egos of these townspeople is evident in their assumption that local people had no names for these places. Glenn Creek might have been Anderson Creek had it been left to these tourists!

A Trip To The Golden Falls, by Edmund A. Anderson
(from the *Coos Bay News*, August 11, 1880, page 3.)

On Monday, Aug. 2nd three of us — T. Hirst, E. A. Anderson, and Dr. Golden[3] — started on the steamer *Bertha* for Coos River to visit the great falls; the weather was propitious, a gentle health-given breeze coming from the northwest and a cloudless sky, the heat of the sun was so temperate as to be just delightful. As we had a late start we arrived at the forks of the south branch of Coos River (which is the head of navigation)[4] only in time to make our campfires, eat our supper and retire to our open air beds, and those who have never enjoyed the luxury of a nights lodging in the open air in Coos county, under a group of wide spreading myrtle or giant firs can scarcely appreciate the health giving pleasure and enjoyment after sleeping in such an extensive bedchamber, his lungs and whole breathing apparatus rejuvenated, and such an appetite, could everybody enjoy such health-giving sport I fear the doctors would feel like Othello when he exclaimed, "Othello; occupation gone."

The sun is up and on his way and it is time for us to follow his example, but not until we halt with our old friend Folk and get a breakfast and a cup of coffee and cream fit for a king. Here we leave most of our load and travel leisurely to Glenn's falls where we halt and catch trout and cook them for our dinner, having in a very short time caught sufficient for our present wants. Our dinner consisted of a number of dishes such as trout, sardines, canned corn, beef, bread, crackers, jellies, etc. provided by Mr. Hirst. After finishing our repast and making our dessert of raspberries growing on the spot and slackening our thirst from the crystal water which flowed over the falls we concluded to leave all but enough for our supper and breakfast and make our way as easy as possible through the tangled mass of salmon brush, vine maple, and other under brush and which we found so dense that it was only with hard labor that we accomplished one mile an hour, and that was made by frequently crossing the river or wading up its bed. After five hours hard labor, we came

---

[3] Thomas Hirst, Edmund A. Anderson, and Dr. Charles B. Golden.

[4] They were actually at the forks of the East and West Forks of the Millicoma River, as it is designated now.

suddenly in sight of the falls, and such a sight! We were in an amphitheater of solid rock rising perpendicularly three or four hundred feet with an even surface at the top leaving only on one side an opening through which the river made its way to join its sister streams on their way to the broad Pacific. At that part of the amphitheater opposite the exit of the river was the falls. The water leaped over the precipice in milky foam in a fall of perhaps three hundred feet, some say nearly four hundred feet; half way down the water strikes a rock and divides into two columns. Just below where the water divides, is a hole or small cave in the rock reminding one of an open mouth in a Griffin's head, and far below the water falls behind and into a mass of huge rocks giving the whole scene an indescribable grandeur so sublime that it was hard to break away from the contemplation.

Others had been there but had left no sign. We were the first party who had ever camped there. We made our campfire and slept at the base of a group of huge myrtles. One of our party said, "as we are the first to camp here we ought to name the falls" and suggested that we name them Golden Falls and then another one coinciding, the motion was carried. The doctor thanked them for their compliment and the honor and said that the title might be contested. It was moved and carried that the branch of the river should be called Anderson river while Mr. Hirst should give his name to a cascade midway between Glenn's falls and the beautiful falls above described.

Perhaps the most beautiful trout stream on the Pacific is this river from the head of navigation to falls. It runs over a rocky bed with numerous rapids and pools which trout delight in. On the next day after our return one of the townsmen caught in two hours fishing, fifty-eight trout. And in the near future there is but little doubt that hundreds if not thousands will go to visit the beautiful spot.

Golden Falls, an amphitheater of solid rock.

Census of 1900
North Fork of Coos River, East Fork of Millicoma

The census taker for 1900 found sixty-two people living on the East Fork of the Millicoma. Of the thirty-eight adult men, thirty-seven were listed "logger" or "lumberman" under occupation. The one remaining man was listed as "farmer." This man was Joseph Schapers, who had the second place above the falls and whose homestead had been "proved up on" in 1898, as was the homestead of his sister, Elizabeth Ott.

Of the women, only one was listed with an occupation other than "housewife." This was Elizabeth Ott, who was listed as "cook" in the logging camp in which her brother Jordan (Jerd) Schapers was listed as "lumberman" and "head of household." Her son, Jesse Ott, was living with them and listed as "school." At this time, Elizabeth Ott was owner of the first homestead above the falls, and Jerd had claim to 160 acres on the East Fork, about halfway between Matson Creek and Beulah Creek. This may have been the location of the camp, but not necessarily. Their brother Charlie, whose address at the time was in Drain, had the adjoining 160 acres.

It appears in this census that the term "lumberman" was reserved for foremen, contractors, or what later came to be known as "gyppo" operators. In any case, seven of the men were listed as "lumbermen." All of the lumbermen were also listed as "Head of Household" and all of them had boarders in the household with them. In some cases, the household was certainly nothing more than a camp bunkhouse. Those who were listed as "lumbermen" included Gustafson, Hendrickson, Peterson, Schapers, and Stemmerman.

There was among the lumbermen and loggers a large percentage who were from the Swedish part of Finland. The name of Gustafson was one such. This name figures prominently in the Ash Valley and Loon Lake area, as well as Allegany and the East Fork. Ash is the first settlement on the Umpqua side of the mountain, as one took the old trail (and later road) from Golden Falls to Loon Lake and Scottsburg. **Otto Gustafson** first purchased forty acres at Ash Valley from the Northern Pacific Railroad in 1898 and so his name goes back at least that far in that area.

John Hendrickson was another of the Swedes from Finland. His homestead and logging show was along lower Glenn Creek. His wife Helma and son Reuben, who was just two years old, were living there at the time of the 1900 census. Reuben lived into his late 90's, all of those years in Coos County.

Andrew Matson and Daniel Mattson were also Swedes from Finland. Matson Creek (sometimes spelled Mattson Creek), the next major tributary of the East Fork above Glenn Creek, bears their name. Dan Mattson came to Coos County in 1888 and worked in the mines and logging camps. In 1893 he took up a homestead on Matson Creek. This was just over the hill from the Upper Glenn Creek Valley, and might have had the same potential for development. In 1906 he sold out and bought a farm on Catching Slough.

The loggers in that 1900 census include many more names that are still locally current. There was, for example, **Albert Gould**, who was raised on the ranch in the middle of the "big burn," on the upper West Fork. This ranch was known as the Elkhorn Ranch and is forever identified with Albert's father, George Gould. It was to the West Fork pretty much what the Upper Glenn Creek Valley was to the East Fork: wilderness places about as far away from the amenities of civilization as one could get. Those two remote locations were actually closer to each other than either of them were to Allegany and were linked by a trail.

The **Stemmermans** were a large logging family on the East Fork, and several 160-acre timber claims on Marlow Creek were in their names at this time. The father, Christopher Stemmerman, came from Germany and then across the plains to Oregon in 1843. He made it to Coos County in 1868. One of his grandsons, George, married Jane Wilkinson who was stepdaughter to Joseph Schapers and was raised above the falls. At this point, it should be obvious to the reader that there was a lot of interconnectedness among the families around Allegany.

There were many members of Stemmerman households on the 1900 census for the East Fork. First was head of household/lumberman **J. Albert Stemmerman** with sons **Robert**, **Renaldo**, **Alonzo**, daughter **Merle** and niece **Luella Hudson**. The dangerous occupation that logging was, and is, really comes home when we consider the fate of this family: Albert was killed in a logging accident in 1909 at age 35. His son Renaldo was killed later in another logging accident, while the other son, Alonzo had his feet amputated in a logging accident in 1951. Head of household/lumberman George Stemmerman was also on the 1900 census with his wife Minny Blake Whitted and her five children by her previous marriage: Ethel, Edna, James, Annie, and Ray.

Alonzo Noah was one of the fifteen children of John W. and Mary Noah. John was a well-known logging bull-puncher who came across the plains in 1853. The various Noahs had several homesteads and timber claims on the East Fork, and descendants still live there. One of Alonzo's nephews, Lewis, married Mable Leaton from above the falls. Another nephew, Harold, in 1946 located a hunter who had been lost in the wilderness between Glenn Creek and the West Fork for over a week and given up for dead. The name of Noah figures prominently in the annals of the East Fork, its tributaries, and the woods beyond.

The census taker found four of the **Schapers brothers**: George, John, Jordan (Jerd, or Gerhard), and Joseph. George at this time had a homestead claim on the 160 acres which now comprise the Golden and Silver Falls State Park. This property adjoined his sister Elizabeth's homestead, which was the first one above he falls.

John Schapers died of appendicitis in camp with his brother Jerd beside him on May 31, 1911. He was forty-six years old. After that tragic event, Jerd lost interest in the East Fork claim and abandoned it. He spent his last years with George and their younger brother Charlie at the homestead of their sister Elizabeth.

Jerd Schapers and his brother Charlie had adjoining homesteads along the East Fork in Sections 8 and 9 of Township 25-10. Jerd's place was patented in 1899 and Charlie's in 1900. Jerd purchased Charlie's homestead at that time for $450. Charlie was living in Drain at that time.

Emmett Pierce Logging Camp about 1905.
East Fork, at Matson Creek

Jerd and his crew built a splash dam across the East Fork at about the boundary between his and Charlie's place, and drove logs down the river to Allegany for a number of years beginning in the early 1880's. At the location of that splash dam, succeeding dams continued in operation until splash dam logging on the East Fork ended in 1953.[5]

In the camp of Jerd Schapers is an interesting crew at the time of the 1900 census. The cook is his sister Elizabeth Ott, who has her son Jesse with her. In addition to Jerd and Jesse, there are thirteen loggers eating there. Among the loggers at Jerd's camp are George Terry, Albert Gould, Alonzo Noah, Daniel Stemmerman, John Schapers, and Alex Evanoff.

The other families are mentioned in other paragraphs, but **Alex Evanoff** is of special interest because his wife was the Princess Lottie, daughter of Chief Daloose Jackson. It was she who the anthropologist John Peabody Harrington interviewed in 1942 and got the story of the big stump that I quoted at the beginning of the book. Lottie was the last of the Coos Indian full-bloods at the time of her death in 1944. Alex himself was Russian-Aleut, originally from Alaska.

Lottie and Alex were very familiar with these backwoods, both the south and the north forks of Coos River. There was a small clearing along the road between the Glenn Creek Valley and Ash Valley — just over the ridge into Douglas County. Cle Wilkinson once pointed that clearing out to his daughter, Alice, saying that it had been the "Evanoff place." It was a small, fairly flat piece of ground, near the head of a creek. Cle mentioned to Alice that Evanoff had an Indian wife. According to Ray Sims' history of Loon Lake,

---

[5] Dow Beckham, *Swift Flows the River*, pp. 73–77.

Alex Evanoff bought land on Soup Creek at Ash Valley as early as 1900, and was in some way connected with the Gustafson's. Both Alex Evanoff and Otto Gustafson were working at a logging camp on the East Fork at the time of the 1900 census.

Boarding separately were several of the Swedish loggers, headed by Herman Peterson and his wife Lydia. The boarders included the two Mattsons, John Johnson, and Alfred Tyberg. **Alfred Tyberg** is of special importance to Upper Glenn Creek because in 1903 he married Elizabeth Schapers Ott, and her homestead above the falls became known from then on as the Tyberg Place. Nearby was Peter Peterson and his wife Ada with eight borders, including George Schapers. The Gustafson family also lived nearby.

One long-time resident of Glenn Creek — possibly its original settler — was notably absent in the 1900 census. This was **William W. R. Glenn** himself. He may have been ill, as it is known that he died the following year. Glenn had homesteaded the southwest quarter (160 acres) of Section 25, Township 24, Range 11. This includes all of the bench land near the confluence of Glenn Creek and the East Fork, on both sides of the river. The location is known locally as Glenn Junction. Glenn's homestead patent was signed in the name of President Chester A. Arthur on March 30, 1882. This means that he had to have arrived there by 1877, which makes him the earliest settler anywhere near Glenn Creek.

Glenn sold the homestead to **James R. Bunch** with a deed dated December 8, 1891. He received $3,000 in gold coin. In 1892 Glenn purchased three acres (more or less, according to the deed) from Bunch further down the East Fork at a location four miles above Allegany, where he retired. That property is now in my possession. He lived there until his death in 1901, and he is buried at the Allegany cemetery.

The East Fork full of logs, 1901.

Census of 1910
North Fork Coos River (East Fork Millicoma only)

The census is a snapshot taken once every ten years. The snapshot taken on the East Fork in 1910 was quite different from the 1900 census. For one thing, the population had increased by almost 250 percent — from 62 in 1900 to 150 in 1910. Most of the increase was associated with two large logging camps. Smith-Powers Logging Company had one at Hodges Creek, five miles above Allegany, and Emmet Pierce had one five miles further up, at Matson Creek. These two camps were significant enough that the census taker divided the East Fork into two parts, one part relating to each of the two camps.

A population of 150 is large enough to look at in the abstract, so to speak. We can analyze the statistics. And the first thing about these statistics that grabs the attention is the acute shortage of women. When we look at it, it becomes clear why only one of the Schapers brothers ended up with a wife, and she by "mail order." This is the way it looked on the East Fork in 1910:

Married women	20
Married men	20
Dependent children	46
Single men	61
Single women	3
Total on East Fork	150

These are pretty stark figures, and they tell the story. On the East Fork there was a very decided gender imbalance. There were not enough single women for the single men.

The families that were there were not particularly large for that time. Four or five children was maximum. The average was only 2.7 dependent children in each of the married households. It was a comparatively young population. The median age was 27 years; the oldest inhabitant was Mathias Roberts at 62. The youngest was Charles Kroeger, seven months old. As of this writing (2002) he still lives on the place where he was born, near Hodges Creek. Second youngest was Suzie Tyberg, two years old at the time the census taker got to the top of Golden Falls.

Oh yes, the 1910 census also shows that the former Elizabeth Schapers Ott is now the wife of Alfred Tyberg. They were married December 23, 1903. Another marriage quite important for our history is indicated in the census: Joseph Schapers was now married to the widow Laura Wilkinson, and her four children are now a part of the population above the falls.

Where did all these people on the East Fork come from? The census tells us something about that. Thirty-three percent of them were born in Oregon. Swedes, Germans, and English born in the old country account for another 18 percent. Twelve percent were from California, and the remainder were from the states of the northern half of the United States, except for one lone Texan working at the Hodges Creek camp.

45

What were all these people doing? What were their occupations, in other words? Well, Nellie Devoe and Lethe Cowes are cooks at the Matson Creek camp. Jerd Schapers, Fred Noah, and Davis Cowan are foremen. Walter Devoe is falling timber along with Clarence Gage, William Doyle, and George Noah. James Wolf, Abraham Matson, Jacob King, and George Floyd are "sawyers," bucking logs. Albert Mullouch must have been a good axman because he was sniper, rounding off the ends of the logs so they wouldn't dig into the ground as they were yarded to the landing in those days before the invention of high lead logging. Running those old steam donkeys were Ray Noel and Robert Frye. Their firemen were Thomas Peterson and Edward Stubbs. James Harrington was chaser while Victor Carlson tended chute. Vern Chandler and Harry Culby were in the rigging, setting chokers one supposes. Oren Totten punked whistle. Bookkeeper for the operation was twenty-two-year-old Lewis Hyde.

Hattie Noah was ten years old, but she remembered the kind of people these loggers were. With her parents, she moved to the Emmet Pierce camp at Matson Creek in 1910. In her memoir, *Reflections of a Logging Camp Cook* (1980), she described them well. In the bunkhouse, she said, was a box partly filled with sand. "Dad forbid me ever to play in it," she said. Loggers would squirt long strings of brown tobacco juice which flew through the air and always landed near the center of that sand box. "Those old-time loggers seemed a breed all of their own," she continued. "They were tough, drank whiskey straight, and fist fought just for the pleasure. They wore heavy, all wool Long John under clothes winter and summer. I believe they considered a hard winter rain storm a clothes wash and a body bath as I never saw them wash clothes or saw any evidence of bathing facilities." One wonders, were the men like that because there were no women, or were there no women because the men were like that?

Quite out of place in this list is the occupation of Bernard Forshay. He was from California and is listed in the census as a piano teacher. Who did he teach? Surely not the loggers. But there were, remember, twenty wives and forty-seven dependent children. Phonographs would have been very rare on the East Fork, and radios and other artificial means of making music were far in the future. To make these steep, damp canyons tolerable at all, music was essential. In those days someone in each family had to be able to make it, and they needed a teacher. At the time the 1910 census taker was there, Bernard Forshay must have been the one.

Logging crew, East Fork, 1903. Standing: Frank Vincamp, unknown, Dave Cowan, unknown, Dan Stienon. Seated: Bob Harrington, George Kruse, Fred Noah, unknown.

Dan Mattson and Gaston's *Centennial History of Oregon*[6]

In Joseph Gaston's four-volume *Centennial History of Oregon* (1912), three of the four volumes are biographical sketches of men who were perceived as representing the essence of pioneer virtue. Families or individuals who submitted their biographies paid to have them included, and the publication of the work was financed in that way. Of the more than 3,000 biographies, only one came from the backwoods of the East Fork of the Millicoma: Dan Mattson. A Swede born in Finland in 1868, he arrived in Coos County when he was twenty. "For some years," the biography tells us, "he was engaged in the logging business." To be "engaged in the logging business" was Gaston's euphemism for saying that he worked in the logging camps. "In 1893," it continues, "he took up a homestead in Township 24, Range 10, Coos County."

Of all the biographies in the book, this is the only one that I found in which the subject's residence was depicted only by township and range. Township 24, Range 10 contains the Golden and Silver Falls, and the three homesteads above the falls that are the main subject of this book. It also includes upper Matson Creek and Dan Mattson's homestead claim was above the Matson Creek Falls. It was every bit as remote as the three homesteads above the falls on Glenn Creek.

"In 1906," the biography continues, "he disposed of that property and purchased a farm of fifty-five acres located . . . off Catching Slough where he now resides. He is successfully engaged in dairy farming and proposes . . . to plant a large orchard . . . and ultimately devote himself to the fruit growing business." The biography concludes with a tribute similar to hundreds of others in the book. It says, "He is one of the enterprising and useful citizens of his county and a man always associated with the advancement of every public measure intended to improve the conditions of the people." Dan Mattson, in other words, was a representative man of his time and place.

The Land Surveys

The thirty-seven and one-half square mile township, which includes the Golden and Silver Falls and the Glenn Creek Valley, is legally described as Township 24 South, Range 10 West of Willamette Meridian, Coos County, Oregon. For short, it's called Township 24-10. Recorded time began in that township in 1879. Before land can be transferred with all legal solemnity it has to be surveyed and recorded. In 1879, W. H. Byars surveyed the west boundary under contract with the federal government. In his field notes he makes no mention of the falls, and points out that "this township contains but little land fit for agriculture." He was certainly correct, but he says very little else of interest. His note of October 6, 1879, says, "Owing to ill health Henry Rhodes quit and James Brown employed as chain carrier." That's about all we can glean from Byars.

---

[6] Gaston, vol. 4, p. 518.

It wasn't until 1896 that the township was subdivided into its constituent thirty-six sections. The surveyors were A. Gosmer and E. O. Worrick, and they give us more interesting field notes than we got from W. H. Byars. Each of the thirty-six sections of a township is ideally one mile square, and each section is usually further subdivided into sixteen forty-acre "forties," giving a total of 23,040 acres to a standard township.

Imposing a rectangular survey onto a spherical world means that from time to time a township has to contain more or less than its ideal 23,040 acres, however, and the west boundary of Township 24-10 was one of the places where such adjustments were made. Gosmer and Worrick, in their re-survey, gave the six sections along the west boundary an additional four forties each, to compensate for the cumulative error due to the earth being round instead of flat. Sections 1 through 5, along the north boundary, were made a little smaller than the standard one mile square, and as a result Township 24-10 contains about 952 acres more than an ideal township, and is a bit irregular in shape. Things up in Township 24-10 are a little bigger than life, and a little out of kilter with the rest of the world!

During the survey, only four dwellings were located: the dwellings of John Hendrickson, Elizabeth Ott, Joseph Schapers, and Joe Larson. These were the only signs of habitation indicated in the entire township of thirty-seven and one-half square miles during the subdivision survey in 1896. There was one more homestead granted later. On March 19, 1904, George Schapers proved up on his claim to the 160 acres, which includes the Golden Falls. Other than his cabin, which was a necessary "improvement" to meet the requirements of the Homestead Act, it seems that nothing was done with his place. Most of it is now included as part of the Golden and Silver Falls State Park.

As they re-surveyed the west boundary, they came upon John Hendrickson's house in Section 19, on lower Glenn Creek. They crossed a fence, then the creek, then located the house, crossed another fence, and then crossed the wagon road and surveyed on north, staying one forty west of the Silver Falls. John Hendrickson proved up on his homestead on September 28, 1904. If his house was there in 1896 when this survey was done, that means he was there at least eight years prior to getting title to the land. The Homestead Act at that time required a minimum of five years.

The survey was approved at the office of the surveyor general in Portland on July 9, 1897. Actual settlers who had been living on the land had three months in which to file their claims. Any land unclaimed after that time could be filed on by outsiders.

Jerd Schapers' splash dam, East Fork T 25S, R 10W

Homesteading on the East Fork
By Emil R. Peterson from an interview with Hanna Stora
From Peterson & Powers, *A Century of Coos and Curry* (1952) pp. 330–31

European immigrants first sought jobs but soon learned that Uncle Sam was offering free farms. Such a one was Alfred Stora. He came in 1881 from Finland, worked for awhile in his uncle Matt Stora's logging camp, and then began to look around for a piece of that free land. He found it on the east fork of the Millicoma River where Glen Creek comes in near the Golden Falls. The place had the making of a good farm, but a bachelor on an isolated homestead finds the long winter evenings rather lonesome.

This was the case with Alfred Stora. He thought of a girl he had known in Finland when both were in their teens. Possibly he sent for her, possibly she just chanced to come to Coos Bay. Anyway, she arrived about 1890. Her name was Hannah Strandell.

Just the other day she laughed as she recalled those days of 60 years ago. She remembered her boat ride up South Coos River to the McKnight place; she remembered how kind Mrs. McKnight was, showing the strange, bashful foreign girl to her room and asking her what her name was. Hannah, not understanding English, just shook her head — "No understand."

In 1893 Hannah Strandell became Mrs. Alfred Stora and went to reside on the Stora homestead near the Golden Falls, 11 miles above Allegany.

Four children were born. Neighbors moved into the community. The Glen Creek school was built.

At first there were no roads, only rough trails that soon were widened into sled roads, and later made passable for wagons.

For a third of a century the Storas lived here. In the early years, Alfred worked in the logging camps while Hannah cared for the home; looked after the children, made garden, milked 10 or 12 cows, made butter which was put up into two-pound rolls and sold at 35 cents a roll, or often put up in tubs or barrels and sold to the logging camps and mills at about 15 cents a pound.

They raised some beef cattle, and sold dressed beef at four cents a pound when they could sell it at all. Once the Storas butchered five small hogs. Mr. Stora hauled the pork 11 miles to Allegany; put it into a skiff; rowed all the way down the river to the bay, then down Coos Bay to North Bend, where he thought he would find a ready market for the pork. He sold half a hog there at three cents a pound. Then he rowed back up to Marshfield, where he made the rounds and managed to sell one hog to a boarding house on time — and the time is still running.

Then he had to row back up Coos River to Allegany, where he hitched up his team and drove the 11 miles, arriving home 24 hours after he had started out. The Storas then had three and a half hogs to salt down for their own use. In recalling the incident, Mrs. Stora said, "We had pork, and pork and more pork."

(Reprinted with permission of Coos County Historical Museum)

The Patient Panther
By Charlotte Mahaffy[7]

It must have been the year 1898. Jesse [Ott] was about twelve years old. He and his mother, blue-eyed good looking Mrs. Elizabeth Ott, were returning from Allegany to their wilderness home beyond Golden Falls. Accompanying the couple was a small cur-dog and two horses, one of which was carrying a pack of provisions.

There was stillness that seemed to possess the earth as mother and son proceeded along the narrow, timbered canyon. Suddenly, like a flash of lightning their dog dashed up the steep, woodsy mountain. there was a bristling disturbance, the dog had espied a panther. At first the wild creature seemed to be petrified; finally, it took refuge on a log which the wind had felled bridge-like onto a green fir tree.

Jesse, knowing that he was only a mile from home, rode horseback for his gun, a 45-70! Meanwhile, Mrs. Ott was waiting with the pack horse as an excited "pooch" stood watch over a tawny-colored animal crouched on the log fifteen feet above the.

Before long, Jesse returned from his mission bringing not only a weapon but also his uncle George Schapers. It was Schapers who took "a bead" on the varmint and then fired the fatal shot.

Jesse Ott, 1886–1989. River-boat captain
and a legend in his own time.

---

[7] From *Coos River Echoes*, pp. 114–5. Reprinted with permission.

PART THREE

THE HOMESTEADS

Joe Schapers Homestead, about 1913.

Home is local historians' measure of every other place.
--Joseph A. Amato, *Rethinking Home*

GLENN CREEK VALLEY

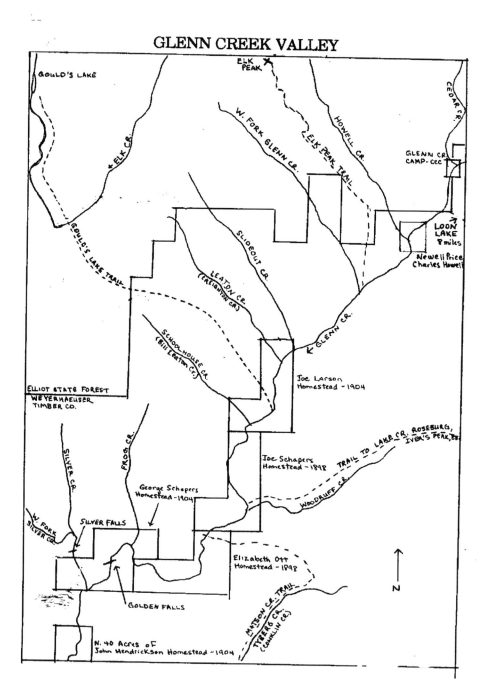

Chapter Four

The Joe Schapers Homestead

Joe Schapers (1857–1939)

At the corner of Sections 7, 8, 17, and 18, the field notes of the original 1896 survey mention Joseph Schapers' house. According to the notes, the soils were both of the "first and second rate." The timber was fir, hemlock, alder, and "chitemwood." The corner was just above the trail, across the field from the house.

According to Joe Schapers' testimony for his homestead proof on the 160 acres, the house was already there when he established residence in July, 1891. It was a four-room, one-story house of 16 x 24 feet. The original settler was said to be a man named Harris. We know nothing about him. He was there several years prior to the government survey and because he was gone before the land could be filed on, his name does not appear on any records connected with it. The story as it came down to Alice Wilkinson Allen is that when Joe Schapers arrived in 1891 the improvements, including the house, belonged to a widow. This would presumably be Harris' widow, and Joe Schapers bought these improvements from her. The land, of course, was un-surveyed government land, in the public domain.

The record is not clear as to what outbuildings and other improvements were there at the time Joe Schapers established residence. In any case, at the time he filed for final proof on the land, there was a barn 36 x 40 feet, a smoke house, chicken house, about one mile of fencing, and an orchard with 120 trees. About forty acres of land had been cleared. He estimated the value of the place to be $1,000 at that time.

Joe Schapers testified that he was absent from the homestead for five months during 1891 and 1892. According to the law, any absence of six months or more might have forfeited his right to the property. Other than that he was not absent more than two or three months at a time, working out for wages. From 1896–98 he was never absent more than a week or so at a time, according to the testimony.

Joe Schapers cultivated crops on the homestead for eight seasons prior to obtaining final proof on it. The first year he claimed cultivation of one-eighth acre, gradually increasing each season until he had about eight acres under cultivation by 1898. An average of one acre increase per year represented more work than it is possible to imagine, when we add to it the building of outbuildings and fences, and slash clearing of forty acres during the same time. Remember, all the clearing was done by hand. There was no power equipment of any kind. The trees were cut by hand, the stumps were burned, the fields were leveled, and an acre at a time the wilderness was converted to a proper homestead.

The witnesses who were listed in potential support of Joe Schapers' claim were William W. R. Glenn, Simon Anderson, Joseph Larson, and Charles Nelson. Only two of the witnesses were required to accompany Joe to Marshfield for the final proof. Glenn and Simon Anderson were the two who went. Both of their forms contained essentially the same information.

Glenn had been living on his own homestead at Glenn Creek Junction in 1891 when Joe Schapers moved in above the falls. In 1898, at the time of Joe's final proof, Glenn was sixty-three years old and living in retirement about a half mile below Hodges Creek, on property which presently belongs to me. Glenn thought Joe Schapers had cultivated four or five acres or possibly more. He added, "Every year that I visited the place, at least three seasons, he had crops on the land. I think he raised crops seven seasons."

Because it was unsurveyed public domain land, residence was allowed prior to filing the homestead entry. Joe had established residence in 1891. The survey had been approved in Portland on July 9, 1897. It wasn't until April 27, 1898, that Joe Schapers filed his homestead entry, application number 9117, for which he paid the required $16 filing fee.

It is my understanding that actual settlers had only ninety days following approval of the survey in which to file their entries. After ninety days, anyone could file. This being the case, Joe had run the risk of someone else filing on his place because it had been eight months since the survey was approved. It may have been that owing to the remoteness of the area the settlers didn't know that the survey had been approved until almost too late. There were already a large number of speculators and agents of railroad and timber companies hovering about the Roseburg Land Office, and it would have been easy to lose out altogether.

Alice Allen and Marvin Stemmerman remember a story that was handed down concerning the filing. There was evidently some excitement about the falls at that time. If the 90-day grace period had passed before the settlers were aware of it, and it seems that it had, then there was every chance that someone else could file on the property. There was plenty of reason for concern. My understanding of the story, when matched with the homestead documents which I have in my possession, follows:

Probably Joe Schapers expected to leave for Roseburg with Joe Larson on April 25, 1898, to file the entry claims on the 27th. It would have taken two days to get there: one day to walk the twenty-five miles to Scottsburg, and the second day by stage coach up the Umpqua through Elkton to Roseburg. In the morning, however, when Joe Schapers got to Larson's cabin, no one was home.

As the story goes, Joe Schapers went inside and found that the stove was still warm. Alarmed at the possibility that his neighbor, or someone else, might attempt some hanky-panky at the land office — and plenty of that was going on at the time — Joe Schapers hurried home, packed some provisions, and walked to Roseburg by the most direct route. This was via the trail up Woodruff Creek to Lake Creek, then over another divide to the Umpqua River somewhere between Elkton and Sutherlin. The walking distance to Roseburg via that route, through the woods, would have been about forty-five miles. Joe Schapers would probably have gotten to Roseburg about the same time as Joe Larson.

Why Joe Larson had left that morning without Joe Schapers we will never know. He might not have known that Joe Schapers intended to go with him. Joe Schapers may have been late, and Joe Larson wanted to be sure to get to Scottsburg in time to catch the stage. Whatever really happened, and we'll never know, the record is clear that on April 27, 1898, both Joe Larson and Joe Schapers filed their entry claims to their respective homesteads. The filings were at the Roseburg Land Office, and they used each other's names as witnesses. One supposes that they returned to Upper Glenn Creek together.

Joe Schapers then placed notices in the *Coos Bay News*, a weekly newspaper published in Marshfield, for the weeks of May 31st to July 19th, 1898. Because this land was unsurveyed at the time the homesteaders established residence on it, and they had more than fulfilled their five years residency requirements, they needed only to publish six weekly notices in the newspaper prior to making final proof of their claims.

The final affidavit was made at Marshfield on July 28. Testimony of the two witnesses, William W. R. Glenn and Simon Anderson, along with Joseph Schapers' own "Testimony of Claimant," was made at that time. The Homestead Certificate, number 4375, was issued later, signed in the name of William McKinley, President of the United States. It was dated November 11, 1898.

Joe Schapers was Elizabeth Ott's oldest brother and his homestead adjoined hers. He received his patent the same day as his sister: November 11, 1898. He didn't tell anyone, but now that he owned his homestead in fee simple, he was ready for a wife. And he got one, a widow with four young children, two boys and two girls. The history of the Joe Schapers place, therefore, is quite different from the history of Elizabeth's place. The Joe Schapers place had three generations of the same family during its sixty years of existence. Neither of the other two places above the falls have that continuity.

Laura Wilkinson Schapers raised her four children on this homestead. The girls, Agnes and Jane, both married boys their age. Agnes married Alfred Leaton from the next place up; Jane married George Stemmerman from further down, on the East Fork. The boys, Robert and Cleland, grew up on the place then married in Marshfield. They moved back up to the ranch at the beginning of the Great Depression in 1930.

Cle stayed, and with the help of his mother Laura, raised his two daughters, Alice and Patricia, on the place. When Joe Schapers died in 1939 he left it to his two stepsons, Cle and Bob. Cle later bought his brother's interest and it has since been known as the Wilkinson Place.

From May 1940, until mid 1945, my dad, George Youst, had a sawmill there. The first setting was on the hill above the county road where he cut forty acres. He then moved the mill into the field, opposite the mouth of Woodruff Creek, where a dam was built for a mill pond. Later, a second dam was built about a half mile upstream so that the timber from the north forty could be logged into the water. No logging trucks, roads, or cats were used in any of this operation. Environmental impact was slight, compared to today's logging.

Cle's daughters grew up and moved on. Alice went to college and married, remaining in Coos County. Patricia went into the army, and then on to make a living. Cle lived out his middle years trapping and picking ferns until, finally, in 1958 the county closed the road above the falls. Cle sold the old ranch to Weyerhaeuser Timber Company, and the bridge across the base of Silver Falls was removed. Cle and his trapping partner, Baltimore Calvert Crane, were the last people to live above the falls.

There is an addendum to this history of the Joe Schapers place, however. In the '60's, Earl Barker arranged a trade with the Weyerhaeuser Timber Company whereby he deeded to Weyerhaeuser the timberland of the old Elizabeth Ott place in exchange for the bottomland of the old Joe Schapers place. The result is that the timberland now belongs to Weyerhaeuser and the bottomland containing the former fields of the two homesteads are in a separate ownership. The current owners of the bottomland are John and Mary Muenchrath.

Left to right: Laura Tomer Wilkinson Schapers and her children Robert, Cleland, Agnes, and Jane, and her husband, Joe Schapers.

Chapter Five

The Elizabeth Ott Homestead

Elizabeth Ott Tyberg, 1864–1939

The first place one arrived after ascending the Golden Falls was the homestead of Elizabeth Ott. The original subdivision survey went right across her meadow, heading north between Section 17 and 18. The survey field notes say the surveyors crossed a cattle trail running east and west, then the creek bottom and a fence, with "Elizabeth's house bearing five chains distant." They left the meadow and crossed the trail which ran northeast. Below the falls, at the Hendrickson place, the trail had become a wagon road by 1896. Above the falls, at Elizabeth Ott's, it was still a trail.

Her brother Joe had walked to Roseburg to make his homestead entry on April 27, 1898. Elizabeth made her entry in Marshfield on May 14. She testified that "owing to distance I am unable to appear at the District Land Office to make this affidavit." She listed Walter S. Bunch, John Brazzil, Simon Anderson, and William W. R. Glenn as potential witnesses.

Joe and Elizabeth made their final proof together in Marshfield on July 28, 1898. This was ninety-two days after Joe had filed in Roseburg and seventy-five days after Elizabeth had filed in Marshfield. They used the same two witnesses, Simon Anderson and William W. R. Glenn.

Elizabeth testified that she had settled on the land commencing May 1891, at which time her house was built. The house was 16 x 18 feet, three rooms, one-story. There were three barns and outbuildings, one mile of fencing, a small orchard, and about thirty-five acres of land that had been slashed and cleared "in part." As to the character of the land, she said it was "covered with brush and timber and moss, valuable for farming and grazing." She estimated the value at $800.

Elizabeth received the patent to her land on November 11, 1898, about sixteen months after the survey was approved. The handsome certificate, signed in the name of President William McKinley, is still in possession of her descendants. Her certificate number is 4374; the certificate of her brother Joe is 4375.

After Elizabeth married Alfred Tyberg in 1903, her homestead became known as the Tyberg place. They had one daughter, Suzie, born May 8, 1908. She died of typhoid fever December 13, 1916. Elizabeth's progeny from her previous marriage to James Ott were living in comparative comfort on the tidewater of Coos River. They evidently had no interest in living on this wilderness homestead, and there were no descendants on the Tyberg side.

Elizabeth died in 1939, her brother Charlie in 1941, and Jerd two years later. At that time the estate was sold to Roy Grant of Allegany, and he sold the timber to Vic Dimmick in 1943. Dimmick put in a sawmill in the field near the old house, built a dam on Glenn Creek, and logged the timber on the south and east side of the creek. The mill was there until 1950.

During the time Roy Grant owned it, Daisy and Joe Morris lived in the old house and picked ferns for a living. The swordferns are used by florists and there has been a market for them through most of this century. Thousands of tons of them have been shipped from Coos Bay over the years. Upper Glenn Creek has been a good place for people who could get by on the cash that ferns could bring in. When Joe and Daisy left, the house was abandoned and was not lived in again.

Later, the place was bought by Earl (Curly) Barker, a Coos Bay businessman. The buildings were all destroyed and a Christmas tree plantation established. Curly flew a light plane and used the meadow as a runway. The Christmas tree plantation was not maintained, and today the meadow is a tangle of non-native species such as Scotch pine and other favorites of the Christmas tree trade.

When Elizabeth's son Jess Ott heard that trees were being planted in the meadow he said that he would not be able to go up there again. It was too distressing to think that after his uncles had spent a lifetime clearing that part of the Glenn Creek Valley of snags, trees, and stumps to make it one of the most attractive homesteads imaginable, a stranger was planting trees back on it. The Christmas tree plantation was no doubt established primarily because of business deductions permitted under the federal and state tax laws.

Elizabeth's homestead, facing north from across Glenn Creek. Elizabeth in foreground; house across meadow.

My Grandmother, Elizabeth Ott
By Harold Ott[1]

My grandmother, Elizabeth Ott, came to Allegany from Drain in 1890 with her sons Sam, age 8, and Jesse, age 4. Jesse said that he couldn't remember much about coming except in crossing the Umpqua River; everyone had to be carried out of the boat. It seems that the route was down the beach and they had to be ferried across each river or bay. After a couple of years, my grandmother homesteaded her place above the falls.

She later married Alfred Tyberg and they had a daughter, Susie, who died in 1916 at the age of 8 of typhoid fever. Alfred's legs were quite crippled and he had to walk with a couple of canes. With the exception of turning the cream separator, it was very hard for him to do much of the farm work, so it was up to "Lizzie" to do most of it including the plowing, planting, fence building, milking and most everything else.

Believe me, she was good at it; she asked no odds of anyone. She proved up on her farm, raised her sons, paid her bills and made a living, even saving a little. (I wish her grandson had her ability!) She once loaned some money with a piece of property in Marshfield as security. She had to take the land instead of the money. Of course that was a long time ago and it wasn't worth what it is now. Hoskings and Gething had their station on the spot later.

She, Alfred, and Charlie went to the Pendleton Roundup one year after she bought a new Ford with a starter, Rocky Mountain brakes and a Rucstle axle. The made it O.K. but everyone marveled at the feat. She survived all the driving and died in her home above the falls after a lengthy illness. She had a lonely life and a couple of instances I believe would not be out of place.

One time when her sons were staying in Allegany to go to school, she was all alone. She was so lonely that she made piles of brush all around and at night she would set them afire and then sit and try to imagine that there were lots of people sitting around their campfires. That seemed to make the nights more endurable. Another time she decided to ask Tom Blaine to let Jesse, who was working for him, to come home for a while to help do some of the farm work. Tom had the place that was later owned by Ed and Rosella Noah. He was a very nice man, but he didn't realize that my grandmother was lonesome for her son, and Jesse was a real good worker, so he sent another boy working for him up to help her instead. Such a disappointment.

About 1913, a stage line was started to take people from Marshfield area to Drain, where the passengers made connections with the railroad for Portland and

---

[1] From "History of Allegany," by Harold Ott, in *Glancing Back (Pioneer Lore)*, Coos County Historical Association, North Bend, 1972, pp. 15–16. Reprinted with permission.

other points. The *Rainbow* would leave Marshfield at 6:00 a.m., arrive at Allegany around seven. The passengers then boarded a stage where they were transported to Scottsburg, by way of Loon Lake and Camp Creek, where they transferred to another for Drain. Meanwhile the steamer picked up freight and passengers and made the regular trip to Marshfield, arriving there about nine. At 2:00 p.m. she started back up the river and at Allegany, unloaded everything and made ready to take the afternoon stage passengers to town. During the season she was a busy boat.

The stages were 1912 Cadillacs. A man named Denny was the first driver, followed by a Mr. Foote. I don't know the names of the drivers that operated the connecting stage from Scottsburg to Drain.

Auto stages on Glenn Creek Bridge, Glenn Junction.

Elizabeth Schapers Ott Tyberg
By Erma Ott[2]

James Pasteur Ott and Elizabeth Schapers were married in Big Spring Missouri. They moved to Americus MO. where Samuel Robert was born in 1881. They moved to Drain, OR. where Jesse James was born in 1886. Jesse was Harold's father. They were divorced and Elizabeth with her two sons came to Allegany in 1890. Her brothers, Joe, Gerhard (Jerd), George, and Charlie Schapers, also came. Joe and Elizabeth homesteaded adjoining property located above the Golden Falls. Jerd and George started prospecting in the hills. Charlie stayed to help Elizabeth get her place in order. Considering all the trees and brush that was growing everywhere this was quite an undertaking. She married Alfred Tyberg a very fine man but terrible crippled with rheumatism. He could hardly walk and had to use a couple of canes to get about but had powerful shoulders and did his part.

---

[2] Written after the reunion picnic on September 14, 1991.

"Lizzie" (as they called her) was the driving force of the family. She was very strong and had the ability to plan things efficiently. They cleared fields, built a house and barn along with other necessary buildings.

They planted fruit trees, apple, pears, plums, cherries, etc. They got some Jersey cattle and some pigs. They were truly self-sufficient, raising everything they needed, having to buy only salt, sugar and flour as a rule. Not only was it an expense, but transportation was non-existent at that time. As they were too far away to sell milk to people, they got a separator and hauled cream on a sled to Allegany about once a week to be shipped to the creamery in Marshfield by boat. That separator was where Alfred shined. He made a sturdy stool about the right height and turned the separator crank. That was his job for many years. They raised pigs and calves on the skimmed milk. The surplus meat was taken to town and sold.

Sam and Jesse meanwhile started out on their own. They began as hired hands for the farmers that needed help. When they got older, Sam started working in the logging camps and eventually became a donkey puncher. Jesse went to work on the sternwheeler *Alert*. He stayed with the boats most of his working days.

The two adjoining farms above continued to provide a living. A sizable creek ran through both places, but the falls stopped any fish from traveling upstream. Such trout that were there had to be planted. A road of sorts was built from Allegany to above the falls, eventually going to Loon Lake. However, only the stouthearted would attempt to drive it. Lionel can tell you about it. Harold would tell me how he enjoyed to visit Grandma Tyberg, so we spent many joyous hours visiting. She possessed such a wonderful sense of humor and always made us feel welcome and glad that we came.

Elizabeth Ott Tyberg (1864–1939), Suzie (1908–1916), Alfred Tyberg (1874–1931).

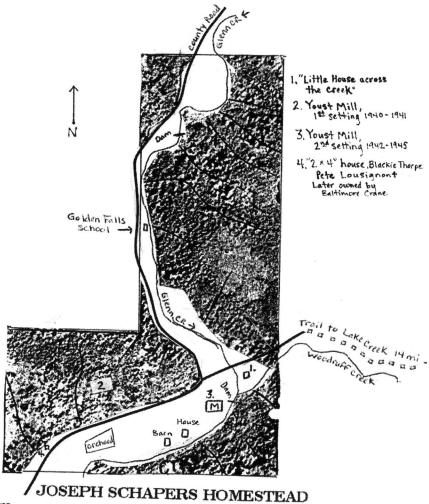

1. "Little House across the creek"
2. Youst Mill, 1st setting 1940 - 1941
3. Youst Mill, 2nd setting 1942 - 1945
4. "2 × 4" house, Blackie Thorpe Pete Lousignont Later owned by Baltimore Crane

JOSEPH SCHAPERS HOMESTEAD
(Known as the Wilkinson Place after Joe Schapers died in 1939)

SE 1/4 NW 1/4, E ½ SW 1/4, SW 1/4 SW 1/4 of Section 8, Twnshp 24S of Range 10 WWM Containing 160 acres. Homestead certificate # 4375. Est. residence July, 1891; Homestead entry April 27, 1898. Final Proof July 30, 1898. Patented Nov. 11, 1898. Willed to Robert and Cleland Wilkinson, 1939; logged 1940–45; sold to Weyerhaeuser 1958. Land exchange with Earl Barker. Current owners of the bottomland, John and Mary Muenchrath. Current owners of timberland, Weyerhaeuser Company. S ½ NE 1/4, Sec. 18 and W ½ NW 1/4 of Sec. 17 of Twnshp 24S of Range 10 WWM. 160 acres. Homestead Certificate #4374. Est. residence May, 1891; Homestead Entry May 14, 1898; Final Proof July 30, 1898; Patented Nov. 11, 1898. Inherited by Jesse Ott upon death of his mother Elizabeth in 1939. Sold to Roy Grant – logged by Vic Dimmick, 1943–48. Later sold to Earl Barker who traded the logged off timberland to Weyerhaeuser in exchange for the bottomland of the Wilkinson place. Current owners of the bottomland, John and Mary Muenchrath. Current owners of the timberland, Weyerhaeuser Timber Company.

62

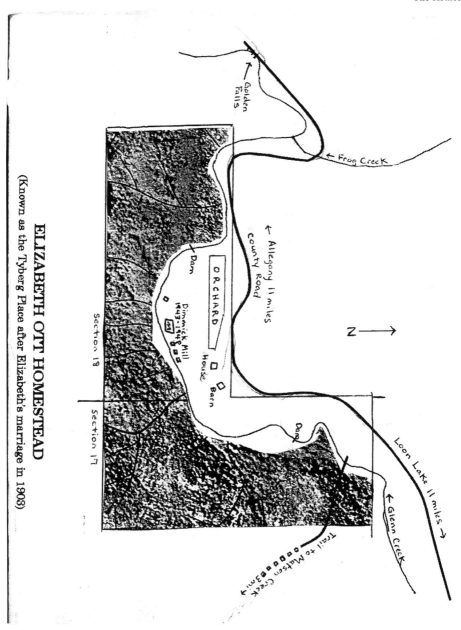

ELIZABETH OTT HOMESTEAD

(Known as the Tyberg Place after Elizabeth's marriage in 1903)

S ½ NE 1/4, Sec 18 and W ½ NW 1/4 of Sec 17, Twnshp 24S of Range 10 WWM, containing 160 acres. Homestead Certificate # 4374. Est. residence May, 1891. Homestead entry, May 14, 1898. Final Proof, July 30, 1898. Patented November 11, 1898. Inherited by Jesse and Sam Ott upon the death of their mother, Elizabeth, in 1939. Sold to Roy Grant, logged by Vic Dimmick 1943–48. Later sold to Earl Barker who traded the logged off timberland to Weyerhaeuser in exchange for the creek bottom of the Wilkinson Place. Current owners of the bottomland: John and Mary Muenchrath; Timberland owned by Weyerhaeuser.

63

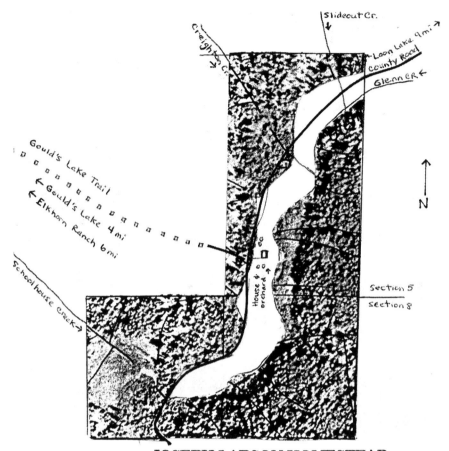

JOSEPH LARSON HOMESTEAD

(Known as the Leaton Place, 1911-1932; Middleton Place after 1932)

NE 1/4 NW 1/4, NW 1/4 NE /4, Sec. 8, W ½ SE ½ SE 1/4 Sec. 5, Tnshp 24S of Range 10 WWM, containing 160 acres. Homestead certificate # 5483. Est. residence Nov. 1894; homestead entry April 27, 1898; U. S. Citizenship Sept. 6, 1902; Final Proof Dec. 8, 1902; Patented Jan. 27, 1904. Sold to C. E. Lennon, Minneapolis, Minnesota, May 10, 1910 for $6,000. Conveyed to Coos Bay Timber Co., later Waterford Timber Co., both of Minneapolis. Leased to William Leaton and family until 1932; then to Slim Middleton until 1939. Sold to Weyerhaeuser Company, 1937. Last tenants, George Youst family, summer, 1941. Current owner, Weyerhaeuser Timber Company. Logged, 1970's.

Chapter Six

The Joe Larson Homestead

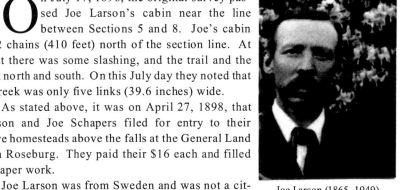

On July 17, 1896, the original survey passed Joe Larson's cabin near the line between Sections 5 and 8. Joe's cabin was 6.22 chains (410 feet) north of the section line. At that point there was some slashing, and the trail and the creek ran north and south. On this July day they noted that Glenn Creek was only five links (39.6 inches) wide.

As stated above, it was on April 27, 1898, that Joe Larson and Joe Schapers filed for entry to their respective homesteads above the falls at the General Land Office in Roseburg. They paid their $16 each and filled out the paper work.

Joe Larson was from Sweden and was not a citizen of the United States. He therefore had been required

Joe Larson (1865–1949)

to declare under oath that it was his "bona fide intention to become a citizen of the United States of America and to renounce forever all allegiance and fidelity to all and any foreign Prince, Potentate, State of Sovereignty whatsoever, and particularly to the King of Norway and Sweden." He had taken this oath previously, October 30, 1894, in obvious anticipation of the day he would file for a homestead. In November of 1894 he had moved onto the property. A copy of his Declaration of Intention was filed with the homestead entry paperwork.

The four witnesses listed by Larson to prove his continuous residence and cultivation of the land were his neighbor Joseph Schapers and fellow Swedes from the East Fork: Knut Nelson, Simon Anderson, and Alfred Tyberg. Tyberg was soon to marry Joe Schapers' sister Elizabeth Ott.

In open court at Coos County on the 8th day of September 1902, Joseph Larson became a naturalized citizen of the United States. John F. Hall and Alfred Tyberg were witnesses that he had been a resident of the United States for at least five years, and within the State of Oregon for one year past, that he had behaved as a man of good moral character, etc. Again, he took an oath "that he doth absolutely and entirely renounce and abjure all allegiance and fidelity to every foreign Prince, Potentate, State or Sovereignty whatever and particularly to that of the King of Norway and Sweden."

The following week the first notice of his intention to file final proof appeared in the *Marshfield Sun*, a weekly newspaper. The notice ran for six weeks, the first on September 18 and the last on October 23, 1902. Publisher Jesse Luce signed the affidavit of publication.

The final proof was presented November 1, 1902, in Marshfield. The witnesses were Alfred Tyberg and Simon Anderson. The testimony indicated that Larson moved onto the land on November 1894, and established his residence at that time. His improvements on the property included a two-room house 24 x 13 feet with a kitchen attached, 16 x 12 feet. There were two barns. One was 20 x 35 feet and the other was 22 x 30 feet. He had one acre of orchard and sixteen acres of land cleared with about 3/4 mile of fence. He estimated the value at $1,000.

The General Land Office was extremely busy in 1902. Agents of the Northern Pacific and Southern Pacific Railroads and of various large lumber companies from Minnesota, along with speculators and crooks of every description were all hovering about trying to capitalize on some of the last and best of the free timberland left in North America. Activities that took place at the Roseburg Land Office around that time resulted in later indictments and convictions in what came to be known as the great Oregon Land Fraud cases.

Because of "land office business" at the Land Office, Joe Larson's final proof was delayed. There is on file a handwritten memo dated December 8, 1902, as follows:

> The honorable Commissioner,
> General Land Office, Wash. D.C.
>
> Sir
>
> We have the honor to report that Joseph Larson made final proof on H. A. 9118 on November 1/02 and the papers were filed November 4/02. Because of the numerous final proofs etc at this office we could not examine said proof until today and therefore the final papers are not until now issued.
>
> Very respectfully,
> J. T. Bright, Register

The Minnesota Connection

The timber resources of the Great Lakes states had virtually been exhausted by the turn of the century, and timber companies in that area looked to the Pacific Northwest for a fresh start. The records of the deeds at the Coos County Courthouse reflect that after C. E. Lennon of Minneapolis purchased Joe Larson's homestead in 1910, it was immediately conveyed to the Coos Bay Timber Company, also of Minneapolis. Lennon was evidently an agent of the Coos Bay Timber Company and his name appears quite often in connection with timberland conveyances in Coos County.

It is not clear from the records at the Coos County Courthouse what happened to the land title during the ensuing years. A deed dated March 24, 1937, shows that the Waterford Lumber Company, a Minnesota corporation, sold the property to Weyerhaeuser Timber Company "for one dollar" as of that date. The document was signed by Emmett Butler, President, and Pierce Butler, Jr., Secretary.

Also during March 1937, H. B. Lennon, widow of C. E. Lennon, conveyed other timber properties within Township 24-10, Section 20, to Weyerhaeuser. By that time, Weyerhaeuser held title to virtually all of the land within the township except the

160-acre homesteads of Elizabeth Ott and Joe Schapers, a few forties belonging to the state and a small parcel belonging to the Butler Corporation. In other words, Weyerhaeuser had more than 23,000 of the 23,992 acres within Township 24-10.

The Larson brothers at Allegany, 1908. Charles Wildahl, P. E. (Ed) Larson, Joe Larson. Cropped from a family photo.

Joe Larson, 1865–1949

Joe Larson's two nieces, Adelien and Florence Larson, lived in Coos Bay and provided me with further information on his life. Adelien told me that Joe Larson came originally to Minnesota from Sweden in about 1886 and was in Marshfield, Oregon, by 1893. He had worked on a jetty somewhere on the Columbia River. When that job was finished he came to Marshfield and the Coos River quarry where he was a powder man on the "first rock for the Coos Bay jetty."

Adelien stated that at his 160-acre homestead above Golden Falls "he had a barn for two horses and two or three cows, and a small house. Apple trees were planted on the hillside. He raised hay crops for his livestock. He bought and raised calves to sell to cattle buyers and to Buckly Bros. He worked on the road over Golden Falls as a powder man." The story of the road appears below under the heading, "Glenn Creek to Douglas County Line Road."

Joe Larson had a sister, Nellie Anderson, who became a widow around 1900. She came to Golden Falls from South Dakota after her husband died. She had four young children, the oldest about eight years and the youngest an infant. These children did farm chores and were sent to Glenn Junction School. The two boys were William (1894–1985) and Dewey (1896–1963). The two girls were Ethel (b. 1900) and Edith (b. 1892). It has been said there was a cabin at Glenn Junction to board the children while they attended school there. Nellie remarried while at Golden Falls, her new husband was Warner Peterson. They had a daughter, Hilda, and a son, Carl.

On May 10, 1910 — Joe, still an unmarried man — sold his homestead to the aforementioned C. E. Lennon of Minneapolis, Minnesota. He got $6,000 for it, which seems to be quite an inflated price. It seems that the Larson brothers had a good sense of business.

Oscar Lundberg was another of the Swedes at Allegany. His daughter Maxine McGuire told me of an evening when her father came into Upper Glenn Creek at the Larson place. For years Oscar was responsible for taking care of the trails into the fire lookouts. He knew all of the Coos River drainage like the back of his hand — North Fork and South Fork. Well, at Larson's no one was home. Oscar, rather than sleep outside that night, went into the house. He told Maxine that when he saw "a picture of the King of Norway on the wall" he knew it was all right. One suspects that some of those Swedes were more loyal to the King of Norway and Sweden than the naturalization oath would have led one to believe!

Joe Larson married a young Swedish woman in 1912 and lived in Eastside for a time. They later moved to Turlock, California, where he and his family had a fine small farm. Joe sold the farm in California in 1929 and returned to his childhood farm near Veinge, Sweden, where he lived twenty more years. He died in Sweden in 1949, at the age of 84. His only daughter, Hazel, was living in Seattle, Washington, in 1991.

Chapter Seven

George Schapers Homestead – The Golden Falls

The bulk of the land which later became the Golden and Silver Falls State Park was originally in the George Schapers homestead. George had proved up on that land in 1904 when he was thirty years old. Harold Ott told me that George was a "geologist," or at least was interested in the economic geology on the area.

George and his brother Jerd are said to have spent a lot of their time prospecting for valuable minerals. They sluiced out tons of sandstone, extracting from it garnet, zircon, and other trace minerals. They were sure that there was gold or platinum present. It is now known that the drainage of the Coos River is virtually all sedimentary sandstone, siltstone, and mudstone. The likelihood of economically valuable minerals is almost zero. On the other hand, Warren Browning (see Chapter 25) told me that he had seen garnets of gem size that Jerd had found, and one wonders how garnets ever got into the formation. George and Jerd were actually not that far off base after all.

Water wheel at the mine of George and Jerd Schapers, East Fork. Virginia and Keith Ott, Jeanne Crane in photo.

The expectation of finding gold or other valuable minerals in the area was very real at the time that George Schapers was homesteading the Golden Falls. A news item in the *Coos Bay Times* dated December 25, 1906, had the headline, "Interest in Gold Find: Discovery Has Caused Many to Take Up Claims on Kentucky Slough." Kentuck Slough is sedimentary, somewhat similar to Golden Falls, except that there are isolated basalt deposits on the headwaters of Kentuck. In any case, there was a small "gold rush" to Kentuck Slough in 1906. The newspaper stated that "all the claims within two miles of the first discovery have been staked out. Over a hundred persons have gone up in the hopes they will find gold. . . . A quantity of ore will be shipped out of here soon and it will be learned exactly as to its real worth. If the find is as big as is thought it will be quite an important thing for the Bay country." Like many another optimistic article of its kind in the *Coos Bay Times* and its successor newspaper, nothing came of it. There was no gold.

Geologically, the Golden Falls is of considerable interest, however. The falls plunge over an escarpment some 285 feet high and is the one location in Coos County where the massive siltstone of the Tyee formation can be observed. The Tyee formation in Coos County, according to the geologist Ewart Baldwin, "is composed of up to 5,000 feet of primarily massive, greenish-gray, coarse to fine-grained, lithic wacke and rythmically bedded sandstone and siltstone." Fossil plant remains are common on some bedding planes, according to Baldwin.

In 1966 J. K. Trigger examined the sandstone of the Tyee formation for his University of Oregon master's thesis. He found that it was 20% quartz, 17% feldspar. "Accessory minerals compose about 10% of the rock and include biotite, muscovite, zircon, garnet, opaque minerals and detrital chlorite." About 32% of the rock is of igneous lithic fragments, mainly andesite. "Other types of fragments and chert . . . Ferromagnesian minerals present in some of the lithic fragments are completely or partly altered to chlorite."

It is possible at this juncture to question whether or not George Schapers took out his homestead claim to the Golden Falls in "good faith," as far as the Homestead Act was concerned. The Homestead Act of May 20, 1862, stated specifically that entry must be made for the purpose of actual *settlement and cultivation.* There were questions to be answered in the homestead proof which asked that the witnesses and the claimant "state specifically the character of this land." The answer would almost always be "ordinary farming and grazing." It would take a considerable stretch of the imagination to make the Golden Falls into valuable farming and grazing land!

Unfortunately, I did not obtain from the National Archives the homestead proof documents for the George Schapers homestead, and so I do not know who the witnesses were and what claims were made concerning cultivation, etc. The documents I received for the other three homesteads, however, included a "Non-Mineral Affidavit" which required that the claimant swear that "the land is essentially non-mineral land, and that his application therefore is not made for the purpose of fraudulently obtaining title to mineral land, but with the object of securing said land for agricultural purposes." In fairness to George, however, it can be said that some of the heavily timbered land adjacent to Frog Creek, in the two north forties of the homestead, are not overly steep, and could, if cleared, have been used as grazing land.

George Schapers cabin was evidently located at the site of the present day parking lot and picnic area of the Golden and Silver Falls State Park. The map of the road survey of 1900 shows at that location the square symbol used for a dwelling. It has the legend, "G. Schapers."

When we combine the homesteads of George with the homesteads of his sister Elizabeth and his brother Joe, we find that the family had 480 acres along Glenn Creek. Their properties ran almost three miles along that stream, from the bottom of Silver Falls to the top of Joe Schapers place. For a time, it was pretty much their empire. Joe and Elizabeth lived on their respective places until they died. Joe Schapers' stepchildren and step-grandchildren were raised on the "old ranch," as they called it. I believe that is what the framers of the Homestead Act had hoped would happen to the land given to "actual settlers."

Molly Stokes, 1892–1986. A Canadian nurse during WWI, she nursed Elizabeth Schapers Ott Tyberg through her last illness and remained above the falls for several more years with her husband Al.

The homesteads of George Schapers and of Joe Larson had fates somewhat different from what the framers of the Homestead Act had in mind. In 1909 both places were sold to C. E. Lennon, the timber speculator from Minnesota. These lands eventually went to the Waterford Lumber Company, also of Minneapolis, Minnesota, which in turn divested itself of the George Schapers homestead to the State of Oregon in 1936, to form the bulk of what is now the Golden and Silver Falls State Park. In 1937 Waterford sold the Joe Larson homestead to Weyerhaeuser Timber Company.

71

Chapter Eight

Neighbors and Successors to the Homesteads

The Price Place

Jesse Ott once told me the names of the places above the falls at the time that he was a young man. He said that Newell Price had the farthest place up. Coming downstream, one would pass the places of Joe Larson, Joe Schapers, and Elizabeth Ott. This matches exactly the map of the road survey of 1900.

In the oral histories I have collected, the Joe Larson homestead is sometimes called the "Price Place," but that is evidently an error, the result of fading memories. By the

The Newell Price cabin and clearing

time I started collecting information on the area, the name of Joe Larson had all but been forgotten. The name of Price is associated with the area, but no one who is living now knows for sure what the connection was.

There was a John Price and his family who settled at Allegany in 1890, and in 1896 had purchased the Bazzell farm at the mouth of Marlow Creek. This property was later purchased by Oscar Lundberg. His daughter Maxine remembers that Mr. Price was diabetic and died in the outhouse at the place. Not much more is known.

The Price who lived above the falls was Newell Price and may have been a brother or other relative of John Price. Newell and his wife had a son and daughter: Hazen and Pearl. Newell is buried at the Allegany Cemetery, but there is no legible date of either birth or death on his grave.

During the county road survey in 1900, Newell Price is shown as having his claim at the mouth of Howell Creek. This is a mile and a half northeast of the Larson place. Charlie Howell lived there for many years, up into the 1940's. If either Price or Howell ever obtained title to it, I could not find the record at the Coos County Courthouse.

After the first edition of this book was published, Benson Judy told me a story of his memory of Mrs. Price. Benson was born and raised at Ash Val-

l to r: Newell Price, Pearl (daughter), Hazen (son), Mrs. Price

ley. His father would sometimes drive the team and wagon the twenty-two miles over the mountain to Allegany to get provisions, and as a child Benson would sometimes go with him. The Price place was on the way, and Benson remembered his father stopping there to admire a strange poultry that Mrs. Price kept. They were Guinea hens, and the elder Mr. Judy was interested in perhaps buying some of them. He asked Mrs. Price how you could distinguish the males from the females. Mrs. Price started to speak, stopped, looked puzzled, and after some hesitation said apologetically, "I can tell it, but I can't say it!" Mrs. Price was not alone among people who lived in the backwoods and who could tell a good many things that they could not articulate. After perhaps eighty years, Benson Judy still remembered that one enigmatic remark of Mrs. Price. We know nothing more about her.

The Leaton Family

William Leaton (1848–1940)

The tenants of the old Joe Larson homestead from about 1909 until 1932 or so were the Leatons. These included old Dad (William) Leaton (1848–1940), who was originally from Kimbolton, England, and his family. He and his wife Hattie Secord and their various sons and daughters came to Coos County from Michigan at various times between 1905 and 1909. I believe Hattie came out in 1907, along with her mother Bridget Rourke, who had originally come from Ireland as a baby. Hattie died in Marshfield in 1909, and her mother returned to Michigan at that time, where she lived another sixteen years.

The years 1909 and 1910 figure prominently for the Leatons, and also for the old Joe Larson homestead. That is the year that Joe Larson was selling the property to C. E. Lennon and the Coos Bay Timber Company of Minneapolis, Minnesota. That is also the year that Martin Leaton, William's second oldest son, married Alma Saling at Eastside, Oregon. I don't know all the connections, but Alma's brother True Saling and their dad Tom were woodsmen who were on the East Fork of the Millicoma. They were no doubt acquainted with the Larsons. Joe's brother P. E. Larson owned the Allegany store and townsite at that time.

The little bit that we can know directly of that period in that place I had to get from Belle Leaton Clarke. She was the only person living who went back that far at the time I was gathering the information. She was the oldest of six children born to Martin and Alma Saling Leaton. Belle's parents were living on the place in 1910, either when Belle was born or immediately thereafter. Also living there was Alma's brother True Saling and his wife Georgina and their daughter Viola. Their son Elwin Saling was born in 1913, while they lived there, but it seems they moved down to Allegany about the

73

time Elwin was born. According to the Leaton family tradition, for many years they paid $50 per year to the timber company for the lease on the 160-acre homestead.

Actually, all of the sons and daughters of old William Leaton lived on that place at one time or another. Bill Leaton (1888–1972) and his wife Bernice Howell (1907–1982) raised their three children, Hattie, Eldin, and Wilma while they lived on that place and at various other locations above the falls. The same was true of Alfred (1894–1968) and his wife Agnes Wilkinson (1901–1977) with their three children, Alfreda, Bob, and Cliff.

Hattie Leaton, 2 yrs old on the cliff road above Golden Falls. Family Model-T in back.

The Leaton men, about 1916.
Clarence, Tom, Alfred, Martin, Bill, William (Dad) Leaton

74

The Middletons and the Last Tenants

The Middleton House, 1940

From 1933 until 1939 Slim and Frieda Milton Middleton, along with a large clan of Middletons and Miltons, lived on the place. They moved over into Ash Valley in 1940, and the next tenants were Al Lively's folks. Following them were George Youst and his family until the summer of 1941. I believe they may have been the last tenants.

The site of the old house has grown over. The apple trees are in an overstory of fir and are growing grotesquely, up into the ever disappearing light. A few of those apple trees are in the open, and they still bear fruit. Those of us who once lived there can recognize the place, but just barely. It is sometimes used as a campsite by elk hunters, none of whom know why the apple trees are there.

On September 25, 1993, we held a reunion picnic at the site of the old Joe Larson homestead. At the picnic were representatives from every family that ever lived there. Adelien and Florence Larson, nieces of Joe Larson; Belle Leaton, daughter of Martin and granddaughter of William Leaton; Hattie and Wilma Leaton, daughters of Bill and granddaughters of William Leaton; Chuck Middleton, nephew of Slim Middleton; Al Lively and his mother Helen; and Lionel Youst, son of George Youst, the last tenants.

P. E. (Ed) Larson

Joe Larson's brother, P. E. Larson, owner of the Allegany townsite and store between 1904 and 1919, had worked unrelentingly in favor of an improved road from Allegany to North Bend. He attended meetings, circulated petitions, and collected data to support such a construction project. For example, he kept track of the traffic in and out of Allegany for the month of June, 1911. His daughter Adelien had his notebook and shared it with me, showing traffic in and out of Allegany June 1 to June 30, 1911.

	IN	OUT
Teams	141	143
Saddle Horses	21	16
Autos	92	86
Totals	254	245

These are pretty impressive statistics. He indicated in his notebook that the county had appropriated $1,450 for the road and spent $1,163.50 on one contract. He noted that this left only $246.50 for the maintenance of thirty miles of road for a full year. One can only imagine the condition of that thirty miles!

P. E. Larson was an artist and one imagines he was a fastidious Swede whose ideas of neatness and propriety contrasted sharply with most of the loggers and homesteaders around him. Harold Ott, who remembered him, told in his "History of Allegany" of the small park and walks, the groups of flowers, and a fountain Larson had put in and decorated with Bluejay Bitters bottles imbedded upside down. Harold said that "they made a beautiful effect."[3]

P. E. Ed Larson, his wife Hilda, and son Edward at Allegany, 1908.

One resident who seems not to have shared P. E. Larson's fastidiousness in all things was Charles Edwards, the riverboat captain and owner of the steamer *Alert*. The few hundred yards of road between the Allegany store and the wharf was littered with wood, cargo, spare equipment, logging rigging, and who knows what else. According to Larson, Captain Edward's steamboat company was responsible for the mess. It detracted from the postcard image that Larson was attempting to create for Allegany.

In any case, Larson circulated a petition demanding that Captain Edwards' steamboat company clean up the mess on the road between the store and the wharf. It was signed by virtually every adult man on both forks of the Millicoma River. We don't know what happened when (and if) Larson presented the petition to Edwards, but we do know that the road was cleared and its appearance improved.

It was in 1904 that P. E. Larson bought the Allegany store and townsite from William Vincamp for $1,500. He made numerous improvements and during his time at Allegany the place was booning with several large logging camps. The largest was Buehner Lumber Company's railroad camp on Marlow Creek, which employed almost 250 men. Larson sold the Allegany site for $15,000 in 1919. He was father to Adelien and Florence, who were born during the time he was at Allegany.

Photography

P. E. Larson was a photographer of considerable talent and accomplishment. He had spent several years in the Klondike during the gold rush of 1898. During that time he was partner in a Dawson City photography business under the name of "Hegg and Larrs," then later "Larrs and Duclos." He went by the name of P. E. Larrs while he was in the Klondike, changing to Larson in 1904. His daughters have donated his Klondike photographs to the Alaska Historical Library in Juneau.

---

[3] Harold Ott, "History of Allegany," in *Glancing Back*, p. 15.

Clark and Clarence Kinsey, brothers of the famous Seattle photographer, Darius Kinsey, had a photography studio at Grand Forks, Yukon Territory, during the gold rush, and their mother ran a boarding house there for a few years. P. E. Larson knew them before he departed for the Klondike and he maintained the acquaintance. Clark Kinsey later had contracts with the West Coast Lumbermen's Association for whom he photographed extensively. One of the members of this association was Buehner Lumber Company of Marshfield, with their large logging camp at Allegany.

In about 1916, Clark Kinsey came to Allegany to photograph those operations. He stayed with P. E. Larson and his family at the Allegany Hotel during that time. The negatives of Kinsey's photographs of that period are at the University of Washington (Special Collections).

There was a gold rush at Goldfield, Nevada, in 1904, and P. E. Larson went there from the Klondike. His Goldfield photographs are among the most famous in the history of Nevada. A large number of them are in the P. E. Larson Collection of the Nevada State Museum in Carson City. Those classic photographs continue to appear in publications down to the present time. Many of Larson's Coos County photographs have appeared in publications, but none have been credited to him. His Coos County photographs have never been assembled into a collection.

Steamer Alert at Allegany, at mouth of East Fork. Note passengers disembarking from bow. Photo by P. E. Larson

In 1919 P. E. Larson sold his Allegany townsite to Mr. Hedrick for $15,000. Following is his description of the property, from his advertising flyer:

Allegany Oregon Offers the Best Bargain in the State

A fine improved place in the most delightful summer resort section imaginable, surroundings ideal. This property is for sale cheap at a sacrifice.

A 40-acre Tract of land including Lots and Townsite of Allegany. Located at the headwaters of Coos Bay.

Mail service twice daily. Launches and steamboats ply the waters at all hours. Stage connections via the Overland Stage Route and Loon Lake Valley and near the Horse Shoe Bottom Basin where the Oregon Protected Wild Elk Herds are having their Feeding and Breeding Grounds. Also near that Old Indian Historical Hunting Grounds, Elks Peak, and that Wonderful Beaver dam noted for its great trout fishing.

There are no better Hunting and Fishing Grounds anywhere. Two of the most picturesque and powerful waterfalls in Oregon are within a short distance of Allegany – Golden and Silver Falls. This farm consists of the following:

Every department of the land well fenced.	13 acres of choice garden truck land.
5 acres of pasture land.	5 acres of prime bearing fruit orchard.

5 acres of park recreation ground, containing clear running streams, native trees grove, picnic grounds, and trout ponds and fountains.

9 acres of forestry park and springs of live fresh water, also stocked with game, deer and birds, etc.

2 acres of garden, fruits and berries. Private water system with a concrete reservoir. Fed by a large, live spring with a service pipe to all parts of the premises. Also a new 3-inch pipe line of water power system for electric power and irrigation.

The buildings, improvements consist of a hotel, 35 x 55, two stories, well furnished and modern, two dining rooms, two kitchens, two reception rooms, and a number of guest rooms, a store building and a stock of goods, general line of merchandise.

Automobile garages.

A livery stable, including horses, buggies and harnesses and stage, wagons, etc.

All necessary farming implements, for a well regulated farm.

Also livestock of cattle and hogs and poultry, large variety of fowls and several colonies of bees.

Allegany is located on two rivers at the forks of Coos River Head of Navigation of Coos Bay and terminus of Coos Bay and Hudson Bay Continental Route.

Allegany has a	
Post Office.	Steamboat Landings.
Hotel.	School House.
City Hall and Club House.	Several private homes.
	3 new bungalows well furnished.

This is an exceptional opportunity for a good business proposition to acquire a fine property. The title is first-class and has merit to it and will stand close inspection. More and fuller information may be obtained by calling on or addressing:

P. E. Larson, Allegany, Oregon

SCHAPERS/WILKINSON KINSHIP CHART

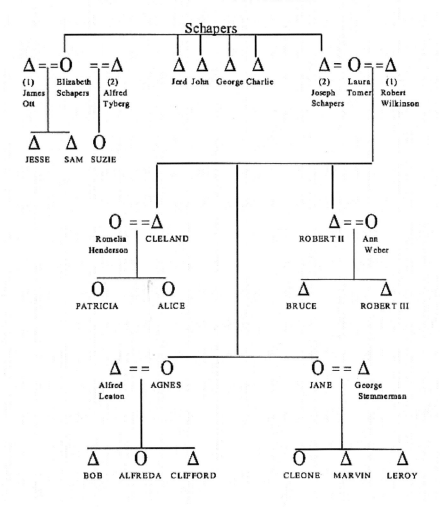

LEATON FAMILY KINSHIP CHART

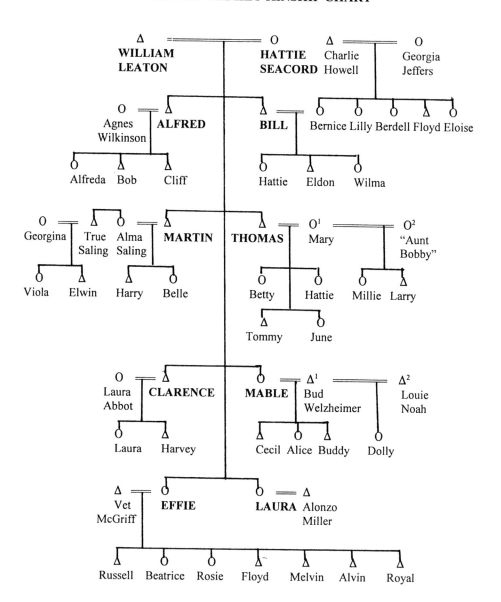

PART FOUR

THE GOVERNMENT

The road at the top of Golden Falls, circa 1909. Men in the back are widening the road under contract with the county. This is the first wheeled vehicle over the falls road. Joe Larson, driving. Baby in arms is Hilda Peterson Coffman. Her mother, holding her, is Joe's sister Nellie. Photo by P. E. Larson, courtesy Alelien Larson.

Telling local stories requires acknowledging distant forces.
--Joseph Amato, *Rethinking Home*

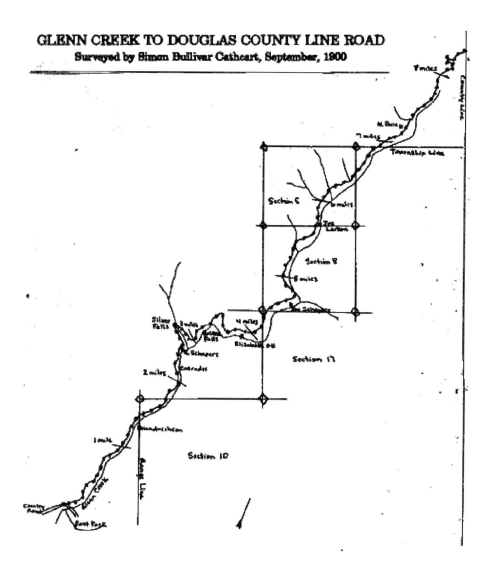

GLENN CREEK TO DOUGLAS COUNTY LINE ROAD
Surveyed by Simon Bullivar Cathcart, September, 1900

Chapter Nine

The Road

Apetition and affidavit to establish a county road was filed September 5, 1900. It asked for a road from the bridge at Glenn Creek Junction "by the most practicable route through Glenn Creek Valley above Golden Falls and to terminate on the summit of the dividing ridge between the waters of Glenn Creek and the waters of Loon Lake Creek." There were fifty-five signatures on the petition.

Among the signatures were those of Joseph Schapers, Jordan (Jerd) Schapers, Joe Larson, N. Price, and E. Ott. These represented the head of each of the four households that were above the falls. The homesteaders below the falls on Glenn Creek and the East Fork also signed. There was John Hendrickson, Otto Gustafson, J. R. Bunch, A. G. Noah, R. Rodine, and W. W. R. Glenn, among others. Folks further down river also signed. The names of Edwards, Michelbrink, Stemmerman, Terry, Piper, Rooke, Blake, Blaine, and Landrith, for example. Some of those folks lived far down on tidewater. A vehicle route from Allegany to the Umpqua River was in everyone's interest.

The county commissioners approved the affidavit and ordered the county surveyor, Simon Bolivar Cathcart, to meet with the petitioners at Allegany on September 17. He did so, made the survey, and submitted his report back to the commissioners, who met on it December 28, 1900. It was ordered "that the viewer's report, survey and plat be recorded and that said road as viewed out, surveyed, and platted be declared a public highway and the road supervisor open said road for public travel."

The actual survey was made in September, 1900. Below the falls, it passed John Hendrikson's place about a mile and a quarter from the point of beginning at Glenn Creek Junction. One and one half miles beyond Hendrickson's, at the present location of the Golden and Silver Falls State Park parking lot, was George Schapers' claim. Cathcart indicated a cabin there with the notation, "G. Schapers." As I mentioned above, George obtained his homestead patent on the 160 acres that include the Golden Falls on March 19, 1904. He had to have lived on the property at least part of each year for the previous five years.

The road survey proceeded up the right bank of Silver Creek, and ascended at a grade of "about 11 percent" to the level of the top of Golden Falls. At that point the survey field notes state that there was an "impassable bluff of rock. As it is impossible to chain the next course I retraced my line S 60" W 1.28 chains and ran transverse line as follows . . . to the top of Golden Falls."

Cathcart later notes the entry to "Golden Valley," by which he obviously meant Glenn Creek Valley. Within Glenn Creek Valley he noted, in order, Mrs. Ott's house, Joe Schapers' house, Joe Larson's clearing, and Joe Larson's house. About a mile and a half above the Joe Larson house, he noted the "N. Price claim." The road survey stopped at the boundary line of Coos and Douglas County, almost exactly at the corner of sections 27, 28, 33, and 34, Township 23S, Range 10 W. W. M.

Coos County, having declared the survey and plat as a "public highway," was unwilling to go to the expense necessary to convert the "impassable bluff of rock" into a road. That was where Joe Larson came in. He had worked as powder man in rock quarries and knew that there was no reason why he and others couldn't blast out a road by themselves. He talked George Schapers into it. George owned the Golden Falls. Joe also worked on his fellow Swedes Alfred Tyberg and John Hendrikson. The four of them together agreed, and in fifty days during the summer of 1901 they blasted out a pack trail across the face of the cliff connecting the Golden and the Silver Falls.

John Hendrikson's son Reuben told the story to Charlotte Mahaffy for her book, *Coos River Echoes* in 1966 (pp. 5–7). He said that his dad gave twenty-five days labor while Tyberg, Schapers, and Larson gave fifty days each. He said that in the morning each man would carry fifty pounds of dynamite to the top of the cliff. They would then let themselves over the cliff on ropes, and with a hammer drill would make six-foot holes for the charges. At noon they would load the holes, set them off, and go back to the bottom to carry another fifty pounds each of dynamite back to the top for the afternoon's drilling. At the end of the day they would set off the charges again, and the next day repeat the process. By the end of the summer they had their pack trail through.

In 1906 the county allotted $1,000 for getting the road finished. The bid was for a contract for grading and the road was to be completed to Loon Lake. According to Mahaffy's book, Sherman Cutlip got the contract to widen the pack trail across the cliff.

In 1909 the width of the right of way for the Glenn Creek to Douglas County Line Road was established at forty feet. Contracts were let again in 1910. On April 12 the county court appointed Joe Larson as Special Road Master for Road District 6. His responsibilities included calling for separate bids for rocking, planking, and grading. The bids were to be opened by the county court at 10 a. m. May 5, 1910. From the records I could not find evidence that bids had been received at that time. By then Joe Larson was selling his homestead to a Minnesota timber company, and his interest in these matters was probably not as intense as it once was.

Road at top of Golden Falls, 1940.

Improvements were made, however. A photograph taken in 1911 by P. E. Larson shows a team and wagon driven by Joe Larson and loaded with members of the Price, Larson, and Peterson families. In the background are ten men working on the road. It is at the cliff at the very top of Golden Falls. After the road was improved in 1911, J. J. McDonald put in a sawmill at Loon Lake. He needed a steam boiler to power the mill and he was able to move it from Coos Bay over the Golden and Silver Falls road. Jack Baker contracted to do the job. A postcard photo taken at the bridge at Silver Falls shows an eight-horse team pulling the eight-ton boiler on a wagon. There are six men in the crew. How they got it around the switchback and steep grade between Silver Falls and the top of Golden Falls is a wonder.

The road was good enough by 1912 that an auto stage line was put into operation, which ran until 1916 when the railroad was finally completed from Eugene to Coos Bay. During those years there were two steamboat runs per day between Allegany and Marshfield. Passengers could leave Marshfield at 5 a. m., arriving at Allegany by eight. At Allegany they would transfer to the auto stage, a 1912 Cadillac, and if all went well they would be at Scottsburg by 11:15. At Scottsburg passengers would change stages again, and would hopefully arrive in Drain by 3 p. m., in time for the afternoon train to Portland. Another stage departed Drain at 8 a. m., getting to Scottsburg at noon.

The Allegany stage picked up those passengers, getting to Allegany in time for the afternoon boat, arriving in Marshfield at 6 p. m.

The *Millicoma* heading upriver with a Ford athwart the stern.
August 4, 1914.

85

In good weather there was not a better way in and out of the Coos Bay area. In bad weather, and when the roads were wet, it was not very reliable. Wilber Gorst told of taking thirty-six hours to go the thirty-six miles when he was a child coming into Coos Bay with his parents. Most of the time was spent pushing the car through the mud.

During those years, Elizabeth Ott Tyberg's place was considered the "Halfway House," and the stages often stopped there for rest and refreshment. If the stage was very late, they would sometimes stay overnight. If there was no room at Tyberg's, passengers would sometimes stay at the adjoining Joe Schapers place. I doubt that passengers or drivers wanted to go over the Golden Falls section of the road after dark.

After the railroad came into Coos Bay in 1916, it seems the county lost interest in maintaining the road. The part from the bottom of Silver Falls to the Douglas County line was maintained by the people who lived there. During the 1930's the county would give warrants for labor expended by the residents, and those

Team and wagon on Silver Falls bridge, about 1911. P. E. Larson photo.

warrants would be sold at about fifty cents on the dollar. Later, when the county had money, the warrants were redeemed at full value by those who had bought them. Later in the 1930's some of the maintenance was done by the Civilian Conservation Corps (CCC), the subject of the next chapter.

During the 1940's while my dad, George Youst, had his sawmill on the old Joe Schapers place, he had to do all the improvements and maintenance on the road himself. I remember that the county loaned him an old horse-drawn road grader, which he would tow behind the lumber truck to grade the road. He got rock out of the creek, and cut planks for it in the mill. When the Silver Creek bridge collapsed with a load of lumber in 1941, he rebuilt the bridge. By the time Vic Dimmick put his mill in on the old Tyberg place in 1943, the road was in fairly good shape, comparatively speaking.

By the summer of 1958, the old Silver Creek bridge was long overdue for replacement. Cle Wilkinson was the only person still living up there. His daughters had long since moved on, the Tyberg place was in the hands of an absentee owner, and Weyerhaeuser wanted the road closed. That was the year that Cle sold the old ranch to Weyerhaeuser and the county closed, and later removed, the bridge. It was the end of an era.

Chapter Ten

The CCC Camps

At the worst of the depression of the 1930's some relief came into the county through the Civilian Conservation Corp (CCC). There was an immediate and positive impact upon the community. The *Marshfield Sun*, May 19, 1933, had the following announcement:

> Two CCC camps will be located in Coos County, one 3 miles east of Golden Falls and the other, 6 miles southwest of Reedsport on Schofield creek. Ten men have been selected by Judge Thompson to work in the forest camps. Coos county's full quota is 59.

Upon arrival of the CCC, on July 25, 1933, the superintendent of the so-called "Camp Loon Lake" asked the Coos County Commissioners for permission to use the labor at his disposal to repair the Coos County part of the road. Permission was granted:

> August 1, 1933, In the Matter of the improvement of the County Road above Silver Falls to Douglas County Line:
>
> It will be their order that C. J. Budelier, the Camp Superintendent be authorized to make such improvements on the County [Road] as he desires after consultation with General Road Patrolman, W. D. Leaman.
>
> Authority is also given C. J. Budelier to remove any timber he may find on the right-of-way providing that notice is first served on the owners of such timber for a period of 15 days, notifying them that should they desire the timber it is at their disposal. If they fail to take the timber away within 15 days, it will be removed from the right-of-way and placed on their property.

Since the first edition of this book, Jerry Phillips did exhaustive research into the history of the Civilian Conservation Corps as it related to the Elliott State Forest and recorded his findings in *Caulked Boots and Cheese Sandwiches* (1997), pages 26–108. Jerry was able to clarify some of the rather dim memories of the CCC camps with an impressive array of documented facts. He discovered that much of the confusion resulted from there having actually been two camps on Glenn Creek, over a period of nine years, each of them with more than one name. And so it is no wonder that some of the memories of the period seemed to contradict each other. Jerry's book should put to rest any confusion on the issue, and all I can do is summarize some of his findings.

In March 1933, Congress passed the Emergency Conservation Work program, creating the Civilian Conservation Corps. It was designed to enroll "unmarried, idle men between the ages of 18 and 25" to work in the "national forests, national parks, Indian reservations, state forests and parks" and so on. Their objective was to "improve, develop, and protect the forests." Barely two months after passage of the act, Coos County had already selected ten men to work at the Glenn Creek camp.

Jerry Phillips found that the first camp on Glenn Creek was actually on Weyerhaeuser property at the mouth of Howell Creek. It was usually known as "Camp Loon Lake" because Loon Lake was the closest known landmark, but it was also sometimes called the "Golden Falls CCC Camp," and its official designation was apparently #S-201. It was only in existence for about four and one-half months, but was the first of the CCC Camps in the Elliott State Forest. Construction of the camp began in late May 1933. A month later it was activated with the arrival of 185 men of CCC Company #1726 from St. Louis, Missouri, and twenty-eight "experienced men" from Oregon. By October 2 the company had been shipped back to Little Rock, Arkansas, and "Camp Loon Lake" was abandoned. But in their short time on Glenn Creek, they accomplished quite a bit. According to Phillips, they built the first four miles of road in the Elliott, running from the county road north onto Umcoos Ridge. The camp was abandoned before the rains began, but the buildings stood for many years and Charlie Howell later leased them from Weyerhaeuser, living there until 1942.

Aside from building and maintaining road, the CCC built fire lookouts and strung telephone lines to them. In the Glenn Creek area, there had been a lookout of sorts at Elk's Peak since 1915, but by the early 1930's the new timber growing up in the burn of the old Coos Bay fire of 1868 obscured the view to the north, and a new lookout was needed. Cougar Pass, just on the east slope of Umcoos Ridge, was chosen and in 1935 it was the CCC that built the sixty-foot tower with the cabin on top that Alice Wilkinson manned for a number of summers. It was an exceptionally important lookout, and although it was aband- oned for a few years, it is now again re-built and in use.

By 1938 the old CCC camp at Howell Creek was not the only camp on Glenn Creek. The State Camp, so called, at the mouth of Cedar Creek where it enters Glenn Creek, was built that year on Weyerhaeuser property and was a source of confusion in the narratives of the old timers. It was often called the CCC Camp, probably because the CCC moved in after its original purpose of serving as a forest camp for prison parolees had been abandoned by the

The "State Camp" at the mouth of Cedar Creek. Built to be used as a prison parolee camp in 1938, it was a CCC side camp, 1939–41.

State Board of Prison Terms and Paroles for lack of funding. It had been built to give prison parolees a transition between prison and civilian life. They were to do forestry work and were to be paid $75 per month, with $25 deducted for room and board. It was evidently the only such camp built for parolees in the state, and was very short lived. It seems not to have made any impression at all upon the people who lived above the falls, inasmuch as none of them could remember it having been used for that purpose. The records are inconclusive, and it may never have had a parolee in residence.

The CCC moved into the camp immediately after the parolee plan was abandoned. A CCC road crew of about thirty men lived there during the summer of 1939, and it was evidently used by the CCC during parts of 1940 and '41. In November 1941, the Reedsport CCC Company was disbanded, and the following month the Japanese attacked Pearl Harbor. The CCC ceased to exist a few months later. But it made its mark on Upper Glenn Creek, in the construction of roads and trails, the laying of telephone lines, and building fire lookouts. Some of the buildings of the State Camp stood well into the 1950's, before they rotted into oblivion, or were otherwise salvaged.

Chapter Eleven

The Golden and Silver Falls State Park

The road between Allegany and the Umpqua River, over Golden Falls, had been open to vehicular traffic since 1909. The road from Allegany to Marshfield opened in 1929 and later became a county secondary highway. There was much hope locally that Golden and Silver Falls should become a state park because then, the argument went, the state would have to take care of the road. There were even dreams that an actual highway might be built.

The Golden and Silver Falls State Park was established after negotiations among the State Highway Department, Coos County, Weyerhaeuser Timber Company, and the Waterford Lumber Company. As part of the package, the County transferred some land to the State and the State agreed to spend $10,000 to improve the road.

The forty that includes the Silver Falls was not in the old George Schapers homestead. It had been part of the timberland that Northern Pacific Railroad had acquired in 1902 and sold immediately to Weyerhaeuser. In 1935 the first transaction toward forming the park took place. Weyerhaeuser subdivided that forty and deeded the 17.27 acres that included the Silver Falls to Coos County for one dollar. There were several stipulations.

First, the 17.27 acres "must forever be to the use of the public as a public park." If the vendee or its successors sell or attempt to sell any other than "down or dead trees" or permit any business or occupation for private gain or profit, then "the vendor may at once re-enter and retake possession of said premises without notice or declaration of forfeiture." The deed was signed August 6, 1935, by J. P. Weyerhaeuser Jr., Executive Vice President.

A curious additional exception was that Weyerhaeuser reserved a right-of-way for a logging railroad "not over 50 feet wide." At that time Weyerhaeuser was primarily a railroad logging outfit in Washington, and big-time loggers were not yet taking truck loggers seriously. The head office had not yet come to grips with just how rugged the Coos River drainage is and how impractical railroad logging would be here. That same year, 1935, below the falls at Glenn Creek Junction the first logging camp on the Millicoma River that used logging trucks had just started. That was Brady and Neal Logging Company.

The first land acquired by the State for the park was 112 acres from the 160-acre former George Schapers homestead, which at the time belonged to Waterford Lumber Company of Minneapolis, Minnesota. This occurred on June 29, 1936. This piece of land included the Golden Falls and what is now the parking lot and picnic area of the park, but did not include the Silver Falls.

Things were moving pretty fast at this time. Just nine weeks later, on September 7, Coos County deeded the 17.26-acre Weyerhaeuser tract to the State Highway Commission. The deed states, "It would be in the best interest of both the County and the State that Golden Falls Park and the Silver Falls Park be united and developed as one unit." For the first time, the Golden and Silver Falls were in the same ownership.

Once the park was established, not much changed at all. The Civilian Conservation Corp (CCC) from the Glenn Creek camp above the falls did some work in setting up the picnic area and the trail to the base of Golden Falls. There was much discussion about improving the road so that the timber from above the falls could be hauled by truck, but by 1940 that idea had been completely discarded. The U. S. Geological Survey established bench marks in 1941. They found the elevation at the picnic area below the falls to be 309 feet; the elevation at the top of Golden Falls was found to be 686 feet. That is a drop of 377 feet, top to bottom.

In 1955 the County deeded to the State a 28-acre timbered area which completed the park as it appears today. The total area is now 157.27 acres. That is only 2.79 acres less than the 160-acre homestead that it started with! On August 3, 1961, there was a formal dedication, at which a bronze plaque was installed near Silver Falls. The plaque credited Weyerhaeuser for giving the park to the state, but its wording was such as to imply that the entire park, not just the 17.27 acres of Silver Falls, had been donated by Weyerhaeuser. This was certainly good for Weyerhaeuser corporate relations, and for thirty years it has been assumed by thousands of visitors that they have Weyerhaeuser to thank for the entire park. During the heavy rains in the winter of 1982 a mudslide buried the plaque, probably forever.

Silver Falls

91

Chapter Twelve

The Elliott State Forest

Prior to 1929, the mostly burned-over land to the north of the Upper Glenn Creek Valley fell within the boundaries of the Siuslaw National Forest. That land had been considered to be of no particular value by the settlers. Oregon's first State Forester, Francis Elliott, recognized that there would be plenty of value, once the new growth of trees was mature and ready for market. He

Logging on the Elliott, 1958

advocated trading all the State lands within Oregon's National Forests for a block of National Forest land, so as to create a contiguous forest that could be managed for the benefit of the State's Common School Fund. Finally, in 1930, the trades were complete, and Oregon created that state forest, believed to be the first of its kind in the nation. Francis Elliott died that same year, and the forest was named in his honor. It initially consisted of 70,000 acres, mostly lands burned in the old Coos Bay fire of 1868, and straddling the boundaries of Coos and Douglas Counties. Its southern limit was near the Upper Glenn Creek Valley.

Initially, nothing was done in the way of forest management due, primarily, to the Great Depression. Nature was left to her own as the naturally re-seeded trees grew toward maturity. No roads were built; no timber sales were laid out. The trees just grew, silently but inexorably, putting on value year after year. Then, in 1955, three years after Jerry Phillips went to work in Coos Bay for the State Forestry Department, the first timber sales from the newly activated Elliott Forest management began to take place. Some of the mature timber stood on Cedar Creek, a little north of the old State Camp on Glenn Creek. There was more to the west, on Howell Creek and the adjacent drainages, and Jerry Phillips was there, helping to lay out those first timber sales. Following is his story in his own words.

The Upper Glenn Creek Valley
As Remembered By a "Pot-Bellied Plutocrat"
by Jerry Phillips

My name is Jerry Phillips, and I am a recently retired Forest Manager for the Oregon State Department of Forestry in Coos Bay. I feel truly honored by the opportunity to contribute to this book, and hope that the following pages will prove to be of interest.

Jerry Phillips

Memories are one of our most pleasurable gifts, and, although they are occasionally imperfect, what joys they hold for us! As a native Oregonian, I came to Coos County forty years ago with my wife and firstborn child, fresh out of Forestry School at Oregon State College, at age twenty-five. The year was 1952. My first professional Forestry assignment here with the State Department of Forestry was that of being a Logging Inspector for northern Coos County and western Douglas County. My first day on the job involved a training field trip with my supervisor from our main office. I've remembered that day for these forty years.

One of the first logging operations we came to was in quite a remote location. My task was to inspect this gyppo logger's equipment and layout for compliance with State laws involving fire prevention and control. This logger (who shall remain nameless), upon being told by myself that his operation had certain deficiencies, literally exploded. I was, he said, a "pot-bellied plutocrat" who had no right to invade his operating area. When I retired, forty years later, that same supervisor repeated the story, to everyone's amusement. So much for my introduction to the world of Coos County logging!

Two years later, in 1955, I met Lionel Youst's father, George, under somewhat similar circumstances. He had just completed his construction of a new sawmill on the Ash place, across the West Fork of the Millicoma from the Old Stone House. The Oregon Legislature, in its infinite wisdom, had just passed a new law which prohibited any woods sawmill from open-burning its slabs and sawdust; instead, a steel "wigwam burner" must be used. George's mill was built on the edge of a deep draw on the side of the hill, and was designed to open-burn all waste materials in that draw. My obvious duty was to tell him about the new law. I fully expected him to reach for a 2 x 4, but, to his credit, after thinking it over for a few minutes, he said he thought he *could* "turn the mill around" and run his slabs and sawdust into a burner. I felt great respect for his innovativeness (and self control)!

93

Well, talking about George Youst leads my memories on up Glenn Creek, and back to the year 1952. I had reported to work here on March 1 of that year, and was assigned to a variety of tasks relating to forest fire prevention and control, under direction of the Coos Forest Protection Association. The 1952 fire season was very severe. The regular field fire warden for northern Coos County was very ill that year, so I was to fill in for him. One of the first fire starts in the season was reported on the Cle Wilkinson place on Upper Glenn Creek. It seemed he had been "smoking out some honey bees" in the old George Youst millsite, and had started a fire in the big sawdust pile. As a twenty-five year old, green, Portland-born "kid," my job was to take a 1941 Chevvie pickup pumper truck and a small fire crew up over the Golden and Silver Falls County Road and extinguish that fire. The courage I developed in the Marine Corps was helpful in driving that road. People today are disinclined to believe there ever *was* a road there, but it was not too bad as long as you kept your rig in compound low gear and kept your eyes on the road. Lionel Youst's mother must have had "ice-water in her veins" to drive truckloads of lumber down over Golden Falls every day when their mill was operating.

George Youst viewing a recent clear-cut on the Elliott, 1967.

My incompetence as a fire fighter became clear when it became necessary to make a trip every week that summer with that little pumper truck and fire crew to work on that same fire in the sawdust pile. We would put a pump in Glenn Creek, string hose up to the sawdust pile and pump water on it for several hours — then come back the following week and do it again. And that was my introduction to the Upper Glenn Creek Valley.

In 1955 the Oregon Legislature decided that the Elliott State Forest, 92,000 acres lying between Glenn Creek and the Umpqua River, should begin to be managed. It had been acquired from the Federal government in 1929, but, since most of the timber was comparatively young, had remained wild and un-managed. However, the Oregon Constitution required that forest to be developed someday for financial support of Oregon's public schools, so, since it was reaching maturity, management was scheduled. My college degree was in Forest Management so I was asked to transfer into that activity, and it did become my long-term career. Not surprisingly, a lot of the early work was in the area north of Glenn Creek, because that timber was old-growth, a high priority for harvest by all owners in the 1950's.

And so, between 1956 and 1966 I spent a lot of time working between Glenn Creek and Elk Ridge, to the north. Of course, timber sale activity goes on year-round, and, while the Upper Glenn Creek Valley was a beautiful, peaceful, quiet series of meadows in the midst of a 200-year-old forest during the summer months, it was stormy, muddy, and dangerous the other eight months of the year. Coos County had long ago stopped doing any maintenance work on the County Road, and the Coos Forest Patrol did only what it had to in order to keep the road passable to fire equipment during the summer. The mud holes were so big and deep, and so much of the roadbed was only deep ruts full of water, that our State Forestry crews got to calling it "County Road Creek," and during the winter months everyone got lots of practice digging and jacking and using old planks to get even the four-wheel drive trucks unstuck. Our forestry short-wave radios could not reach the Coos Bay Office from there, and it was a long walk to Allegany, so you *did* dig yourself out when you got hung up in a mudhole. Having to ford Glenn Creek every day during the winter was tough on brake linings and truck bodies, too, and we figured that a normal life for a new 4 X 4 International carryall was one year. And every strong wind would leave big windfalls across the road!

As I remember it, not much was left of the old homesteads by 1952. We would stop and pick apples at the old Tyberg place. Cle Wilkinson was still living on his place, and there were the remains of some old buildings at what we called "Glenn Creek Camp" up near the head of the valley, where the Douglas County line crosses the road a short distance away.

This camp setup was also known as "The State Camp." The CCC Crews had built some 30 miles of roads between 1933 and 1941, providing access through the Elliott State Forest between the head of Glenn Creek and the Walker Ranch on Schofield Creek, via Cougar Pass and Dean's Mountain. Then they cut thousands of large snags along those roads, and the Coos Forest Patrol built a ground telephone line along the same route, linking the lookouts and the Elkhorn Ranch with Allegany and the outside world. Still, that left a lot of work that could be done for the public good around that area, and what better source of additional labor during the last few years of the Depression than prison labor! Or so the thinking went in 1938.

A site for the prison parolee labor camp was chosen at the extreme upper end of the Glenn Creek Valley, some three miles above the Tyberg place, and just below where the County Road left the valley and climbed up through a couple of switchbacks to the divide. The camp was right at the mouth of Cedar Creek. Construction of the cookhouse, the cooler, the two barracks, the power house, and the shop was done in 1938, on what was believed to be Elliott State Forest property. Imagine everyone's chagrin, then, when a check of the property line showed the camp to be actually located on property belonging to the Weyerhaeuser Timber Company! Fortunately, the Company was willing to be cooperative, and sold ten acres of their timberland to the State in September, 1939, for $150, or, $15 per acre. (Since there was at least three hundred thousand board feet of good fir timber on it, the timber alone would have been worth some $60,000 when prices in recent years have run around $200 per thousand board feet for stumpage. The sale was a cooperative gesture, and recognized, no doubt, that the State did not have the money in 1939 to pay true market value, anyway).[1]

The State Camp operated later as a CCC Camp, and was in use from 1939 through 1941, when World War II started. All such camps seemed to have closed in 1942. The

---

[1] Stumpage prices in 1939 were only about $1.50 per thousand. 300,000 board feet would thus have only had a market value of about $450 at that time.

crews from the camp on Glenn Creek built the original road linking the County Road with the top of Elk's Peak, which had been a U.S. Forest Service lookout site (using a tent) back in the 1920's. Duffy Lewis, from Reedsport, was one of the men who occupied that lookout. When I worked as a timber cruiser and sale layout man for the State Department of Forestry on the Elliott State Forest in the 1950's, the Glenn Creek State Camp was a place we used as a base camp. We would camp there for a week at a time, and prepare timber sales in the stands of 200-year-old fir timber on Cedar Creek, Howell Creek, Leaton Creek, and Slide-Out Creek and West Fork Glenn Creek.

The policy of the State Board of Forestry was to cut the oldest timber first, and that meant that our 36 million board feet per year of annual cut from the Elliott Forest had to come from the Glenn Creek slope, Schofield Creek, and the Marlow Ridge, Mill Creek, and Silver Creek stands. The rest of the Elliott Forest had been heavily burned over in 1868, so it contained primarily 75-year-old timber. A lot of the 8,000 acres of over-mature Elliott timber lay on the north slope of Glenn Creek.

In 1956, all that remained of the Glenn Creek State Camp was the cookhouse, the cooler, one barracks, and part of the truck shop. Some of our men slept in the cookhouse, but I didn't like the rats and mice in there, so I always slept on the ground outside. Later, the remaining buildings were salvaged, and today it is very difficult to even locate the campsite. With great difficulty, I did find the old concrete foundations for the cookhouse a few years ago, but one would never believe today that a forest labor camp with some six or seven buildings ever existed there.

Another good memory I have of the Glenn Creek Valley in the 1950's is that of using the old trapper's trail from the place where Elwin Saling was born,[2] up the ridge to the north and over the top of Elk Ridge, dropping down into Elk Creek and serving "Baldy" Crane's Cabins on both Elk Creek and the West Fork of the Millicoma (known as Pheasant Cabin). This was a very good trail, and we used it many times before any of our logging roads were built into the Elliott State Forest in the 1950's and the 1960's. Today, logging roads have replaced almost all of the historic trails in northern Coos County, and we have lost a little bit of our heritage in the process. Small segments of the original Gould Trail on both sides of the Elkhorn Ranch still exist, but one must hunt hard to find them.

Although my memories of the Upper Glenn Creek Valley go back only forty years, my imagination can still run wild. What I would give to have had one ride on the stagecoach that ran from Allegany to "the railroad at Drain," via Tom Fool Creek, Camp Creek, Jimmy Creek, and Scottsburg! Those were the days.

Jerry Phillips
Coos Bay, Oregon
November, 1991

---

[2] This is the "Middleton place," earlier known as the "Leaton place," and was originally homesteaded by Joe Larson.

Old-growth Elliott timber (220 years old)

DRAIN–MARSHFIELD ITINERARY
From the Pacific Coast Automobile 1915–1916 Blue Book
Page 539–40

Miles	Going
0.0	DRAIN – Leaving depot, go south along Main St.
4.1	SUNNYDALE – Keep left fork. 25% pitch. Cross covered bridge, then up winding 6–15% grade. Summit (11.1), then down 8% grade.
15.6	ELKTON – From here on to Scottsburg the road is easily followed, winding close along River through the beautiful Umpqua Valley.
35.3	SCOTTSBURG – Turn left and cross Ferry just beyond town. Turn Left after leaving Ferry and follow along river to
35.8	Turn Right at Bridge and up winding 6–18% grade. Summit (38.3). Elevation 1200 feet. Then down 15% grade to (40.7).
41.8	Turn right at small Bridge. Cross Bridge and up 15% grade. Summit (44.0). Elevation 1200 feet. Down winding 18% grade. CAUTION for sharp Turns.
47.4	Right fork at small Bridge. Cross Bridge (49.1). Up long 6–15% grade (50.0). Summit (53.7). Down narrow, rocky 10% grade. Cross Bridge at Waterfall (60.1).
62.9	Right fork at small Bridge.
70.3	ALLEGANY – Post Office. Keep Left for boat landing. From here on the river boat will carry machine and passengers to Marshfield after a three-hour ride on the picturesque Millicoma River. Distance 18 miles.
70.3	MARSHFIELD

Miles	Returning
0.0	MARSHFIELD – In order to complete the trip from Marshfield to Drain by daylight, it will be necessary to take the early boat, leaving Marshfield 5 o'clock a. m. and reaching Allegany, a distance of about 18 miles, by 8 o'clock.
0.0	ALLEGANY – Leaving boat landing, proceed to Post Office where take Right-hand road.
7.4	Left fork at bridge. Cross Bridge in front of Waterfall (10.2), then up rocky grade from 8–15%. Summit Elevation 1200 feet, then down winding 8–15% grade, partly on plank road. Foot of descent (20.3). Cross Bridge.
22.9	Left fork at small Bridge.
23.1	DANGER – Sharp Turn. Up long 6–18% grade. Summit (26.3). Elevation 1200 feet, then down similar grade. Foot of grade (28.5). Cross Bridge and Turn Left. Up 10–15% grade. Summit (32.0). Elevation 1200 feet. Down 6–18% grade. Foot of grade (34.5). Turn left along River.
34.8	Ferry across Umpqua River. CAUTION for steep approach.
35.0	SCOTTSBURG – From here to Elkton the road follows close along Umpqua River. Cross covered Bridge (46.7).
54.7	ELKTON – Proceed direct across covered Bridge. Take left fork at end of bridge.
55.0	Right fork. Up short 18% grade (55.2), then down 6–10% grade to (56.0). Up 6–8% grade. Summit (59.2). Then down 6–15% grade. Cross covered bridge (60.0). 25% pitch (63.3).
66.2	SUNNYDALE – Right Fork.
70.1	Direct at Sign. (Turn Right here for Roseburg)
70.3	DRAIN –

HOTEL
(Perkins Hotel)

PART FIVE

THE SCHOOLS

The Golden Falls School, May, 1941: The Last Day. Pat Wilkinson, 3rd grade; Lionel Youst, 1st grade.
Outhouse, far right; lean-to at right of building was the woodshed, but teacher Franklyn Smith lived
there.

*Simultaneously the object of the most profound feelings, the subject of
the greatest nostalgia, and a topic for a lifetime of re-thinking . . .*
--Joseph A. Amato, Rethinking Home

Golden Falls School
Known Students and Teachers

Years	Teachers	Students
1916-17	Dora Brown	Suzie Tyberg, Belle Leaton
1928-32	Anna Mary Weber	unknown
1932-33	Lilian Austin	Bob, Alfreda, & Cliff Leaton Freddie Middleton, Alice Wilkinson
1933-34 1934-35	Lilian Austin Grace Gray	{Bob, Alfreda, & Cliff Leaton {Hattie & Wilma Leaton {Freddie Middleton, Alice Wilkinson
1935-36	Grace Gray	Freddie Middleton, Alice Wilkinson
1936-37	Marjorie Baird	Freddie Middleton, Alice Wilkinson
1937-38	Bernice Reames	Hattie, Wilma & Eldon Leaton Freddie Middleton, Alice Wilkinson Donald Gardner
1938-39	Miss Diurks	James*, Don, & Charles Knight Hattie*, Wilma, & Eldon Leaton Freddie Middleton, Gloria Diurks Alice and Pat Wilkinson
1939-40	Lynette Hagquist	Freddie Middleton*, Alice Wilkinson* Pat Wilkinson, Carol Youst
1940-41	Franklyn Smith	Pat Wilkinson, Al Lively Carol* & Lionel Youst

* Graduated from eighth grade that year

Chapter Thirteen

Backwoods Education

The one-room country school disappeared in Coos County a generation ago, or more. It was one of the many casualties of the "progress" we have experienced since World War II. The professional school administrators who took over at that time hated anything as decentralized and apparently anarchic as a little school out in the woods someplace, out of their direct control.

The frontiersmen and recent immigrants who homesteaded the marginal lands above the head of tidewater on the Oregon Coast had not themselves received many of the blessings of an academic education. Nearly all could read and write, but few had attended school beyond about the third grade or so. That was enough to get them by, but they understood perfectly that their children deserved better. Schools, it turns out, became extremely important to them.

There was kind of a class distinction between these backwoods homesteaders and the established gentry who lived on tidewater. The gentry themselves were only a generation or less removed from the backwoods, but they had quickly established their differences. To be a "Mason, a Republican, and a Presbyterian" (or perhaps Methodist, Episcopalian or United Brethren) became the norm for these tidewater farmers. The homesteaders in the backwoods wore none of those labels.

The tidewater farmers were dependent on the daily run of the river boat, and were integrated into the larger economy. The folks above the falls were self-sufficient and their need for cash was limited to such things as taxes, kerosine, coffee, sugar, and cloth. Most of the cash came out of the woods, through the sale of furs, ferns, chittam bark, and sometimes illegal meat and whiskey.

Religion

With the notable exception of Laura Schapers, the people living above the falls were not known for their attention to religion. If they had religious convictions, for the most part they kept them to themselves. The Schapers were originally from a Catholic German community in Missouri, and were nominally Catholic. Joe Larson and his sister Nellie, as Swedish immigrants, were nominally Lutheran. I have never heard what religious background any of the others above the falls might have had. It did not seem to be a major part of the lives of any of them before Laura Schapers came onto the scene.

Missionaries would show up on the East Fork from time to time. The United Brethren, the Methodists, and the Seventh Day Adventists seemed to be the most active. Of the three, the only one that made inroads into the population above the falls was the Seventh Day Adventists. This happened during the 1930's through the missionary efforts of Fred Noah's ex-wife Amelia and the abiding faith of Laura Schapers. It was probably the only religious education any of the children of Upper Glenn Creek ever got.

All of the children from above the falls, however, were educated in the 3-R's. The education they got was perfectly adequate for the time and the place. In fact, Charles Middleton observed that the school above the falls "turned out more solid citizens per capita than any other school in the world!" Following is the story of the schools, insofar as I can piece it together.

School: The early days

At the beginning of the homesteading above the falls, the only children (as far as we know) were Elizabeth Ott's two boys, Sam and Jesse. This was in 1891. Sam was ten and Jesse was five years old. School was at Allegany, School District 45, which had been organized in 1880. It was eleven miles away. The boys boarded at the Blaine Ranch at Allegany while attending school there. When Jesse graduated in 1898, he was the first of four generations of Otts who graduated from the Allegany School.

The next children from above the falls who needed to be educated were nieces and nephews of Joe Larson. Joe's sister Nellie Anderson had become a widow a little after 1900 and came to Joe's homestead above the falls with her four children. The oldest was about eight and the youngest an infant. By this time a school had been built at Glenn Creek Junction. Nellie's children, including Edith (b. 1892), Bill (b. 1894), Dewey (b. 1896), and Ethel (b. 1900) attended there. It has been said that there was a cabin for the pupils to live in, because the walk from Joes's homestead to Glenn Junction was about fourteen miles, round trip, down over the Golden Falls road.

The cabin at Glenn Creek Junction.

In 1909 Joe Schapers married the widow Laura Wilkinson, and she and her four children moved in above the falls. The oldest was Bob, and he had already finished third grade in the East. As a result, he didn't go to school anymore. Cleland, Jane, and Agnes, however, attended school at Glenn Creek Junction. They were old enough to walk the ten mile round trip from Joe Schapers' place to the school and back each day.

Other children at Glenn Junction School at that time would have been from the families of Crane, Bunch, Devoe, Noah, Hendrickson, Stora, Calhoun, and others. The Glenn Junction schoolhouse was built in 1905 or earlier. John Hendrickson, whose son Reuben and daughter Agnes needed to begin school around that time, is said to have furnished the lumber and served on the school board of the newly formed district. This was School District 76, the boundaries of which extended from Glenn Creek Junction to the Douglas County line. It comprised about fifty-six square miles of timber, a half dozen homestead ranches, and a fluctuating number of logging camps on the East Fork.

School at Tyberg's Apple House: 1916

The next children that we know of who were living above the falls and needed to go to school were two girls who were ready for the first grade in 1916: Suzie Tyberg and Belle Leaton. It was too far for first graders to walk, all the way down over the falls to Glenn Junction. It would have been a fourteen-mile round trip for Belle. To solve the problem, Elizabeth and Alfred Tyberg converted a room of their house into a school room. The teacher, hired by the Glenn Creek School District, was Miss Dora Brown. Belle Leaton Clarke, at eighty-two, remembered Miss Brown as a pretty lady, tall and dark. She lived with the Tybergs and, as Belle remembered it, "There was a nice little room for the school."

Bob Wilkinson, Dora Brown,
Joe Schapers

Typhoid

School began in September of that year. In November Suzie Tyberg became ill with typhoid fever and she died December 13, 1916. They never knew where the typhoid germ came from. It is associated with feces-contaminated food or water, but no one else came down with it. If there had been drinking water drawn from Glenn Creek, it could easily have been contaminated because there were the two homesteads upstream from the Tybergs, and there was a certain amount of traffic along the road from Loon Lake.

During the previous summer Elizabeth and Alfred had taken Suzie to the World's Fair at San Francisco, and there was some speculation that she might have gotten the germ along the route. This is unlikely because it normally only takes about two weeks for the typhoid symptoms to show up. It can take longer, but I don't think it would be as much as three months. In any case, it must have been a shock to all of the people living in the wonderfully healthful Glenn Creek Valley to have had a case of typhoid in their midst.

Typhoid at that time was not all that uncommon in the United States. Deaths from it ran about 30 per 100,000 population. Five years earlier, in May 1911, Grace Woodruff (daughter of George Gould, on the West Fork), contracted the disease from a sailor she was caring for as a nurse in the hospital. She died, as did another nurse, Marguerite Mauzey, and so the people of Allegany were aware of typhoid.[1]

I'm sure that people above the falls were conscious of the dangers. Years later when Cle Wilkinson put indoor plumbing into the Tyberg house, the pipes evidently went first to the bathtub, then to the newly installed flush toilet, and finally to the kitchen sink. Alice Allen tells the story that Suzie's uncle Jerd Schapers would only drink from water at the bathtub because he knew the pipes went by the toilet before reaching the kitchen. This would be a funny story if we didn't know about the typhoid and the very imperfect understanding of germ theory that Jerd must have had.

Typhoid is quite rare nowadays, but still shows up from time to time. I remember in 1976 or '77 when a little boy at Broadbent came down with it. His sister worked with me in North Bend, and I don't remember a case of illness that had such an emotional impact on the community. After two weeks or more of intensive care at Bay Area Hospital, he pulled through. The family suspected contamination was from the water supply at Broadbent, which came from the South Fork of the Coquille River. They moved as a result.

After Suzie's death, Belle's parents Martin and Alma Saling Leaton moved to Glenn Creek Junction and Belle attended school there. Her teacher was Theresa Sandberg, from North Bend. Later they moved on down to Allegany proper, where her grandfather Tom Saling and her uncle True Saling ran the store at that time. The way Belle remembered it, the school at Tybergs ended after Suzie died. Of course, it did end for Belle because her family moved to below the falls, but the school evidently continued at least through the rest of the year.

Charlotte Mahaffy, in Coos River Echoes, tells of Miss Brown having six pupils there, from the Leaton and Wilkinson homes, and tells of a hike Miss Brown had with her seventh-grade pupil Agnes Wilkinson on January 13, 1917. They got lost in the woods and had to remain out overnight, and were found the next morning by a large search party of loggers.

The history of the Upper Glenn Creek school during this first period is pretty murky. Belle is sure that there had been no school there before Suzie was ready to go in 1916, and that fits with what we know of the Wilkinson children going to Glenn Creek Junction. The information in Coos River Echoes is about the only other source we have at this time, and it is not clear as to what years (other than 1916) school was held there.

---

[1] Aileen Rickard, *The Gould's of Elkhorn,* p. 105.

Upper Glenn Creek School
by Charlotte Mahaffy

Children of school age in the Glenn Creek District in 1916 were living beyond Golden Falls and so Upper Glenn Creek School was organized. It was a six-month school, and was held in the apple-house that was just across the yard from the Alfred Tyberg home. The improvised school room, attractively curtained, was headed by a small stove.

One of the first teachers was teenager Dora Brown (Mrs. Guy Churchill), who had six pupils registered at the same time. One of the primary youngsters, Susie Tyberg, died during the school year. Children attending this school were from the homes of the Wilkinsons and the Leatons. School board members were Mrs. Bunch, Fred Noah, and Mr. Neece.

It was on Saturday of January 13, 1917 that Miss Brown, with her .22-rifle and her seventh grade pupil, Agnes Wilkinson (Leaton), went for a hike in dense timber beyond Silver Falls. At night, when the hikers didn't return home, an alert was sounded. (Here was where rubbering on a country telephone had its merits.) The adventurers, after realizing their plight, hesitated about maneuvering in the woods, for they knew that somewhere in the vicinity was a dead fall. This was an Indian-dug pit which, when covered with brush, was used to trap deer and elk.

The night was crisp and clear; in fact it was the coldest one of the year. Now and then the plucky teacher would signal by firing shots from her rifle. Then to break the monotony, she would tell stories to her companion. The two, void of fear, paced under a roof of firs. Finally day dawned. The long night had passed.

The girls were found and led from the forest. They were overly embarrassed at finding themselves confronting fifty solicitous loggers. These men had left the Saturday evening dance at nearby Allegany to join the party for the lost teacher and her pupil.

(from *Coos River Echoes*, pp 45–6, reprinted with permission)

Glenn Junction School about 1912. Art Stora, Hattie Noah, Agnes Wilkinson, Fred Noah, Sanne Stora, Jane Wilkinson, Sigrid Stora, teacher.

105

Glenn Junction School Closes

By the mid-1920's there were no more children of grade-school age living either above the falls or at Glenn Creek Junction. The crisis occurred near the end of the school year 1924–25. It hit the papers, and fortunately for our history, Harold Ott saved the clippings. He made them available to me, and from them I will summarize what happened.

It seems that during the previous school year, 1923–24, there were only two students at Glenn Creek Junction: Amanda Noah and Los Angeles (Lossy) Crane. If it hadn't been for Lossy's name, which caught the attention of the newspaper reporter, there would probably not have been a record of this history.

Lossy's father Charles Crane evidently wanted a record of his westward migration and so he named some of his children after the cities in which they were born. One son was born on Calvert Street in Baltimore, Maryland, and so he was named Baltimore Clavert Crane. He figures quite prominently in our history of Upper Glenn Creek, because he was Cleland Wilkinson's trapping partner during the last years that anyone lived up there. One daughter was born in Los Angeles, California, in 1910 and she was named Los Angeles, Lossy for short.

Amanda Noah, daughter of Fred and Amanda Bunch Devoe Noah, quit school and got married, according to the newspaper article (*Coos Bay News*, May 8, 1925). That left only Los Angeles, a seventh grader, by herself for the 1924–25 school year. Amanda's sister-in-law, Amelia Noah, was the teacher. The controversy concerned the question of whether or not the school would run during the following year, with Lossy in the eighth grade, and the only student.

The school board consisted of Mrs. Baltimore Crane, Lossy's sister-in-law; Amanda Bunch Devoe Noah, mother-in-law of the teacher; and Mrs. James Fisher. Mrs. Fisher was the odd person out. She thought it was "a waste of public money to employ Mrs. Fred Noah, Jr., at $150 a month to teach one student." This attitude was most impolitic, and as a result Mrs. Fisher resigned from the board.

Mrs. Fisher's vacancy was immediately filled by the appointment of Mr. Alonzo Crane, one of Lossy's brothers. The newspaper caption on May 26, 1925, announced, "Los Angeles Wins Private School Through Brother. Alonzo Crane Named To Succeed Mrs. Fisher In Glenn Junction." At the same time, Mrs. Charles Crane, Lossy's mother, was named as Clerk of the School District. With these appointments, the Glenn Junction School District 76 became a family affair!

The newly constituted school board immediately signed a contract with the teacher, Mrs. Amelia Noah. The contract was for Mrs. Noah to teach Los Angeles through the eighth grade at $150 per month. This would keep the Glenn Junction School running with the one student for another year – until May 1926. The total cost of keeping the school open for one year was about $1,500. The controversy escalated, however, and it was not to be.

The following news item from the *Coos Bay News* tells the story of the controversy:

Glenn Junction to be Combined with Allegany

Coquille, June 5, (Special to *the News* – The Glenn Junction school, district 76, which has long been the private and exclusive educational institution of little Los Angeles Crane, will immediately be combined with the school at Allegany, district No. 45, the district boundary board meeting here today decided. The boundary board consists of the county court and C. E. Mulkey, county superintendent of schools. The decision of the board was unanimous.

A delegation appeared at the meeting from Allegany and urged the consolidation. Mrs. James Fisher, former member of the Glenn Junction school board who resigned because she regarded it as a waste of public money to pay Mrs. Fred Noah Jr., $150 a month to teach one pupil, was also present at the meeting in favor of the consolidation.

Although the present school board in Glenn Junction, consisting of relatives of the lone pupil and the teacher are said to be opposed to the consolidation, they did not register themselves at the meeting today.

A contract has already been signed in the district with Mrs. Noah to teach during the present season, and if this contract is legal she may be transferred to Allegany with her only student.

I have no record of whether or not the newly consolidated district at Allegany had to honor the contract with the teacher, Amelia Noah, or not. But beginning with the school year 1925–26. the Glenn Junction School was a thing of the past. In 1935 Brady and Neal Logging Company moved a large camp to the site of Glenn Creek Junction. When that camp closed in 1941, my family moved into the house Roy Neal had previously lived in. The Glenn Junction School building was still very much intact, after being vacant fifteen years, and it was one of the many places I played in while we lived there.

Golden Falls School

Probably in 1918 or '19 a new schoolhouse, called the Golden Falls School, was built at the upper end of the Joe Schapers place. It was built with donated labor and materials on land donated by Joe Schapers. This school ran off and on during the 1920's and continuously from 1928 until May 1941. During those years it had an enrollment that fluctuated from a low of two students to a high of ten.

After 1925 the Golden Falls School operated as part of the Allegany School District 45. In other words, there was only one consolidated school board. It was composed of three members, one of whom would be from above the falls. The teachers were hired by the school board. The old Glenn Creek District 76 with its fifty-six square miles of timber was now within the Allegany District 45. This was a very good thing for the Allegany district and made its per pupil assessed valuation the highest in the state!

After the 1940–41 school year there would have been only one student left at the Golden Falls School. As mentioned above, my family was living at Glenn Creek Junction at the now inoperative Brady and Neal Logging camp. I was in the second grade, attending Allegany School. My sister Carol was in high school at Coos River and my brother Laurence began first grade at Allegany the following year. Only Pat Wilkinson was left above the falls. She was in the fourth grade and went to live with her Aunt Jane and Uncle George Stemmerman so that she could attend Coos River School. The Golden Falls School was now a thing of the past.

The Consolidation of Schools

In 1941, the Golden Falls School was closed. At the same time the West Fork School District 87 (which had been formed in 1911) consolidated with Allegany. A 'C' was added to the number for the Allegany district, making it District 45C, for consolidated. The consolidation of four schools brought thirty students for the 1941–42 school year. A declining enrollment was due to Brady and Neal Logging Company ceasing operations at Allegany, and demographic changes caused by the advent of World War II.

After the war, enrollment went up again. Morrison and Knutson Construction Company had a large contract to build the logging roads for the impending Weyerhaeuser operations. Weyerhaeuser began its first logging at Allegany in July 1950, and enrollment at the school went back up to about fifty students in first through sixth grade. It remained fairly constant at that number for the next thirty-three years.

During the period 1948 to 1950 there was a big push within Marshfield School District 9 to consolidate with all of the rural school districts. This would do two things: it would give District 9 access to the immense revenue base that a half million acres of timberland would provide — timberland that was then within the boundaries of the rural school districts — and it would give the administrative bureaucracy more power and control. Newspaper articles and editorials of the time suggested that all of the school districts in Coos County should be consolidated with the implication that District 9 would be in charge. The District 9 administration threatened the people of the outlying

108

districts into believing that the state was going to force them to consolidate if they didn't do it voluntarily. This, of course, was pure bluff. Even forty years later, in 1992, Ash Valley still had its own elementary school district, as did several communities in Curry County.

As it turned out, the outlying districts that were more or less forced to consolidate with District 9 were Millington, Englewood, Delmar (Greenacres), Sumner, Coos River, and Allegany. District 9 officials promised that the schools in those consolidated districts would never be closed, as recorded in the minutes and reported in the newspaper. In elections held during 1950 all of those districts except Allegany voted to consolidate with District 9. Allegany alone voted not to consolidate.

In 1950 Weyerhaeuser moved a number of families into its camp across the river from Allegany, and there was a large influx of other Weyerhaeuser employees within the voting precinct. It has been alleged that not many of them voted in 1950 in the first (defeated) election for consolidation. We have no proof of this, but it has been alleged that prior to the second election, in 1951, Weyerhaeuser supervisors actually told their employees who were living within the Allegany voting precinct to vote in favor of consolidation. In any case, there was a larger turnout in the second election and the vote in favor of consolidation passed by a narrow margin. In 1952 District 9C had a new school building constructed at Allegany, at a cost of $90,000.

In November 1985, well into the school year, the D-9C school board unceremoniously and with no discussion voted to close Allegany School, effective immediately. There had been three years of increasing tension between District 9C and Allegany. This was the final blow.

District 9C had sold the school properties at Sumner, Coos River, and Greenacres for a pittance to private interests. To prevent that from happening to the Allegany school property, the Millicoma River Park and Recreation District was formed by a vote of the people of Allegany on November 4, 1986. The hope was that by forming a taxing district, Allegany could eventually gain title to the school property for use as a community center and thus avoid the disintegration which plagued all of the other rural communities in the area after they lost their schools. In the fall of 1991 the park district was able to purchase the site from District 9C for $64,000, and the old school continues to this day as a community center.

The Students and Teachers Speak

On the following pages are narratives, letters, and other first-person accounts pertaining to education and the Golden Falls School. It begins with the most senior of the students, Belle Leaton Clarke, who attended in 1916, and includes narratives from two of the teachers, and several of the students.

Chapter Fourteen

Belle Leaton Clarke's Early Memories
(Recorded at her apartment in Eugene, Jan. 12, 1992.)

I lived there [above the falls] soon after I was born. I was born in Eastside, Oregon, at my Aunt Effie McGriff's place [in 1910]. We moved back up above the falls and lived there until I was seven years old.

Suzie Tyberg and myself were the first students above the falls, and that was in 1916. Our teacher was Miss Brown, a pretty lady, tall and dark. She lived with the Tybergs and we had a nice little room for our school. We went to school every day, as we did later on in life.

There had never been a school above the falls before. I don't know how the children got to school before. It must have been down at Glenn Junction. I think when Suzie died that was the end of it. There was just the two of us. They didn't want to keep the school for just one child. Suzie and I were both the same age.

Belle Leaton Clarke (1992)

Our only pleasure was meeting with the Tybergs, who lived in the third residence above the falls. [Actually, the first residence above the falls; Leatons, where Belle lived, was the third as you went upstream]. It was always a pleasure to go there. Until we moved down below the falls, that was the greatest thing that happened, to play with Suzie. I used to play with Suzie, and then we had school. There was only Mr. and Mrs. Tyberg and Suzie. There could have been others [living there] because I was never there in the evening. If they were working out during the day, I wouldn't have seen them.

We had to go to town [Allegany] with a horse and buggy all the time I lived there. There weren't cars in that time. My grandfather Tom Saling was the first one to have a car in Allegany. That was about 1917 or 1918. Where the Sneads lived there was a road going down to the pasture and a barn. He [Tom Saling] put on the brake yellin', "Whoa, Whoa!" But we went down and I went through the windshield and I have a little scar yet.

I can remember when I was small that cougars would come down and steal our little pigs or cattle or chickens or turkeys that they could get from us. I also remember that we had a turkey that I didn't miss when they got him! He used to flog me every time I went out into the yard. My, they're strong. Beat you to death, if they get a chance.

110

It was hard to be the only child. I'm five years older than my brother Harry. At that place I got my first whipping from my mother. I bit my brother. They made me rock the buggy and I thought he was asleep and started out the door and he started crying. I had been rocking him for about a half an hour to get him to sleep. I thought he was asleep but Mom gave me my first whipping that I can remember. Actually she didn't give me many. I guess I was pretty good.

They [the Leatons] farmed a little land and made their own living almost. I think all we ever had to buy was flour, salt, pepper and this sort of thing, coffee. Water came from the creek behind the house. [Hattie: "I remember the drinking water coming out where the Gould's Lake trail came down. It was gravity feed and it came down in cedar troughs that were up on cross bars.] We also could catch fish in the morning and have them for breakfast or lunch or whatever.

Hunting was excellent and most all the men that didn't have a specific job trapped for the animals in the wintertime. I can still see them putting the hides on the little slabs of wood to stretch them so when the pelts dried they'd be right.

My mother's brother True Saling and his wife and their daughter Viola lived with us from the time I was born until I was about three. They moved into Allegany before us. Our neighbors were the Wilkinsons and my father's brother married Agnes Wilkinson, one of the girls of the Wilkinson family. They had a very nice, large family.

Grandad [William Leaton], he lived with us, and his son Tom lived with us from time to time. The men did a lot of trapping, and they always worked for the forest service in the summertime. In the wintertime they would trap. We had hunting dogs.

William Leaton was born in 1848 [in England] and passed away in 1940. He would have been 92, right? As long as I knew him he was very active, right up to the very end. He had plus personality, slow and easy going. He was a pleasure to have around.

I think the son, Martin, moved up there first. Then Uncle Bill and Uncle Alfred and all of them was up there a bit after that. Grandpa lived with us when we lived in Lundberg's house, and next he lived with us when we lived right across from the park [at Allegany]. Oscar [Lundberg] wasn't married at that time. Soon after we left down there, he got married. He had children, evidently, right?

Glenn Creek Junction and Allegany

Then we moved to below the falls and I believe it was called Glenn Junction. My teacher there was Theresa Sandberg, from North Bend, Oregon. When we moved below the falls to Glenn Junction our neighbors were Birches [Bunches?] at that time. The Noahs lived on up beyond the school.

When we moved to Allegany proper I went to school there until 1923, when I was thirteen years old. I was born February 28, 1910. I don't think I can remember the children's names. The picture I have is of the school at Allegany when I was in the eighth grade. There was Marie Michelbrink and Davey Robinson and the Ott children. And there was the Campbell girls too. Lee and Maureen and Ida Campbell. There was a Jack Piper I remember going to school with at Allegany.

My uncle True [Saling] and his wife had the store at Allegany and the hotel. My father and mother ran the park. People would come up from Coos Bay on the weekend and swim and have dances. That was the way they'd take a trip, particularly in the fall when the hunters all come up.

My father would take them hunting and my mother would do the cooking and take care of the people that were there and pack their lunches and keep them the week or so they were up. Then just as we were leaving in 1923 they started putting a road or a highway from Coos Bay to Allegany.

The sad thing, or frightening thing was the War [World War I]. We were all blessed because Uncle Alfred came home. But the family went through a lot at that time when he left. Of course we didn't get any word from Washington D. C. and the world day by day. It would take months before any news would seep through to us. In fact, I don't think we ever had a newspaper when we were there. We'd get mail every day at Allegany, because we had to take milk into the creamery, but not when we lived above the falls.

Dr. Horsfall was the MD that delivered me at Aunt Effie's house. His wife also gave my two aunts and myself music lessons. We would take the whole day taking the *Alert* to Marshfield. We'd be in town from about eleven till two. It would be about six or seven, depending on the tides, coming or going.

One of my desires is to see Loon Lake again. I haven't seen that since I was just a child – 1921, I think.

Chapter Fifteen

A Teacher's Memories

A Letter from Lillian Austin Edghill for the picnic of September 14, 1991.

Kings Beach, CA
September 7, 1991

Lilian Austin Edghill (1992)

Dear Natives of Golden & Silver Falls:

Warning: It's best you get a clown to read this epistle. Was great to talk to you Lionel Youst. Regret that I didn't have him as my 7th pupil back in the early 30's.

As I recall I applied for the vacancy at Allegany school but because of no experience, I was given the school above the Falls and, as I recall, over the objections of board members (Cle Wilkinson who wanted someone else) but as the story goes, after my resignation at the end of two years he goes to Martha Mulkey, Co. Supt. of Schools, and asks for a teacher just like Miss Austin. (Pardon the puffed-up stuff).

From there I taught first and second grades at Coos River – then on to Multnomah Co. where I taught in three different places and served as President of Multnomah Co. Primary Teachers Assn.

My last two years there, I fulfilled my desires to teach in Junior Hi, then I quit to be married. I could have said to my principal, "No more teaching, for fear I may end up an old maid like you." We had two boys, moved from Portland to Mill Valley, Ca. where Miles was Asst. manager of a chemical company in S. F. From there to Sacramento, Colorado back to Sacto., Chico, Fresno and here at Lake Tahoe all in my 81 years.

I've enjoyed excellent health and I thank the good Lord for His constant loving care. I praise Him for restoring my life after a Greyhound bus accident in which for one hour I was given up for dead.

Enough of that — now back to memories of my first school. I stayed with Grandma Tyberg, her Model-T Ford, brothers George and Jerd. Jerd, if you knew him, should have been in the movies portraying the good 'ole days in Virginia City, NV. Grandma too was something out of the story books. As Harold Ott would tell it, she would speed up on the blind curves going to Allegany trying to get around them before the other fella got there.

113

I had five students, namely Bob, Alfreda and Clifford Leaton; Alice Wilkinson, Hattie and Wilma Leaton, my first years. Freddie Middleton became my sixth the second year there.

People tried to warn me of Bob's distaste towards teachers. I'd say, "Ah, shut up, they're all Bobs." But, the first day of school he challenged me with a stick of wood. Guess what? I stepped right up to his face. I knew I had to overcome this problem so later I made up Arithmetic problems for him involving hunting, fishing, etc. He liked that. That won him.

Alice, are you there? Remember the time you had a loose tooth and I bravely tied a string around it and pulled. The tooth never gave way but you did a beautiful swoon. I haven't seen a better one in the movies today. I wasn't an accredited piano teacher like Harold Ott but Grandma Schapers and your daddy encouraged lessons. How come I've never read of an Alice virtuoso.

Hattie's mom and I finally got Hattie's mouth taped (not really) so timid Wilma could talk & share.

Bob Wilkinson would come once a week to keep my potbellied stove supplied. He would always ask, "What did Cliffy do or say this week?" You, Cliffy, never missed a thing said in the other classes when you were supposed to be working on your own assignments. Remember how I would make you write words missed in Spelling 10 X's. You looked up at me with venom in your eyes when you had only 5 cats instead of ten cats and said aloud, "I'm going to get a gun and shoot you."

Martha Mulky, Coos Co. Supt. of Schools would visit often. Who wouldn't find an excuse to view God's splendor.

Much to my regrets, that first year "they " replaced phonics with Dick & Jane's "see it and say it." I was horrified so, sneaky me, was incorporating phonics (sounds) into everything I could. I got caught. Martha walked in one day and after observing work on blackboards said, "Why Lillian, are you teaching the children phonics? Didn't you know that is regarded as old fashioned?" I believed so strongly in what I was doing – my retort was, "Don't you know I'm old fashioned?" The very same day a chord from my little 1800 A.D. organ brought the kids to their feet and they marched out to the music. Ditto when they came in from recess. Again, Martha, "Lillian, don't you understand, we aren't doing those formal things now." You guessed it – my answers.

I had no car, so my means of getting to and from the area could have been a problem. It wasn't. I'd short the kids noon hour on Friday, don my boots and trousers and strike out to catch Sam Ott's school bus which came as far as the Silver Falls. It's almost unbelievable how, without warning, different cars from the valley would come around the bend – "Hi, I came to pick you up."

Making it to school seemed likewise simple. I'd either get to Allegany Sunday eve or Monday morn – Sunday nights spent with Erma Ott's gracious mother Ethel Weaver or my brother Walter Austin would take me Monday morn to catch Sam.

Cattle rustlers! Yes, I had a taste of them. One Monday morn as I was hiking along, perhaps singing Joyce Kilmer's "I think that I shall never see a poem lovely as a tree," I rounded the bend and saw smoke rising from the schoolhouse. Yes I had laid the fire before I left Friday. Upon arriving I could see footprints in the snow. The Wilkinson brothers had lost their young stock but found the hides drying on the fence some distance away. Justice was dealt to the culprits. I lack the ability to make this story a "thriller-diller" but it was frightening.

Pat Wilkinson, you weren't out of the cradle when I taught at the school. My second year I lived with Grandma and Grandpa Schapers, your daddy Cle Wilkinson, sister Alice and you. Everyone knows times during those years were rough. Grandma would cook beans in many savory dishes but you still seemed to know *they were* beans. One time she brought a dainty little dish of them to your high-chair. I hardly realized you could talk but you opened your mouth, "I tired beans" and with one mighty thrust beans and dish went sailing through the air.

I'm determined to make the Coos River reunion next year. Won't it be fun to again see all your bald heads.

My prayers are that we're all in good shape spiritually and ready to meet the Lord when our time comes.

Love you all sincerely,

Lillian Austin Edghill

Lillian attended our picnic September 26, 1992. Here she shows the author where the Golden Falls schoolhouse was when she taught there 1932–34. Marketable second growth Douglas fir are growing in the old school yard.

Chapter Sixteen

The Golden Falls School
by Alice Wilkinson Allen

The first year I went to school we had five students. There was myself and Freddie Middleton, who lived on the place above us, and my cousin Clifford Leaton, his sister Alfreda Leaton, and his older brother Bob Leaton. Neither Clifford nor I were old enough, really, to go to school. We were both five, and would not be six until long after school started. I would be six in January following and I believe Clifford would have been six in March. But Miss Austin said that if we wanted to come to school she would be glad to take us and try to teach us, and we could at least try. So both of us decided, yes, we would like to go to school. Well, I did pass the first grade that year but Clifford had to repeat the first grade. He was almost a year too young, where I was only six or eight months too young

Class of 1932–3
Alfreda, Cliff & Bob Leaton, Alice
Wilkinson, Freddie Middleton

to actually start school that year. And generally girls are ready for school sooner than boys. Anyway, we had a nice school year that year. I think that as we didn't have such a thing as kindergarten in those days, we had what you might call a kindergarten education that year, plus whatever else we could absorb.

It was about a quarter mile from our ranch house up to the school house. The school house sat on some land that my step-grandfather, Joe Schapers, had donated for school purposes. The school house was erected with local lumber and local labor. It was stipulated that if school was not held for a certain number of years, then that piece of land would revert back to the ranch.

It was just a little one room school. It had probably a dozen desks in it, and a blackboard and a heating stove, some hooks on the wall where we hung our coats, and a bench to set the water pail and the dipper on.

The water was fetched from the creek behind the school, which was referred to as Schoolhouse Creek. We all drank from the same dipper, and all the classes sat in the one room. We had windows on one side for light, and fortunately it was on the side that faced the creek, so if you weren't too interested in lessons you could look out the window and watch the creek go by and daydream, which I think all of us took our turns doing.

There was a big maple tree across the creek from the school house that leaned way out over the water and was covered with moss. As a special treat, quite often after noon hour we would all go across the creek and perch in the maple tree, all of us including the teacher. She would bring a book and read a chapter of a story to us; something like *Alice in Wonderland* or *Treasure Island*, some of the real classics. We were very, very anxious and sometimes we could talk her into reading us a second chapter if the first one was rather short and it left you at a real exciting place. She could be persuaded on occasion to read the next chapter before we had to go back and resume our studies.

I went all eight years to that school, and graduated from the eighth grade there in 1940. The only other person I know of that went all eight years and graduated was Freddie Middleton. He and I were always in the same grade together and went all through grade school together. We had some happy times at the school house, lots of games during recess and noon hour. Everybody played: anyone who was in the first grade clear up through the eighth grade. The largest student body we ever had was ten pupils one year. The smallest was two, when there was just Freddie and I a couple of different years.

Alice & Pat Wilkinson, Freddie Middleton

The winter of 1936 was one of the hardest winters up there as far as weather was concerned. We had a fairly good snowfall that year and it lasted on into the spring. I remember when it began to snow. It first hailed and put a good coating of ice all over the ground several inches thick. Then it started to snow, so the snow had a good bed of ice to lay on and it didn't melt for a long time.

We generally wore galoshes to school, but with that snow the snow came way over the galoshes. Daddy took some old inner tubes and cut them up and made leggings to go on above the galoshes, so that our feet and legs would not get wet from walking through the snow. I remember the very first school day after the heavy snow. He went ahead and broke trail for us so that we wouldn't have to be worn out by the time we got to school. I think I was probably about in the fourth grade that year. None of the children were very old. He broke the trail for us and after that we could do pretty good on our own after the first real heavy snowfall.

I know around the stove there were coats and mittens and wet shoes and socks. It seems everybody got dried out before it was time to go home. Then, of course, when you got home you'd have all the things to string out and dry again. Almost everybody wore gum boots during the wintertime at the ranch because the mud in the corral was pretty deep where the stock had been wading around. There were rivers to wade across and that type of thing. Around the heating stove there was always a whole row of gum boots sitting back there steaming and putting out their odor and drying out.

117

I know I never did have a pair of gum boots that didn't leak. The water always seemed to come over the top, somehow. I did find that if you faced upstream when you were crossing the creek that the front part of the boot had a little scallop on it and you could take maybe another thirty seconds before the water would pour in the top, if you faced upstream. Whereas if you walked straight across, the water always came in the back of the boot. It was sort of a challenge to see how far across the creek you would get before the water would come in. This was something that my grandmother knew but never seemed to really understand. Somehow, it always happened.

One of the big events at the school was always the Christmas program. Everybody in the valley came to the schoolhouse on that night. I can't ever remember anyone missing it. There was always a little box of candies and walnuts that came from the Tyberg place. They were put in a little pasteboard box and each child had one. They had pictures of Santa Claus and red and green stripes on the boxes. Once in a while there would be oranges if someone had been to town and been lucky enough to have enough money to buy an orange apiece for everyone. Every child had something to do in the program. A little poem to recite, or we all sang Christmas carols together, and at the end it was always everyone singing "Silent Night," the audience and all.

This was pretty much of a social occasion. The other time at school would be the program at the end of school, which again was recitation by all the students, but it didn't quite have the spirit of the Christmas program.

Chapter Seventeen

Christmas, 1940

Alice mentioned the Christmas celebrations at the school, and that reminded me (Lionel) of my first Christmas above the falls. I am the youngest of the alumni, having been only in the first grade the last year the Golden Falls School was open. It got me off to a good start. Like most people who attended one-room schools, I have only fond memories of it, fond memories that extend beyond the school to home and neighbors.

Cle's cabin: the little house across the creek.

I was six years old that first year. It was May when my dad put in the mill. It was on the hill above Cle's field and the slab chute ended above the road a little east of the orchard. We lived in Cle's little cabin across Glenn Creek from the main place.

One thing about that valley that I remember so well is that once the sun goes down, it's dark. The hills go up fairly steep on each side, and the timber was about 200 feet tall and came right down to the edge of the fields.

The little cabin was crowded at Christmastime. It wasn't very big in the first place, and there were five in our family. There were several single men from the mill who had no place to go, and they were with us for Christmas. There was Bud Huff, Vic Graham, Charlie Strack, Sam Spearbeck, and maybe others. They were my buddies, and always talked to me just like they would to a grown-up.

Before the days of electricity there were little candle holders that were used on Christmas trees. Candles, about like the candles for a birthday cake, fit into those holders, which then clamp onto the boughs of the tree. We had those kinds of candles, and my mother would light them at a certain time when everyone was looking. If you weren't careful and happened to have a candle under one of the upper boughs, it could easily cause a fire.

After Mom lit the candles, we were distracted by something else and one of the boughs did flare up, causing a little excitement. My dad yelled irreverently, "Put those damned candles out!" Fortunately, there was no damage, and Christmas continued.

The men from the mill were talking about how far they could see in the dark. There was no consensus. One said twenty-five feet, another thought fifty feet, and so on. One of them asked me how far I could see in the dark. I thought about it, and trying to be conservative in my estimate, said that I could see a thousand feet in the dark.

Well, the men subjected me to considerable ridicule over that. How, they asked, did I think I could see a thousand feet in the dark? I answered, "If you put a thousand feet of lumber out there in the dark, I can see it," There was much laughter and my quick answer satisfied them and certainly elevated my status in their estimation. They never knew that I, growing up in a sawmilling family, didn't know that "a thousand feet" could also be linear measure. I thought "a thousand feet" always referred to a unit of lumber!

As I said, the mill was built in May and the slabs, edgings, and other waste from it was shot down the hill into Cle's field, where they took up a lot of room. This slab pile couldn't be burned during the summer, of course, nor in the early fall. Now it was December and there was an enormous pile of slabs. I suppose it took up two or three acres, and was thirty or forty feet high.

On Christmas Eve they set it afire. In a few hours it lit up the entire valley brighter than it had

The slab pile in Cle's field, summer 1940.

ever been. Pat Wilkinson remembers that she could read newsprint on their front porch from the light of it. It was a remarkable display for the occasion.

But what I remember most about that Christmas is not the slab fire with all its brilliant light. It is not Christmas presents, nor the ornaments on the tree, nor the light of the candles. What I remember most is the warmth of that little cabin across the creek at Cle's: the family, my parents, my brother, my sister, and the men from the mill. It was a good time for a little kid.

Carol Youst & Alice Wilkinson, 1940

Lionel and Laurence Youst, 1940

Chapter 18

A Stranger in the Night at the Golden Falls School
by Franklyn E. Smith

I received my teaching certificate from Ashland, Oregon's Southern Oregon Normal School in 1938 and signed my first contract to teach at a one-room school at Agnes, Oregon, up the Rogue River from Gold Beach. After spending two years there I came to Coos County and signed a one-year contract to teach the little one-room school at Golden Falls, above Allegany. I had not seen the school nor had I ever been to Silver Falls, but jobs were scarce so I really took the position sight unseen when I signed the contract at Strickland's store in Allegany. My friend and former schoolmate Norman Hamilton who was teaching at the Allegany School and who later became principal, drove me up the narrow one-lane road to Silver Falls where I found a place to board and room at the Stoke's home. I was not completely happy there so asked the school board for permission to remove the wood from the shed that leaned against one side of the schoolhouse so I could fix it up for living quarters. The school board condescended, and I put in a floor with some green un-planed lumber which I purchased from a nearby mill. The Allegany School had an old cook stove which the school board let me use, and after buying a small cot, a table and kerosine lamp and a few cooking utensils, I was finally settled rent free in my new living quarters for the ensuing school year.

Franklyn Smith, taught at Golden Falls School 1940–41.

When school opened on September 3, 1940 there were three students: Carol Youst, eighth grade; Lionel Youst, first grade; and Pat Wilkinson, third grade. Allen Lively was to arrive later. Needless to say, teaching was practically on a one-to-one basis and fortunately my students were all quite intelligent, eager to learn and discipline problems were unheard of since they all brought a deep respect from their homes. All five of us seemed like a family.

One day I was preparing Lionel for reading the story about Peter Rabbit and Farmer McGregor's Garden, and as we discussed the pictures above the story we came to the last one where Peter Rabbit stuffed with cabbage, sees the farmer looking over the fence at him and he starts to run towards the hole he had crawled through to get to the garden. At this point I asked Lionel what he thought Peter Rabbit was thinking at that moment. He looked at me with his big sparkling eyes and ever-present smile and said, "I'll bet he's wishing he could empty himself out in a hurry." The manner in which this little boy expressed himself that day long ago still brings a smile as it did then.

Life at Golden Falls was very lonely for me but on Wednesdays and weekends I'd hop into my 1936 Chevrolet with rumble seat and drive down to Allegany to get my mail and groceries and visit with my friend Norman Hamilton and also with Ella Noah at whose home he boarded.

One evening during the late spring, Carol and Lionel's parents invited me to dinner at their home which was a short distance up the road from the school. I arrived there about dark and we all had a lovely evening dining, conversing and enjoying ourselves and I left with my flashlight about ten o'clock. Next day it was school as usual and as evening darkened I lighted my kerosine lamp, turned on my radio and began correcting some papers and planning the next day's lessons, when out of nowhere a loud knock came to my door. Upon opening it I was confronted with a wild-eyed sort of person who introduced himself as "BLACKIE." This person was a total stranger to me as I had never seen him before. He asked me if I was Franklyn Smith the teacher and he also wanted to know what I was doing at Carol Youst's house the night before. I asked him how he knew and just what business it was of his. He looked at me with a smirk on his face and said, "I'll have you know I am in love with Carol, and I plan on taking her out to sea and marrying her someday as I have a boat captain's license which allows me to do so." This statement made, he informed me that he had been hiding out in the bushes near Carol's house, watching every move that was made and that I'd better not get any ideas in my head about her. At that moment in time I realized there was something seriously wrong with this person so I used a little psychology by asking him to sit while I tried to convince him he was wrong regarding his thoughts about Carol, and that my relationship with her was purely a teacher-student one. After this he seemed to mellow a bit and then went into a very lengthy dissertation about the fact he had been involved in a bank robbery with another fellow in Sacramento in which a policeman was killed and he himself was beaten over the head. He parted his hair to show me the scars. He also stated he had spent some time in prison.

Well, here I was, no phone, no nearby neighbors, and alone with this obviously mentally unstable and self-admitted ex-convict with a very shady past which I previously knew nothing about. I was frightened beyond words but I tried to cover it up with conversation. The long confession finally came to an end when he got up from his chair and stared at me once again with his beady eyes and said, "Well, Frank, I think you are a pretty good sort of person." In reply I asked, "And just what would you have done had you not thought so?" With this he reached into his pocket and pulled out a revolver and twirled it around his finger without another word. He turned towards the door and disappeared into the darkness of the thick Oregon forest and I never heard of or saw him again until I read Lionel Youst's father's narrative about him which Lionel just sent me here in Paradise during the month of July 1991.

Needless to say, on that frightening night at that isolated little schoolhouse I spent a sleepless night and the next day early in the morning I put a note on the door that there would be no school and I headed for Allegany where I told school board member Mrs. Noah and my friend Norman Hamilton of my experience and that they were to keep it a deep secret because I was afraid if the word got out I might get shot somewhere along the road or some night at the school. They kept the secret. I prayed for my safety and that of my students and finally, I completed my term of teaching at Golden Falls at the end of May, 1941.

Now on this 30th day of July, 1991 I relate this secret to Lionel Youst, his sister Carol, Pat Wilkinson and Allen Lively who I'm sure never knew about this incident.

In April, 1996, Mr. Smith's entire class of 1940–41 showed up unannounced at his house in Paradise, California, to present him a myrtlewood plaque. The inscription read, "We voted Mr. Franklyn Smith the best teacher we ever had," signed by the entire class. Left to right: Pat Wilkinson, Lionel Youst, Franklyn Smith, Carol Youst Baughman, Al Lively.

Allegany, Oregon
August 6, 1991

Dear Mr. Smith:

I was fascinated by your story of "the Stranger in the Night." It must have been terrifying beyond imagining. You are correct – I knew nothing about that. I read it over the phone to Carol this evening, and she didn't know about your episode either, but she did know about Blackie's designs on her. She told me that Blackie used to come around the house at night and blink a flashlight outside. Because of that, my parents sent her to our grandparents in Centralia, Washington, a few weeks before school ended that year. That must have been very shortly after the incident you had. She told me that Blackie followed her up there, and that he blinked the flashlight outside Grandma's house, and that my uncle Charlie called the police and put a stop to it. I never knew about that until tonight! Quite a story unfolding.

Sincerely yours,

Lionel Youst

Paradise, California
August 22, 1991

Dear Lionel:

Thank you for your nice letter of Aug. 6. Am so happy you were so pleased with the pictures and the little story about Blackie. I'm just glad I didn't know then what I know now after reading your father's account or I no doubt would have quit my job at Silver Falls School and hightailed it out of there. Seems I do remember your mother asking me to let Carol leave before the term ended. It all fits into place.

Franklyn Smith

———————

Excerpts from the Teacher's Contract between Franklyn Smith and the board of School District 45C, dated August 29, 1940: ". . . said teacher is to teach in the elementary grades of the above district for a period of 9 months for the sum of $810 in twelve installments, commencing on the 3rd of September, 1940." Chairman of the school board was Roy Strickland (who was running the Allegany Store at the time), and signing as clerk was Rose A. Stivers. Mr. Smith said that it came to "$67.50 per month + $5 janitor fee, and at year's end I bought a new Pontiac coupe for $595."

124

Chapter Nineteen

The History Of Allegany
(Original Project , English IV, Marshfield High School, Oct. 14, 1931)
by Elwin Saling

Allegany received its name from an old settler who came from Alleghany, Penn. His education was very limited and he did not know how to spell the word as it was spelled in Penn. so he did the best he could and "Allegany" was the result. It has always gone by that name and probably will always continue to do so.

About forty-five years ago there was no roads in Allegany except a sled road which ran above Allegany on the east fork of the Millicoma. To state the exact spot, the road extended to Marlo Creek. From there on the settlers used a pack horse trail which wound around the river and many times directly up the bed of the stream. Their produce was freighted to Allegany on a pack-horse and then shipped by small steam boats to Marshfield or Empire.

Elwin Saling (1913–1989)
High school graduation photo.

On the west fork of the Millicoma there were no roads and no outlet but a pack trail. This trail ran as far up as Elkhorn ranch which is a distance of about twenty miles by river.

In that day and age most of this country was open except for patches of large timber. The west fork country was especially open without any trees whatsoever because of a great fire which had gone through that section and burned north almost to the Columbia River. It was possible to see for miles and to ride a horse where ever you might chose. Grass grew very plentifully on all the hills and the country was almost overrun with game.

The story has been told that during this great fire the Indians, who were nearly the only ones to witness it, would get in the river but the heat of the water was so terrific that many were killed. It is also stated that wild animals were in the river with the red people and that most of these terror stricken beasts swam into the bay near Cooston at Crawford Point accompanied by many of the suffering savages.

There are several burial grounds of the red men in this vicinity and skeletons and Indian pottery or arrow heads may still be found. The Empire tribe of Indians made trips up the river after fish and clams in large canoes. One tribe that had their camp at Elk-horn were going to drive the whites out and had guns to do it with, but the whites soon put down the insurrection. George Gould was the owner of the Elk-

125

horn ranch and when he first came to that place there were Indians camped near his homestead. They soon moved on and the last that anyone saw of them was several years later when out hunting Gould met a small band of buck Indians riding across the mountains. Gould made his living by hunting and he had his own saw-mill and built a three story house which still stands. They even packed in an organ on horses. He reared a large family at Elk-horn and they were all excellent hunters.

During the time Gould lived at his homestead there was a large slide that they heard in the night. A whole mountain side slid in and damned up a creek, which then formed a lake. At the time they did not know what the strange noise and shake was but later they discovered the lake and named it Gould's Lake. It is beautiful little body of water in a tiny valley shut in by the mountains. It is almost a quarter of a mile in length and about seventy-five yards wide. At certain times of the year it offers excellent fishing, and I have known of two or nearly three hundred fish being caught in one day.

A few years ago it was attempted to plant bass in the lake but the trout killed them out. Many people think that it was better to have the trout kill the small bass because as soon as the planted fish grew to any size they would do away with all of the mountain trout.

The first logging camp in Allegany was the Porter Mill Logging Company. They logged with oxen on Laird Creek which joins the main river a half a mile from the boat docks. Just below the mouth of the creek there is a large bend in the river which is called ox-head bend. It received its name from an old ox head which still hangs there on a tree. This was placed there by the lumbermen when they killed an ox which was too mean to handle and fastened its head to the tree. Their logging works extended back to Smith Basin.

Vincamp ran the first hotel which still stands although it has been repaired and has an entirely new foundation. This building was later a school house and still later it became a hotel and a saloon where the first dances took place upstairs.

A man was shot in one room after two fellows had been quarreling. As one walked out of the door he shot back, but missed his foe and killed old man Micelbrink who was sitting there reading a paper.

Harris was the first settler above the Golden and Silver falls. The trail which led over the falls was very steep and dangerous. At that time there were no fish above the Golden falls, but later the inhabitants caught fish below the falls and carried them in buckets up to their homesteads and planted them there. Numerous trout may be found in the creek now. After a number of years the road was completed to Glenn Junction which is seven miles from Allegany. Later they finished the road from Loon Lake or Ash Valley to Allegany.

Horse stables, hitching rails and watering troughs were to be found for the accommodations of the people who came to "town," as it probably was called.

The first car was brought to this community in about 1910. It was a very strange looking vehicle compared with our automobiles today. A stage line was then established from Loon Lake to Allegany and also to Scottsburg by a man named Foote.

The old road wound around over the hills to make a shorter distance but the present road follows the river and omits most of the steep grades.

The fire patrol was established in this community about 1912. It was a small affair at that time and consisted of one man only. Since that date they have been enlarging the patrol to a great extent. Now there are many firewardens and lookout stations on the highest and most suitable peaks. The highest mountain around the Allegany section is named Ivers Peak. Fire patrol trails extend all through the forest and are kept in very good condition so that in case of a fire it will be (nearly) easy to reach by some of the numerous trails.

Much of the timber belongs to State forest reserve. Each year state foresters make a tour through this region to see that the trails, telephone lines, etc, are kept in excellent condition.

Oscar Lundberg is the head firewarden of the Allegany district. He is a very capable man and has held the job for a considerable number of years.

The patrol owns pack horses which are used to carry the food and other supplies back in the hills to the wardens. These wardens are under the supervision of Oscar Lundberg and during the summer they seldom leave their stations.

The look-out men do nothing but watch for fires from one day to the next. They are equipped with an instrument called a fire finder, by which they are able to locate the exact district of a fire. They immediately telephone the head office and report the blaze. The head office is in Marshfield and is run by J. A. Walsh.

The first public dance hall was built in 1912, but in a few years it fell down and was later replaced by a hall at what is now called Nowlin's Park. This hall burned down a few years ago and was replaced by the building which stands there today.

The new school house was constructed about twelve years ago and it stands on the hill just above the store. It was but one large building at first with only one teacher in charge but this soon proved to be unsatisfactory and a petition was placed through the center and two teachers were hired to instruct the pupils.

The road to Marshfield was completed a little more than a year ago. This was the greatest event in the history of Allegany because it gave the people a chance to go to town and come back when they wished. It takes about forty minutes to go from Allegany to Marshfield in a car and this includes the crossing of two ferries. It took from two to three hours on the boat and you could not come home until the boat left town which was at two P.M. It reached Allegany at about five.

The mail is still carried by the boat and also much of the freight including milk.

At one time about five years ago the river froze over as far down as the forks and for nearly a week communication with the outer world was cut off. We received no mail although the Mecca, which was the freight and passenger boat at the time made several attempts to break through the ice. Two logs were fastened along side the boat and came to a point a few feet from the bow. The boatmen would back up as far as possible and then go ahead in an attempt to break their way through, but it was all in vain. The ice at Allegany was thick enough to hold a man's weight.

The largest logging camp in this community was Buehner's camp which was later taken over by Stouts. They employed from two hundred to two hundred and fifty men. One phase of their entertainments was a show which was held every Friday night. This camp was located in Marlo Creek and the logs were transported to the log dump just below Allegany with trains or shays as they were called. The logs were then taken to Marshfield in rafts which were towed by launches or tow boats.

Trapping has been one of the leading industries during the winter. This was especially so in the past when game was much more plentiful. Years ago beaver ranged this country and on the West fork of the Millicoma river about ten miles above Allegany they dammed up the river and made a large hole which was named beaver hole and it is known by the same name today. Marten were very plentiful but in recent years are getting scarce. Fisher, like the beaver, were trapped but at present neither of these animals may be found in this community.

One of the principle occupations in summer was, and still is, the pealing of cascara bark. Hundreds of tons of this bark has been shipped from this district.

The elk have been protected for many years and are increasing very rapidly. Now we have one of the largest herds in the state of Oregon in this vicinity.

In the past years salmon were extremely plentiful. The rivers were alive with their bodies and especially just below a falls or rapids, but they are getting fewer from year to year.

Two of the most picturesque and powerful waterfalls in Oregon which are about ten miles above Allegany are named the Golden and Silver falls. It is hoped that someday this will be made into a state park and Allegany will consequently acquire a state highway.

(The end)

Teacher's notes: Material interesting; Form excellent.
Very fine work. Unusually interesting and Assembled. A+

Oscar Lundberg, left; Jim Nowlin, right. Dogs are Spot, Duke, & Ranger. Large black bear across hood of Model-T Ford and hide of very large cougar draped over the roof and windshield.

PART SIX

LIVING ABOVE THE FALLS

Joe Schapers homestead from the road, about 1913

Local history . . . confirms the idea that one's own home is worthy of study.

--Joseph A. Amato, *Rethinking Home*

Chapter Twenty

The Old Ranch
By Pat Wilkinson[1]

It's October 17, 1991. I'm in Hillsboro, Oregon, and my name is Patricia Jacqueline Wilkinson. I was born on July 1, 1932, at the old Keiser Hospital in North Bend, Oregon.

My mother died when I was born. I wasn't expected to live, but I'm still here, almost sixty years later. Anyway, the first eighteen days of my life I spent at the hospital. Then I went home to our ranch above the falls, and that's the area I'd like to tell you a little bit about.

The falls that I refer to is the Golden Falls, in Glenn Creek. The falls is located about twenty-five miles east of present day Coos Bay, in the coast range of mountains. Above the falls is a little valley usually referred to as the Glenn Creek Valley.

The first place above the falls is known as the Tyberg place. It was a homestead of 160 acres. The second place above the falls was the Schapers place, later the Wilkinson place, and that's where I went home to. It was also a homestead of 160 acres. The third place above the falls was the Price place, and later the Middleton place, and that was also a homestead of 160 acres. A couple miles above the Middleton place was the Howell place. It was a very small place, and I don't know how the land was acquired. About a mile above that was a place that is referred to as the old CCC Camp by many people. I knew it as the State Camp. It was originally built as a state prison camp for convicts, and the convicts worked on the road and in the Elliott State Forest.

I think the first homesteaders in the valley were the Tybergs. At that time you had to come from Coos Bay, which at that time was called Marshfield, up Coos River by boat to Allegany, and from Allegany by trail up the river to the falls, and up over the falls – all the way by trail. Now, the Tybergs: there was Mr. Tyberg; Mrs. Tyberg (Elizabeth Tyberg); and four of her brothers: Joseph Schapers, who was my step-grandfather; Charlie Schapers; Jerd Schapers; and George Schapers; and I believe there may have been another brother living at that time. Anyhow, they homesteaded the first place above the falls. They planted a large orchard, cleared the fields, built a house, and had a small dairy herd. Also, Jerd and George went out from the homestead over into the Matson Creek country and did a lot of prospecting

---

[1] Transcribed from audio tape and edited by Lionel Youst

for minerals. They trapped there for a number of years, and supplemented an income that way. Mr. and Mrs. Tyberg had a daughter named Suzie, and I believe she was born sometime between 1900 and 1905.

Joseph, or Joe, or Dad, as many people called him, went on above their homestead. He wanted to homestead there, but there were already homesteaders there: a man and a lady, and the man died. I don't know whether Joe bought the homestead from her or whether he just bought the improvements. At any rate, he acquired the land there. That gave them two homesteads.

I don't know what the time period was when the place on above was homesteaded. I believe it was homesteaded by people by the name of Price.[2] I don't know their names; I do know they had a son named Hazen, and he was born sometime between 1898 and 1905.

When Tybergs first came to the valley, I believe was in 1889. In 1909 a wagon road had been built from above the falls down to Allegany. This was quite a project, and of course there was no modern equipment. It was all done by manpower and horse power, and a lot of dynamite was used because they had to carve a trail right up the rock walls of the falls. This road went way on up Glenn Creek, up past the headwaters, and over the divide and down into Lake Creek, and Loon Lake, and connected with the road that went over to Scottsburg and Drain.

Mrs. Tyberg was quite a ruler over her brothers, and they did just about exactly as she said. Of course when Joe went up and homesteaded the place above there, it was more or less to increase her holdings in the valley. Well, unbeknownst to her, he corresponded with a woman in the East through a matrimonial association.

This woman was a widow lady with four children. She was my grandmother. Her husband had died and left her alone to raise four children. Her name was Laura Alice Tomer Wilkinson. Her oldest son, Robert Wales Wilkinson II, was born in 1898. The next child was Agnes, born in 1900. The third child was Jane Elizabeth, born in 1902. Her fourth and last child was Cleland Tomer Wilkinson. He was my father.

I've always sort of thought of my grandmother as being just a bit of a "woman's libber." At least I'd like to think she was, because of my father's name. I believe she named him to preserve her maiden name and her mother's maiden name. His names,

Joe and Laura Schapers family on the road above the homestead.

---

[2] Actually, the place above the Joe Schapers place was originally homesteaded by Joe Larson. The place which was a half mile above it was first settled by Newell Price and his family. It was later known as the Howell place.

Cleland Tomer, were taken from their last names. Cleland was her mother's last name; Tomer was her last name.

I'm not sure just why both of them were writing to a matrimonial association. I suspect that Joe had found that homesteading all by himself was a very, very big job, and he needed help. I know that my grandmother was having great difficulty trying to raise four children by herself. Anyhow, they corresponded, and he sent her train fare and boat fare to bring her out here to the West Coast. I'm not sure where she was living at the time, but I believe that she was living in the Shenandoah Valley in Virginia.

Anyhow, she and her children came out here by train to Portland, and from Portland they caught the boat to Marshfield. There was no highway or raod that went through from Portland to Marshfield. Anyhow, he met them at the dock where the boat came in, and literally, they were married on the dock. Then they made the journey up to the Glenn Creek Valley.

Well, Mrs. Tyberg had no idea of what Joe was up to. She didn't know my grandmother was coming, or that he had any plans to bring anyone else up there. Of course, she was very, very put out with the turn of events, and she and my grandmother were never very close. They were not enemies, but yet they were never really very good friends.

Joe was about fifty-two years old when he got married, and I believe my grandmother Laura was about thirty-two years old. This was a real change for her. She had been a city girl most of her life. She was born in Pittsburgh, Pennsylvania, and I believe all of her children were also born in Pittsburgh. After her husband died she lived several different places. I think she lived in Maryland for awhile; she lived in Virginia; for awhile in Pittsburgh; and I believe she lived a little while in Kansas. She made her living primarily by taking in washings and doing housework for other people.

Joe had been living in a one-room cabin. When he knew a family was coming he made quite a large addition to the cabin: an upstairs and a downstairs. The shack that he was living in became the kitchen. The downstairs of the new building was a living room and a storage room and then there was an open upstairs.

Life on the homestead was hard. There was land to clear, animals to care for, fences to build. They had a small dairy herd, chickens, pigs, turkeys, some ducks, and of course horses. My grandmother did a lot of the sewing, made a lot of the clothes. Some of the furniture was homemade. The beds had cornshuck ticks. That is, you take dried cornshucks and stuff them in blue stripped ticking material and put them on the beds rather than mattresses. Coal oil lamps —and this was really quite a change for my grandmother. Everyone worked.

The kids did go to school at Glenn Junction. That's the point where Glenn Creek runs into the East Fork of the Millicoma. There was a school there, a one-room school. All of the children attended that school at one time or another. This school was about five miles from where the ranch was. That was a long trip for kids to make every day, a ten mile round trip. And so, later on, in about 1914 or '15 or '16, for a few years a school was held in Tyberg's apple house. All of my grandmother's children went there, also Suzie Tyberg went there for awhile. I think she died when she was about eleven or twelve years old. She died in about 1916. I think she was just the same age as my dad, who was born in 1905.

Glenn Junction School, 1913. Small boy in front, left, is Cle Wilkinson; two girls behind him are his sisters, Agnes and Jane.

After that, my grandfather gave to the school district one acre of land on his property. Everyone got together and built a little one-room school there. My dad helped to build the school. Later he went to school there. I think the first class was held in 1916 and the first teacher there was Dora Brown.

It was a long, hard trip from up there into town, to do any sort of business or any trading. They had to go by wagon down over the falls to Allegany. At Allegany they caught a boat and went to Marshfield, usually staying over at least one night, then back on the boat to Allegany and back up over the falls by wagon. It wasn't until I think 1930 a road was built from Allegany on down the river to Marshfield, so that you could go all the way by wagon, or in that period, by car.

As time went by my grandmother's children, one by one, started getting married, leaving what we always referred to as "The Ranch," or "The Old Ranch." The first of her children to get married was Agnes. She married Alfred Leaton shortly after World War I. The second to get married was Jane. She married George Christopher Wesley Stemmerman. The third to get married was my father. He married Romelia Henderson in 1925. The last to get married was Robert. He married Ann Weber, I believe her name was.

So my grandmother and grandfather were left for a few years by themselves on the ranch. But when the depression came, and times got very hard, first Robert came back, I think it was about 1929 or '30, and stayed in the original ranch house. A little later my father and my mother and my sister, Alice Ann Wilkinson, came back up there. My father built a little cabin or small house over by the mouth of Woodruff Creek. Others came to the valley then too, trying to do something to weather the hard times of the depression.

When I was born in 1932 and my mother died, my father didn't know what to do. He thought of trying to find someone to adopt my sister and I, but I was a sickly little child and no one really wanted to adopt me, and he didn't want to separate us. My grandmother, who was about fifty-six years old at the time, agreed to take on a second family and raise us herself.

I'd like to say a little something about the people who lived in the valley as I knew them when I was growing up, mostly during the 1930's. There was Mrs. Tyberg, Elizabeth Tyberg, who lived on the place below ours. As I remember her, she was really quite a character. She sort of ruled the roost over all of her brothers. There are many, many stories about her, like before women were able to vote she would go to the polls with her brothers. When the election officials objected to her going into the voting booth with her brothers, she explained she had to, because otherwise she didn't know how they would vote!

She was a very hard working woman. She worked a lot in the fields, and I believe she was the only person that lived on that place who knew how to drive a car. I believe Mrs. Tyberg must have been in her seventies one morning when I went down with some letters for them to mail, because they were going to town. Just as I got to their place, Mrs. Tyberg was loading the cream cans into the trunk of their Terraplane. She had a five-gallon cream can in each hand. As I got there, she swung first one up and put it in the trunk, and then with the other hand swung the other one up and put it in the trunk of the car. I don't believe there are a whole lot of women her size and her age who could have done that.

Then there was Charlie Schapers, who lived there also. He was the youngest brothers. He was a very kindly man. He loved children. I remember that he used to come up to our house every so often, and he always had something for us kids. It might just be some walnuts off of their tree. Our walnut tree never had any walnuts, so walnuts were quite a treat for us. Of all the kids, he had a favorite, and that was my sister. He would hand walnuts out to the kids and he'd always be sure she got the largest ones, or an extra one; if he handed out candies, that she got one or two more. I can remember that he had a crippled hand. He would set us on his knee, and we would go "ahhhhhhhh" while he thumped us on the back. I can remember how that crippled hand of his felt on my back, as he would pat me on the back so that the long, drawn out sound would sort of waver.

Then there was Jerd, her other brother that lived down there. He made pipes out of apple wood, out of the limbs of apple trees. He had quite a large collection of them. Some of them he smoked, and he wanted to make pipes and give them to us kids. Well, my grandmother wasn't very approving of this, but he said to tell her that they were bubble pipes, not pipes for smoking. At one time I had two or three pipes that Jerd had given me. Also, in spring I would make a pilgrimage down there to visit Jerd. They had apple trees that were early transparent apples, and we didn't have any. I would always take a small gunny sack and a little piece of rope down with me, and I'd say to him, "Well, Jerd, how do you think your apple crop is going to be this year?" He'd sort of chuckle, and he'd say, "Let's go see." We would go to the orchard, and what really fascinated me is that he'd take a small apple and put it in the lower corner of the gunny sack. He'd tie a rope around the apple in each corner, and then tie it around the top of thesack with the apples in it, and make a little pack sack that I could take home with me.

Then of course there was Joseph Schapers, my step-grandfather, who homesteaded the place we lived on. He was to me a very strange man, but also a very, very good man. It seems as though I was his favorite. I can remember he did a lot of work with the wheelbarrow, always hauling something somewhere on a heavy, homemade wheelbarrow. I would watch him working from up on the hill or wherever I was playing. If he

Laura Tomer Wilkinson Schapers with her husband Joe Schapers & her children, Cleland, Robert, Agnes, and Jane Wilkinson.

started out with the wheelbarrow toward home, usually from the direction of the orchard, I would start running toward the wheelbarrow and he would see me coming and he would stop. No matter how heavy a load he had on that wheelbarrow, he would let me climb on top of it and then give me a ride the rest of the way home.

All of the Schapers, I believe they were born in a German community in Missouri, spoke with a German accent and they also read German. I remember newspapers the Tybergs used to get and then send up to Joseph that were written in the old, hard to read, German script. He would occasionally read those. He had a lot of funny ways. Once my grandmother told him that she would like to have a new watch. She had been looking in the catalog. Nothing happened, and nothing happened. She didn't get a new watch. The one she was looking at cost two or three dollars. Then, one day, he flipped a twenty dollar gold piece into her lap and he said, "There, Aunt Hanner, there's that watch you been wantin'." And where in the world he ever got the name of Aunt Hanna, or Aunt Hanner, for her, I will never know.

After the first addition to the house had been made, the original cabin that we referred to as the old kitchen was really falling into disrepair. She asked him if he would replace that and build her a new kitchen. Well, she had waited a long time and he had made no efforts toward building a new kitchen and she had sort of given up on it. Then one day he asked her, "Would the measurements 20 by 30 be about right?" "Of course," she said. "That would be fine," because she didn't want to do anything to discourage him from getting around to building her a new kitchen. Well, out of the new kitchen we got a very large dining room, a bathroom, a large kitchen with a pantry, and a small bedroom, plus a full upstairs. So, quite an addition was made to the house at that time.

Also, one time, in a little publication known as the *Oregon Farmer*, that most farmers in Oregon got, there was an advertisement. If children could get subscriptions to the *Oregon Farmer* they could win prizes, and the prizes for little girls were what they called "Betsy-Wetsy" dolls. My sister and I decided that we would like to have these dolls, so we would sell subscriptions. We went to our neighbors who, of course, knew we were trying to get these dolls. We sold two or three subscriptions to every household, they knew we wanted these dolls so bad. At

135

any rate, we did get enough subscriptions, so finally, our dolls came. The thing that was so special about these dolls is that they came with a little bottle. You could feed the "Betsy-Wetsy" dollies water out of the bottle and it would go through them. There was a little hole in the bottom of the doll and they would wet their diapers. When my grandfather found what those dolls did, somehow he seemed to think that they were really quite obscene. He went to my grandmother and he said, "Aunt Hanner, you ain't gonna let them little girls play with them dirty pissin' dolls, are you?"

Dad, as almost everyone in the valley called him, was always busy doing something. He, of course, helped in the fields; he helped every morning and every night with the milking; he did all the pruning that was done in the orchard. He was always making things out in the woodshed on the shave horse with the drawknife — pegs and door latches and I don't know what all. He made many, many things with that drawknife. He sometimes helped with the separating and mending of the harness and just always, always busy doing something.

Then of course, there was my grandmother Laura. There is so much I'd like to say about her. She never really had a very good life. She worked terribly hard all her life, and she did so many things there: all of the cooking; the housekeeping. She made a lot of our clothes; she worked in the garden. I don't think she ever worked out in the fields or in the barn very much, but she did so very many things — even making our soap out of lye that she leached out of the ashes from the stove and mixed with beef tallow and made it into cakes. And I'll tell you, that was good soap. It would bleach things clean and it would also take the skin right off your hands sometimes! We used it sometimes for everything: for washing clothes, washing dishes, washing ourselves, and even our hair with it. She did a lot of canning. She would put up hundreds and hundreds of quarts of fruit and vegetables and meat.

She was a very, very religious woman. I don't think she was ever a member of any particular church, but her beliefs were very much like those of the Seventh Day Adventists. Being up there, she of course had no church, no support in her beliefs, except reading her Bible, which she did nearly every day. She was not a well-educated woman. I believe she completed the third grade, but she read her Bible nearly every day. I'm sure she felt a lot of isolation from the things she believed in. And then of course, after having raised her own family, she had my sister and I to raise. I know, in my case at least, that was a very big job.

And then, of course there was my dad, Cle Wilkinson, who did a lot of work on the farm. During the depression he sometimes worked on the road. I believe the men were making four dollars a day then, being paid by warrants from the county. They could sell the warrants to anyone for whatever the person would give them. The county was not able to honor them. But if you held them long enough, until the county could pay, they would pay a hundred percent of the face value plus a fair rate of interest. The usual amount that people could sell them for was fifty percent, so actually people were working on the road for two dollars a day.

When he was younger, and also later in life, he worked some in the logging woods. I think where most of his cash money came from was from trapping in the winter. He had trap lines on a lot of the ridges and up several of the creeks. He trapped for a long time out over the divide toward Lake Creek. He built a little cabin of mostly scrap material on Bear Creek. He also stayed in Guerin's cabin, up the hill. That's one on the cabins that was built by what we called the "Lake Creekers." People had gone in there — actually they were speculators — and they had taken up timber claims. Each family had built a cabin and Guerin's cabin was one of those. He [Cle] also built a cabin on Matson Creek, and later on he and Baldy Crane built two trapping cabins over on the West Fork. One they named "Pleasant Valley Manor." It was completed on 10-10-46. The other one was called "Pheasant Cabin," on down the West Fork, and it was completed on 12-12-47.

Each winter he would go out on the trap lines and be gone for several days a week, during which time my grandfather and my sister and my grandmother and I would do the milking and the chores around the ranch. He trapped mainly for martin and for mink. Occasionally he would catch a bobcat. There were no beaver in any of the streams then, and I believe that during that time it was not legal to catch beaver.

He also made some money by peeling chittam. That was really quite a job. You had to peel the bark off the chittam tree, chop the tree down, peel the bark up until the limbs were, oh the size of your finger. Then you had to roll all that up and pack it out and spread it out on the roofs or the ground to become thoroughly dry, then gather it up from there, crack it on a device that was made for cracking up the bark into small chips, stuff it into bags, and take it to town. The bark dried out about fifty percent. If you peeled a hundred pounds of chittam bark, by the time you got it dried and cracked and sacked you would probably have fifty pounds of it. Of course you had to pack all this out of the woods. Sometimes the price for a pound of dried chittam was one cent, which meant that you would have to go out and work nearly all day to make just fifty cents.

Bill and Bernice Leaton lived in the little cabin near Woodruff Creek with their children, Hattie, Wilma, and Eldon. That was mostly during the depression years. Charlie Howell lived about three miles up the road on the Howell place. I don't believe it was a homestead, because it was very small, only a few acres. One of the main things I remember about him was his team of mules. When haying time came around and all the neighbors got together at each place to put up hay, everyone wanted Charlie Howell to come. Not only with his team of mules, but to load the hay because he was one of the best hay loaders in the country. He could get an awfully big load of hay onto a hay wagon.

On the place above ours lived Slim and Frieda Middleton and their son Freddie. I always called them Aunt Frieda and Uncle Slim. They also had dairy cattle, they picked ferns, peeled chittam, raised crops — about the same thing as the other people who lived in the valley.

My sister, of course, lived with us on the ranch. I remember that she did an awful lot of work around there. Every morning and evening she would be sort of in charge of separating the cream from the milk. The buckets of milk would be brought from the barn up to the separator house. She would run it through the separator. These old separators were rather complicated affairs. They had a number of disks inside them, which had to be washed after each morning and evening's separating, and that job seemed always to fall to my sister.

137

Another job which fell always to her, and I know she was not fond of, was sprouting the potatoes. We had a potato house and it was very dark; it had no windows. There were bins on the dirt floor, and dirt that partially covered the potatoes to keep them from freezing in the wintertime. Periodically she would have to go into the potato house to pick up any potatoes and break off any sprouts that were starting to grow so that we would have potatoes enough to last us until the new crop. It was very cold and very dark and very smelly out there but that job seemed always to fall to her. She helped sometimes in the fields at haying or harvest time, and also did a lot of things around the house.

She went to school, all eight years of grade school, at the little Golden Falls School. I don't remember who all of the teachers were, but there was Miss Lillian Austin, Grace Gray, Marjorie Baird, a Miss Reames, Miss Hagquist, Mrs. Diurks, Franklyn Smith. It was a small, one-room school. The most children that ever went to that school was ten, and that was in 1938 and '39 when I was in the first grade. There were ten children in the school that year.

The farms in the valley, each of them had a small dairy herd. I believe everyone sold cream to the creamery in Marshfield. I don't think much milk was sold. Only the cream was taken to town. We had quite a large flock of chickens at one time, leghorns. We sold eggs, we sold cream, we grew beans — mostly bayo beans — and we sold them. We sold potatoes and some other produce out of the garden. Occasionally a calf or beef would be sold.

We had pigs, but I don't remember of ever selling any of the pigs. They were killed and the hams and the bacon smoked for our own use. I can remember them sticking the pig. Then we had a great big log that was hollowed out that would be filled with water. Then a fire was built, and rocks heated in the fire. The rocks would be lifted out of the fire and into the tub of water to heat the water, and the pig would be rolled in there and scalded so it could be scraped and butchered.

A lot of our meat came out of the woods — deer and elk. Some of them may have been killed during a hunting season, but most were not. Some of this meat was made into jerky and taken to town and sold. My dad and my uncle Bob and Charlie and Jerd and I think nearly everyone in the valley was also engaged in a moonshining operation making whiskey and selling that to bring in a few dollars.

All in all, I think the people living up there during the depression were much better off than those who lived in town and could not find any work and couldn't live off the land or out of the woods. We had our own milk and eggs and vegetables and fruit and meat. We didn't buy very much from town: soap and lots of sugar for canning, coffee, sometimes lard and spices and flour.

I remember when I was small, a conversation I overheard one time near the end of the year. My dad and my grandmother was talking, and my dad said to her, "We have done pretty well this year." I think the year must have been 1937 or 1938. There were five of us living there at the time. Anyhow, he said, "We have done well this year. We have made three hundred and sixty dollars." And as I sit here and figure it out, that is approximately one dollar per day, or twenty cents per person per day. That bought everything. It bought the oil for our lamps, our clothing, the

groceries that we had to buy; anything and
everything. So I do feel that the people in the
valley up there did live better than those in
town during the depression.

I recall a few incidents from my
childhood. Once when I was about four or five
Mrs. Tyberg came up. She and my
grandmother were working on making rag rugs,
and they were talking about women of "ill
repute." I was fascinated by the talk of the way
these women dressed. It really fascinated me.

Alice and Pat
"where the road comes down the hill"

Out in our dining room there was a row of nails driven into one side of the wall and
that's where everyone hung their spare raingear, sweaters, jackets. The wall was just
filled with all kinds of gear like this. Well, I took all this stuff down from the wall
and took it out into the yard. I was dressing up in it, pretending I was a woman of ill
repute and dressing the way I imagined they dressed. My grandmother came out and
she said, "My goodness, what's all this mess? What in the world are you doing?" I
said, "I'm playing that I'm a woman of ill repute." Well, my grandmother went into
high gear and made a beeline for me for taking all the coats and stuff off the wall and
having them all out in the yard, so I gathered them all up and took them back into the
house. It wasn't until many, many years later, when I found out how women of ill
repute actually made their living, that I figured out why I had gotten a spanking that
day.

Also, when I was about five years old, a missionary lady named Amelia
Noah, who may have been connected with the Seventh Day Adventist Church, came
up and spent most of the summer there. I think this was a good time in my
grandmother's life. It's the only time that I know of while she lived up there that she
had anyone to talk religion with. Anyhow, Amelia Noah organized meetings at least
once a week and held services at the various houses. She used to take us kids down
by the creek and read us Bible stories. Before she left, a number of people were
baptized in Glenn Creek. I think this was really a good time in my grandmother's
life.

Once my sister and I were playing out in front of the house in the field
where the road came down from the hill, across the field to the picket gate around our
front yard. I don't know whose idea it was, but one of us would go up to the road up
the hill and close their eyes. The other kid would stand down by the front gate. The
one up the hill would start running with their eyes closed, just as fast as they could,
down the hill and across the field. Just before they got to the gate, the one standing
by the gate was supposed to yell at them to open their eyes. We had done this several
times each. Why someone didn't fall on the way and break their neck, I don't know.
Anyhow, my sister was up the hill with her eyes closed and I decided it would be neat
to find out what would happen if I didn't tell her to open her eyes. I guess I thought
that somehow, miraculously, she would know when to open them. I wasn't mad at
her, I didn't intend for her to get hurt. But anyhow, she was coming down the hill
and across the field just as fast as she could go, and wham! right into the front gate,

which was made of rough picket boards. She didn't open her eyes in time, and she really hit the gate. I don't remember if they had to take her to the doctor or not, but I do know she will bear the scars to her grave.

Another time, we had gotten a wagon for Christmas. It was a wagon we were to play with and to help us do our chores. Since she was a little older than I, my dad explained to both of us that we were each to be in this wagon half of the time. It was to be shared between the two of us. A few days later we were playing this game where she would get in the wagon and I would pull her to the top of the hill

Pat and her dad

on the road, then we would both get in the wagon and coast down the hill. She would then get back in the wagon and I would pull her back up. I complained that she should be pulling me up part of the time. She said, "Oh no. Daddy told us that we were each to be in the wagon half of the time. Though you're not in the wagon while you're pulling me up the hill, you are in the wagon coming down the hill, so your are in the wagon half the time." I was quite satisfied with that explanation.

After the Yousts came to live up there, I remember a couple of incidents in playing with Lionel and Laurence. One of them, Lionel and I were going on a picnic. My grandmother had made something for me to take and Lionel's mother had made something to eat for him to take. We went up Woodruff Creek a little ways and we ate some of our picnic. There was plenty of food left over, so we decided we were going to become cooks.

We got a large flat stone and put it on the ground, and that was our stove. We put a little of this kind of food, and put it on the stone, and a little of that kind, and maybe add a little water and a little dirt, and stir it, and play that we were cooking. Suddenly Lionel turned to me and he said, "You know, my mom will be real mad when she finds out we wasted this food." I thought, "Yea, my grandma too." I guess we felt we had to hide the evidence, so we started digging a hole. All we had to dig with was our hands and some sticks. Anyhow, we must have spent an hour digging this hole, probably two or three feet deep, and we buried the evidence so that no one would ever know we had wasted all that food.

Sometimes my dad would take my sister and I on walks during the weekend or on summer days. We would take sandwiches or something to cook and nearly always a little bit of coffee and a can and something to drink out of and hike up the road or up the trail. He would build a little fire and we would brew up coffee and maybe cook something over the campfire and have a little picnic of our own. He always talked a lot about his trap line, and how the creeks ran, and how the ridges would curve around. He would draw maps, either just in the dirt or perhaps on a piece of paper. I think his great love, and also my sister's and mine, was when we were out in the woods.

I think that I had a very good childhood. I always had chores to do around the place, but there was time for playing in the creek and fishing and hunting

140

squirrels and that type of thing. In the spring my dad would go out with me, usually up Woodruff Creek, and select a tall, straight hazel pole that would become my fishing pole. I didn't have a lot of fancy gear, and never had a reel that I can remember of, but the fishing in the creek was pretty good, and the playing in the creek, the swimming, catching crawdads. There was a little gravel bar that ran out into the creek where I was allowed to build fires. I used to build fires down there and cook chipmunks that I had killed with my BB gun and generally had a real, real good time when I was a kid.

My grandfather died in 1939. Actually, he died in Marshfield of a stroke, and he had willed half of the ranch each to my father and my uncle Bob. Also, he had willed $500 each to his two stepdaughters, Agnes and Jane. There was not money to pay the girls their inheritance, and also I believe the taxes on the ranch were somewhat behind. So, they decided to sell the timber on the place.

They sold the timber to a man named George Youst. George Youst had to do a little bit of work on the road, which was not in good shape, especially down over the falls, and very wet and slick around the Frog Creek area. After improving the road, George Youst brought some equipment up and he set a mill up on top of the hill and built a lumber chute across the county road and it ended near where the orchard is. Then he built another chute, also across the county road, to chute the slabs down, and they landed in the middle of our field. Every once in awhile it was necessary to burn the slabs, before the pile got too large. This was usually done at night, and it was quite an event in the valley. I remember we could stand on our front porch and read a paper from the light of the fire at night. Everyone would come to the burning of the slab pile, partly I think for safety reasons, and partly because that was really a big attraction.

The lumber that went down to the dock was loaded onto trucks and trucked to Coos Bay. Doris Youst, George Youst's wife, was one of the truck drivers. It was unusual for a woman at that time to drive a lumber truck, and she also, I believe, drove log trucks. At that time these trucks were not as automatic and mechanical as they are nowadays. They had mechanical brakes, and Doris Youst was not really a very large woman. But she drove truck down that road that many people would not dare to take their cars over. She drove down there every day.

The loggers and some of the men who worked in the mill built little shacks, most of them down near the orchard. They lived there at least during the week while they were logging or working in the mill. After most of the timber was logged off in that area, George Youst moved the mill from up on the hill to down in one of our fields near Woodruff Creek. He also built a dam there so he could have a mill pond.

He logged some of the area around there. As he went up the creek, he built another dam, a splash dam, and sort of sluiced the logs from the upper end of the property down the creek and stopped them at the mill pond near the mill.

I think that George Youst first came there in the latter part of 1939 and ended his operation probably sometime in 1943.[3] For awhile he and his family lived in the little house near Woodruff Creek.
Later on, they moved up to the old Middleton place.

Pleasant Valley Manor – Cle and Baldy's cabin on Elk Creek

In 1940, my sister graduated from the eighth grade and had to leave that fall to go to school at Coos River. In 1940 when the school started there were four students: Carol Youst, who was in the eighth grade; myself, who was in the third grade; Allen Lively, who lived with his grandparents Al and Molly Stokes down on the Tyberg place. Mrs. Stokes was taking care of Mrs. Tyberg, who was very ill at the time. And Lionel Youst, who was in the first grade. Our teacher was Franklyn Smith.

After the end of the school year in 1941, the little school up there closed. In the fall of 1941 I had to leave and go and live with my aunt and uncle on Coos River so that I could attend school. I came back to the ranch every summer, when school was not in session. When I was living in Coos Bay, Marshfield as it was at that time, many times I would walk home on Friday night and then walk back to town on Sunday afternoon. Once in awhile I would catch the school boat in Marshfield and ride it up to the end of its run near Allegany.

Some of the years, during the winter, I had a little short trap line that I ran up part of Woodruff Creek. When I was home on the weekends I would tend to my trap line. It was about twenty-seven miles from the ranch down to where I lived in Marshfield.

I think that George Youst had a pretty hard time keeping a crew together because the war had come and a lot of the men were being drafted. Sometimes my dad worked in the logging woods or in the mill, but he still went trapping nearly every winter. By this time our herd of cattle had diminished or disappeared. New laws about selling milk had come into being and we had no electricity and no way of keeping things modern and up to date and sanitary enough to be able to sell our milk anymore. So, our dairy herd deteriorated and one by one they were sold as beef.

In about 1943 or '44, I think '43, my grandmother moved to town because of failing health and both my sister and I lived with her from time to time. My sister had graduated from high school and went on to college at Monmouth where she received her teacher's certificate, and she married Clyde Allen and they lived in the Coos Bay area. On Christmas Eve, 1948, my grandmother was sitting in my Aunt Jane's living room watching her children and her grandchildren and her great-grandchildren open their Christmas gifts and when she went to get out of her chair,

---

[3] The timber negotiations were in late 1939. The mill was moved above the falls in spring 1940. It was finished cutting in 1945.

she could not rise. It was discovered that she had a mild stroke. She lived until the spring of 1948 when she passed away at a rest home in Myrtle Point.

My dad continued to live up at the ranch. There was a man named Frank O'Conner who came up there. He was a fern picker. He lived there for some time and he and my dad made their living at that time primarily by picking fern. Later on my dad sort of teamed up with a boyhood friend of his, Baldy Crane. They went over into the West Fork country and built a couple of cabins and a trail and trapped on the West Fork during the winter. One of the cabins, that they named Pleasant Valley Manor, was quite a large trapper's cabin. They built a very tall fence around a little plot of ground there and raised a magnificent garden. The deer were kept out of it by the very, very tall picket fence.

They also picked some ferns in there and took them out over a wide trail they had built. They bought a little tiny Caterpillar cat that was, I think, thirty-six inches wide. They built a trailer to pull behind the Cat, and they hauled supplies in that way and hauled ferns out. When my grandmother became ill at the end of 1947, my dad had to pull his traps up and move to town for awhile to help take care of her. I think he never went back into the woods to trap after that. However, he did continue to live up at the ranch and pick fern.

Charlie Schapers and also Jerd Schapers had both passed away and Joe and Daisy Morris moved onto the Tyberg place. They were both fern pickers, also.

In late 1945, not long after the war, a military plane carrying service personnel crashed between our ranch and the Lake Creek county. Quite a search-and-rescue operation was launched. Local people, loggers, soldiers from Camp Adair, all participated in the search for the men who had been on the plane. Most of them parachuted out. Some of them were caught up in the tops of trees and climbers went after them. The pilot and co-pilot were killed. All of the other men except one survived the crash. The one man who was never found, his parents used to come every summer for several years, to the ranch, and go into the area where the plane had crashed to look for his remains. I remember every summer the lady would borrow my leather hiking boots because she didn't have any. To the best of my knowledge, that man has never been found.

In January of 1951 I joined the army and left the ranch, but my dad continued to live there. A lot of the time he lived by himself and he continued to pick ferns. After spending about five years in the army and a couple years in San Francisco, I came back in 1956 and was the lookout at Cougar Pass. Also, I brought an old army friend with me. Her name was Virginia Smith and she was from Boston, Massachusetts. After the fire season ended in 1956, I think it was about October, Virginia and I went back to the ranch and lived with my dad. We picked ferns until January 1, 1957, when I left the old ranch for the last time.

My dad continued to live there and pick fern until 1958 when the bridge across Silver Creek was dynamited. That made it impossible for him to continue to live there. The road from the ranch over to Ash Valley was closed a great deal of the time, and it was a very long route to get out to town. At any rate, he sold the ranch to Weyerhaeuser in 1958. From there he was a caretaker on people's property for awhile. Then he bought a little place down by Myrtle Point where he lived for several years. In 1973 he married Carrie Hicks and went to live with her in Springfield where he passed away in April 1976.

Over the years I have been back to the valley quite a number of times. There are no buildings left in the valley any more. They've all been burned. For awhile the valley was really kind of ugly: all of the scars from the logging of the timber; the fields grown up in blackberries and brush.

But I really don't find it that way the last few times I've been back. As a matter of fact, I can walk along the old county road and look at where the fields were, the fields I used to work in as a kid. I really have to convince myself that I'm back on the ranch and those *were* fields, because they're timber now. There's almost marketable timber growing down in the fields where I used to work when I was a kid. I've noticed the last couple of years that the brush is starting to thin out and it's not as brushy anymore. It's just stands of timber, and the creek had, of course, changed course and looks quite different than it used to. The old swimming hole by the orchard is pretty much still there.

A few of the trees of the orchard both on our place and on the old Tyberg place are still there. On the Tyberg place there used to be a chestnut tree near the barn. It was fair sized when I was a kid, and it is still there. It is absolutely huge now. It is one of the hugest chestnut trees I've ever seen. It's weather-beaten and battered by storms, but it is really a magnificent tree.

At our old house you can still find the flagstones that went between the back porch and the woodshed. The old cherry tree is still there, and the old Maynard plum tree. The small plum trees around the house and most of the plum trees and the plum sprouts, where I used to have to go and cut my own switch when I was a bad little girl so I could get a spanking, are gone. I don't know whether that makes me sad or happy. At least I haven't had a plum sprout taken to me for awhile!

But the beauty is certainly coming back. It used to be a beautiful place and a good place to live. It is becoming beautiful once again.

144

Chapter Twenty-one

Memories of the Old Ranch
by Alice Wilkinson Allen[4]

This is Alice Allen and I'd like to try to record some of my memories of the old ranch up above the Golden and Silver Falls. The ranch was a 160-acre homestead that my step-grandfather had proved up the homestead rights on. It was the second homestead above the Golden and Silver Falls.

After he bought the existing improvements from a widow, he made other improvements and eventually proved up on the land. He decided that he needed someone to help him, so he needed a wife. He corresponded with my grandmother, Laura Wilkinson, who was a widow lady with four small children. My father was the youngest, and he was about four years old when they came out to Oregon by train — and from Portland down to Coos Bay, which was then Marshfield, on a ship. I remember my father saying he was the only one who did not get seasick. He kept beating a path to the door of the kitchen of the ship to fill his tummy up and so one else paid much attention to him because they were all seasick.

The Old Ranch in 1943
Old-growth Douglas fir to the edge of the fields

Anyhow my step-grandfather, Joseph Schapers, met my grandmother in Marshfield and they were married and he moved her and her four children up above the Golden and Silver Falls to the ranch. Prior to that my grandmother had not been very far west. I think Kansas was the farthest west she had been when she was a girl. She had received some postcards from Joseph Schapers that showed some huge trees that she thought surely had to be fakes because they were so large and she had never seen a tree of that size. She couldn't believe that they existed. However, when she got to Oregon she found that they really did exist and that she was living up among them. I don't think she ever did get to see the redwoods, and they far outstrip the Douglas fir, even the old growth that was present on the ranch at the time she arrived there.

---

[4] Transcribed from audio tape and edited by Lionel Youst

Early Childhood

It was always to my knowledge simply called "The Ranch." To me, The Ranch was synonymous with home. I first came to live on the ranch when I was probably about four or four and a half. This was during the depression of the thirties, probably about 1931. My father had a job in town — he was a plumber. With the depression his job went, so he moved his family, which consisted of myself and my mother and him up to the Old Ranch. He built a small cabin out of shakes across the creek from the big ranch house. It was always called "The Little House Across the Creek."

We must have lived there for at least a year because I can remember both summer and winter in the little house across the creek. At one point my mother's father, Grandpa Henderson, came and stayed probably for a week or two with us. I can recall tagging around with him. He loved to fish and to hunt and he would go out and kill rabbits, which were cottontails, the only thing we had above the ranch. He would bring those back to the house and my mother would make rabbit stew and that sort of thing.

I remember one day my grandfather very solemnly told me that he would give me the left hind foot of one of the rabbits to wear around my neck as a good luck piece. As long as I had this rabbit's foot around my neck that no bad could happen to me. He fixed it up on a leather thong and tied it around my neck and I was very proud of it, believed in it. There was a log across the creek that I was afraid to cross, but once I got the rabbit's foot I would stand at the end of the log, grab the rabbit's foot, trot across the log, then I could let go of it on the other side, and nothing ever happened. I did fine.

However, pretty soon the rabbit's foot got to be quite odorous because it had not been preserved in any way. It had just been cut from the rabbit and strung on the thong. My mother, after several arguments with me, finally got the rabbit's foot away from me, I think probably one night when I was asleep, and it just simply disappeared. I was almost heartbroken over it. A few day later I was up the creek fishing with my grandfather and I had taken the family cat, which was one of my favorite toys, because I didn't have too many toys. I was carrying her along with me. Somehow, as I was crossing the creek I fell into a fairly deep hole. By fairly deep in our creek, that would have been a foot or two. I remember holding the cat high above me so that the cat wouldn't get wet and hollering for my grandfather, who came and rescued me finally. I remember him solemnly telling me when we got onto the bank that if I had still had my rabbit's foot, that would not have happened. I believed him.

As I say, I didn't have too many toys when we were there in the little house. It was depression years. I remember two dolls that I did have that my mother made for me. One was made out of a potato that they had dug out of the garden and it had a lot of knobs growing on it, and they looked just like two arms and two legs. My mother fixed up a head and stuck it on top of the potato, and she made some clothes, and I had "Spudora," as long as she lasted, until she sort of withered and went by the wayside. Later on I remember an ear of corn my mother dressed up and made a head on, and that was "Cornelia!"

I don't recall having any real dolls. But I did have some doll clothes and Lady, the cat, was quite willing to have me dress her up if she was in the mood. I'd often dress her up and put her in a little old cart that I had and wheel her around, tuck her in with

The little house across the creek.

blankets, and she put up with all this quite well. I recall that she was a calico cat, not very large. I don't recall what happened to her, but when I think of the little house across the creek I always think of Lady.

As I say, I can remember both winter and summer at that little house. In the wintertime the ponds in the field would freeze over. I remember going out and scooting around on those and thinking I was skating, and looking down and thinking I was skating, and looking down and seeing the bubbles that had been trapped underneath the ice and thinking how beautiful it was. And it was. Those same ponds, in the summertime, I can remember going out and catching a whole jar full of frogs and bringing them in the house and we set them on the table until they kept us awake at night with their croaking. My dad finally had to take them out and get rid of them so we could get some sleep.

Mother

I remember another time, one of my few memories of my mother, probably not too long before my sister was born because we were living there when my mother was expecting her. We had a chair that had a cane bottom. Probably that had disappeared and been replaced with gunny sacks or something like that. Anyway, mother was not a large person and she sat down in the chair and she went down between the wooden parts of the seat of the chair and she became stuck. Probably because she was pregnant she could not get herself out. Her feet were off the floor, and I recall she told me to run down to the creek where my father was fishing and to bring him up to pull her out of the chair. I recall going down and telling daddy that mother was stuck in the chair and would he please come up to the house. Amid much laughter she was pulled out by my daddy and things were fine.

She never came back to the little house across the creek when she went to town to have my sister. It was not too long after my sister was born that mother contracted pneumonia and passed away. It was not so much from childbirth, I don't believe, as from the fact that she did not have very strong lungs. She'd had tuberculosis when she was younger and she had lost one lung prior to that because of pneumonia. So, my sister was only a few days old when we lost our mother.

147

My Sister

After that, Daddy moved into the big ranch house so that my grandmother could help take care of my sister and me. My sister was very fragile; she was very small and quite weak. If you laid her on one side she would turn black and not breathe, so it took very careful treatment to bring her through all of this.

I remember she was on what they called SMA, which was a baby formula of some kind which was supposed to give her extra strength. During this time there was no cash flow at all at the ranch, so my father went out and peeled chittam. I recall him saying he got a penny a pound for dry chittam. To get a hundred pounds of dry chittam it took about 200 pounds of wet chittam. It was then dried and they put it in a crusher and broke it up into small pieces, sacked it into a gunny sack and hauled it to town and sold it. That money all went to the SMA that we had to have for my sister. A little later on when she became more healthy and her appetite began to increase, he couldn't keep up. So, a switch from SMA to cow's milk was made rather slowly and the cow's milk seemed to agree with her beautifully.

Grandmother Henderson
Alice, Grandmother, & Pat, 1933

She became a fairly healthy girl and got into all kinds of mischief. However, up until she was about two or three years old if she would get angry and start to cry hard, or if she would get hurt and cry very hard she would stop breathing. All measures had to be taken and one of the things I had seen my father and grandmother both do at various times when this happened was to throw cold water on her face and she would automatically then sort of take a big gasp and start breathing again; the shock of it, I suppose.

One time, when she was about two or two and a half, she and I were out in the yard swinging in the swing. She was sitting in the swing and I was pushing her. She kept saying, "I want to go higher, higher, higher." So I was very bravely pushing her and pushing her higher and higher and finally I gave one great big shove and what I actually did was shove the seat of the swing right out from under her. Her hands let go of the rope and she landed on her head underneath the swing. I immediately ran over to her and I could see that she was not breathing, that she was crying and holding her breath and turning a little blue. I knew that she would turn black, so I grabbed her by the arms.

At that time I was about seven. I had quite a ways to drag her over to the yard, open the gate, drag her up the cobblestones to the edge of the porch where I left her and ran to the laundry tubs on the porch. There was running water and a dipper that Joe Schapers used to drink out of. I grabbed the dipper and got water in it and got back to her and threw it in her face and thankfully she gave a big gasp, but she was getting pretty black by that time and I was pretty scared.

I had yelled for Grandma, but evidently she was busy in the house and didn't hear me or just figured it was the screams of kids having a good time. This was one of the things she often scolded us about, making too much noise and hollering and screaming out there because she didn't know whether we were in trouble or whether we were just having a good time. This was one of the things she continually cautioned us: not to scream and holler when we were outside because it worried her.

The Outhouse

One other memory I have of the little house across the creek while we lived there was the outhouse. The outhouse stood out on the bank of the creek and the front of it was sort of on the top of a little hill. The back of it hung over the hill, more or less, so that they didn't have to dig as large a hole. The embankment sort of furnished a ready-made receptacle. We did not have running water and that type of thing in the little house. There was running water at the main ranch house.

One evening I had to go out to the outhouse before I went to bed — and again I must have been somewhere around five years old when this happened. It was dark so I had to take the flashlight with me and during operations I laid the flashlight down on the bench beside me. When I got up, I evidently bumped the flashlight and it rolled down into the hole. I don't know whether it was Eveready batteries in there or not, but anyway the flashlight stayed lit and I could look down through the hole and see it lying down there.

I knew that I was in trouble! If I didn't come back to the house with that flashlight I was in trouble. So, I went out around the back of the outhouse and sure enough there was room for me to crawl underneath the boards. By really stretching I could reach the flashlight. I picked it up, very gingerly holding it by the very end, which was the least "mucky," and I, rather dripping with muck myself, with the flashlight held by the end, came up to the house. I had to confess, of course, what had happened. Well, much to my surprise, both my mother and Daddy started to really laugh uproariously. Both the flashlight and I were given a bath and I was put to bed, with no punishment, thank Heaven! I just knew I had to retrieve that flashlight and I couldn't leave it where it was.

The Depression

During the Depression there was quite a population at the ranch house. There was my father and my sister and myself, my grandmother, and Joe Schapers all of the time, and I recall part of the time Charlie Schapers, Joe Schapers' younger brother was there to help on the ranch. For awhile my Uncle Bob and his wife Aunt Ann and their small son Bobby were also living there, so that made quite a few feet under the table. It wasn't too long before Uncle Bob and his family moved back into town, as he had gotten some kind of a job and was able to support his family in town. In later years Charlie Schapers went down to the Tyberg ranch and lived there with his sister Elizabeth Tyberg, who had been widowed. He and another brother, Jerd, lived down on the Tyberg place with her and helped her work her ranch.

Of the products that the ranch produced during those days, one of the main ones was cream that was delivered to the creamery in North Bend. I also can recall during the depression Daddy taking sacks of rutabagas that were grown at the ranch, and potatoes and apples. All of these things were taken into town and sometimes they could be traded for flour and sugar and other necessities that we couldn't raise on the ranch.

We didn't really suffer from lack of food because we had our own chickens, so that gave us eggs and chickens to eat. We had the milk. Nearly every fall a hog was butchered and we had our own hams and bacons that were hung out in the smokehouse. All of our garden stuff — my grandmother canned pears, peaches, cherries, beans, corn, and all kinds of vegetables. I think she probably put up hundreds of quarts of food every fall. This was a lot of our winter eating.

Although it was not lawful, we also had venison and elk meat to eat. I can remember Grandma frying some of the venison and then she would put it down in a crock and pour hot grease over it until the grease covered all of the meat. As we needed it, we would dig out a steak or two and finish frying it in the frying pan. It wasn't as good as fresh, but it was certainly better than all canned meat.

I can remember that I never did very much like to do housework. If I could do something outside and get out of doing the dishes and helping Grandma around the house, I'd always choose the outside chores. Some of my regular chores were getting in the wood, feeding the chickens, going after the cows. I liked to go after the cows. Generally, fairly early in the afternoon, I'd go up to the upper end of the ranch and bring the cows down to the barn so that Daddy and Joe Schapers, whom

Cle with a large set of elkhorns.

everyone called Dad — as if Dad was his name — could milk the cows.

Stromquist

I remember there was a state policeman, who used to come into the area above Allegany and up above the Golden and Silver Falls, whose name was Stromquist. He was not very well liked by most of the local people and he was always trying to find somebody poaching deer or something like that. He sometimes went to quite elaborate means to catch someone doing this.

One time he had picked up my cousin Bob Leaton on the pretext that he was hunting deer, because Bob was carrying a gun, a rifle. Most of us kids above the falls did carry a rifle. We were all taught how to use them fairly early. I used to always carry my .22 rifle with me when I went after the cows.

I remember one time I was going along the county road and Stromquist came along in the state police car and stopped and he asked me if I was hunting. I said, "Yes, I am." He said, "What are you hunting?" I said, "I'm hunting the cows." He said, "Why do you have a rifle with you if you're hunting the cows?" I told him that my daddy never let me go after the cows without a rifle with me because there was a bull with the herd that he wanted me to have some protection against, in case he took a notion to chase me. I think Mr. Stomquist was rather disappointed that he didn't get me to say that I was hunting for deer. It was rather a standing joke that whenever Stromquist came along you better be careful and most of the neighbors always warned each other if they knew he was in the area.

Bob and Cle Wilkinson as teenagers with their 4-point buck.

The chores on the ranch were always done according to the daylight because, as I mentioned before, there was no electricity. If you were in the barn after dark, you had to work by lantern light. In the wintertime the chores were done about daybreak, and then in the evening they were done before it got dark.

Charlie Schapers

Charlie Schapers lived at our place for awhile and then later on moved down to Mrs. Tyberg's. He used to go to town with Mrs. Tyberg all the time when she'd go to town. All of the neighbors would pick up each other's mail and generally when Charlie would come back the next evening he would come up to the ranch and bring our mail. He dearly loved all children. He could always be found sitting a little apart from where the adults were talking, with probably a kid on each knee. He would always have candy when he came back from town, and distribute it among the children. If he didn't have candy, then he would dig in his pockets for pennies and nickels and whatever change he had and distribute those among the kids.

I was always one of the lucky ones who got to sit on Charlie's lap, on one knee or the other because, I don't know why, but I was his favorite. He made no bones about it. He always made sure I had one piece of candy more than what he had given any of the other kids; at least a penny more if it was change he was handing out. After he went down to the Tyberg's, Grandma would gather up whatever he had given the kids and divide it up evenly among us. But he always had to see that Babe, as he always called me, had just a little bit more than everybody else.

151

One of the favorite things for the kids to do while they were sitting on his knee was to play with his crippled hand. At one time Charlie had had one hand injured and it had evidently damaged the tendons and the little finger was curled back against the palm and the next two fingers were curled partially, and it was only his thumb and pointing finger on that hand that were actually normal. But even so, Charlie could milk a cow and he could do anything anyone else could do.

I remember a couple times when I had bigger eyes than what my tummy would hold, and everyone else had left the table and the adults had gone into the living room to visit and talk, and I was still sitting at the table to finish up what I had taken. Well, a couple different times Charlie would sneak back into the dining room from the living room and he would clean up my plate for me. He felt so sorry for poor Babe who was sitting there with tears in her eyes that he would eat the food and then Babe's plate would be clean and Babe could leave the table!

I don't think that Grandma or Daddy ever did catch on to that. I felt very guilty about having Charlie do this, but it was not my suggestion that he do it. It was his own idea. As I said, I was his favorite and he did several special things for me, and that was one of them.

Dogs and Trapping

Cle, with a cougar trap

I don't know what year it was that Daddy got a job trapping for the WPA, which was the Works Progress Administration. He had always trapped in the wintertime for mink, martin, and some of the fur-bearing animals and sold the skins. When he trapped for the WPA he was also what they called a "trapper of predators." This took in cougars, coyote, and that type of thing. He had to make out reports and send in as to what he had caught and so forth.

I remember we always had a dog at the ranch. The first one I remember was King. He was sort of like a shepherd, but he was a shaggy dog. I can't remember any of our dogs ever being really a good chore dog, probably because no one knew how to train them. They were around the ranch, but we couldn't send them for the cows by themselves. The would go with me when I went for the cows.

Another dog I remember was Rowdy. That was the dog that Daddy picked up down at Joe Stienon's gas station one time when he went to town [Marshfield]. He had showed up at the station and seemed to be a stray. Daddy came to town and Joe told him about the dog. He appeared to be rather smart, so Daddy brought him home. I think we were without a dog at that time. He was fairly large, but short haired. We found out that he was really quite intelligent. He knew quite a few tricks. He would sit up, lay down, and play dead. He probably knew some other tricks, if we had known the correct commands to give him.

152

He really attached himself to Daddy, and I think that was Daddy's favorite dog of any I can remember. He took Rowdy with him on the trap line a couple times. One time Rowdy got caught in a trap. He had run ahead of Daddy down the trail and got into one of the traps that Daddy had set. It was something like a mink trap, so it was not large. When Daddy got down the trail to where the dog was, he was sitting there holding his foot up with the trap on it and howling, wanting Daddy to get him loose, which Daddy did. Other than a pinched foot, he wasn't hurt too badly. But Daddy decided that probably it would not be a good idea to take Rowdy on the trap line with him anymore.

The next few times he'd go out the trail, he would send the dog back to the house. About the third time, he went to leave early in the morning and he didn't see Rowdy anywhere, so he couldn't tell him to stay home. He got out the trail about a mile or mile and a half and here was Rowdy sitting in the trail waiting for him. He had been smart enough to know from the signs what was going to go on that morning, and he had gone on out the trail to meet Daddy so that he wouldn't be told to stay behind. Daddy didn't have the heart to send him back, so Rowdy got to go with him. When it came lunch time, Daddy was eating his sandwich and Rowdy was just sitting and looking at him. Daddy knew he was hungry because he hadn't been there when Daddy went to feed him that morning. He hadn't been fed since the night before. Needless to say, Daddy shared his sandwich with him. After that Rowdy was a regular companion on the trail. He had gotten his way.

The last dog that I can recall was Coony. He was a small, tan, terrier-type dog. He was around for quite a number of years. He and [my sister] Pat became really great friends. She would take him out and tell him to "Dig." He would dig and dig and dig until he would get tired, and he would stop and look up at her and she would say, "Dig, dig!" And he would go ahead and dig some more. I don't think they ever got to China, but it wasn't for lack of trying.

I recall one time when the mill was there on the place and several of the mill hands had little shacks down below our orchard. At that time Pete Lousignont was living in one of the cabins. One day he had left the door open a little bit and Coony came down and went in the door and stole a pound of butter from Pete. Of course, that tasted really good, but he had a guilty conscience. Every time he would see Pete he would hang his head and slink away. All Pete had to do was point his finger and say, "Coony, you stole my butter," and the dog would slink away, and did that for several weeks, so they do have somewhat of a memory!

The hay field by the house

Haying

One sort of social time when everyone got together up in the valley was during haying season. Everybody had cows except for Mr.

153

Howell, and he had a horse and at one time he had a mule or two. So everybody had hay to put up. The people would go from ranch to ranch and put in the hay. They'd bring their teams of horses and their wagons and all the women would get together and make a big dinner, sort of a potluck affair. It was always a time for everyone to visit. The day would generally end when everyone had to go home and do their own chores. The cows were waiting to be milked and so forth.

Mr. Howell used to always be the one elected to load the hay wagon. Us kids helped make hay stacks and things of that nature, but we were too small to pitch the hay onto the wagon, so we always got to ride, which was a big treat. I remember one time we were coming across the field between the little house across the creek and the barn and as usual Mr. Howell had loaded the load. He was quite proud of his ability to load a hay wagon to get a lot of hay on it, and the hay would stay. We were coming across this field and the roadway was rather sideways, one rut was down quite a bit farther than the other rut. I don't remember whether they hit a rock or what, but suddenly a flake of hay from underneath where us kids were sitting shifted and fell off the wagon.

The next flake of hay that fell off was the top one we were sitting on, and another one came down on top of us. I can remember Mr. Howell dragging me out by my ankle and all of the men being quite excited and upset. To me it was, you know, over fairly fast and I was not at all frightened. Later on I realized we could easily have suffocated underneath that hay if the men hadn't found us as quickly as they had. That was the reason for all of the excitement. That's the only accident that I can remember.

If company came during haying season, us kids were always glad because the kids got to go out and take their blankets and pillows and sleep in the hay shocks in the field. This was a big treat. If it was a little later in the year when company came, and the hay was already in the barn the kids took their blankets and pillows and went down to the barn and slept and again this was a big deal, you know, because it was something out of the ordinary.

Picnics and Pet Deer

My sister and I used to go out and have picnics in the haystacks when they were out in the field. We would make a sandwich and have some Kool-aid and go out — I guess it would have been the equivalent of other little girls' tea parties — but to us it was a picnic.

One of the treats that we used to have once in awhile in the summertime was a "vinegar fizz." We did have Kool-aid and then there was a sort of a syrup that was put out by Watkins or Raleigh's that you could make a cool drink out of. Those were rather tame, but a "vinegar fizz" was something else again. You took about a half a glass of water, put in a tablespoonful of sugar, then you poured vinegar in until the glass was about two-thirds full, stirred it up well until the sugar was dissolved. Then you'd take anywhere from a third to half a teaspoon of baking soda and quickly stir it in. Of course, it foamed up very fast so you had to drink it quick before it ran over the top of the glass. It sort of tickled your throat and your nose as it went down. We didn't have these very often because Grandma had the idea that they weren't too good for our stomachs and she was probably right, but to us it was, I guess, the equivalent of soda pop.

One time, when we were up at Slideout Gulch, Coony had jumped a little fawn. He chased it up the creek to where I was dipping water to made the coffee. All I had time to do was drop the coffee pot, lean down and scoop up the fawn and put my foot in the dog's face. He had already bitten the hams of the little deer, and it was only a few days old, so we took it home.

We didn't know where the mother was, so we raised it on a bottle there at the ranch. We named the little deer "Muggins" because it was such a cute little muggins! Muggins was around the ranch for probably about a year. One of her favorite things to do was to go out and fight the haystacks, paw them with her little front feet and go "bah" at them. She was finally killed by hunters, or at least that is what we assumed happened to her, as she disappeared during hunting season. She was a joy to have.

Laura Schapers' pet deer

High School Days

In about 1940 George Youst had a mill there at the ranch. This was about the time I had to go to high school. My school year was spent with my Aunt Jane and Uncle George down on Coos River, but the ranch was still home and that's where my vacations and some weekends were spent, back at the old ranch. If I wanted to come home for the weekend, I would catch the boat at the dock at the schoolhouse on Coos River and ride up to Allegany. Then from there I'd either walk home or possibly catch a ride with somebody who was going at least as far as Brady and Neal's logging camp. Generally from that point, which was about five miles from the ranch, I had to walk on

Welcome, milk cans on bow. This was the school bus for the Allegany kids.

home. Quite often the folks wouldn't know whether or not I was coming, so no one would come to meet me. Once in awhile it would be after dark by the time I'd get home.

155

With the coming of Youst's mill to the valley there was quite a boost in the population, and more of a turnover in the population also. Some of the workers in the mill were single men or bachelors, and others had families that moved in or out. The population wasn't nearly as stable as what it had been in earlier years.

Joseph Schapers, My Step-Grandfather

I'll talk about some of the people who lived above the falls. I'll start with Joseph Schapers, who was my step-grandfather. He came there sometime in the late 1800's. As I mentioned before, he bought the improvements from a widow and finished proving up on the homestead rights of the ranch. I remember him as an old man, because he was old by the time I came along in 1927. He was always busy doing something. He was always cutting blackberries or cutting brush. He was the one who always picked most of the fruit on the ranch, stored the apples in the apple shed, and sprout the potatoes in the potato shed. Later on this was one of the jobs that was assigned to me and I didn't like it at all, but that's beside the point. He wore a mustache, as did all of the Schapers brothers that I remember. He had a very heavy head of hair. It was gray when I knew him. On top of his head he always wore an old black felt hat. It had holes cut in it to give ventilation. I'm not exaggerating when I say he even wore that hat to bed, because he did! You very seldom saw him without his hat.

When I was a kid, Dad — as we called him as though Dad were his name — Dad always slept on the cot in the living room. The only preparations he made for bed that I can recall was taking off his gum boots or his shoes, as the case may be, taking off his pants, and laying them over the foot of the cot. Probably his coat would be off, and he would crawl into bed that way, with his hat on his head. He liked to read the paper in the evening, especially if the mail had just been brought up. Normally, we received mail about once a week, whenever one of the neighbors in the valley or ourselves would go into town. We would pick up all the mail, and we took the *Coos Bay Times*, which was the daily paper.

I used to like to follow the funny papers, and some of the ones I liked in particular were Alley Oop and Prince Valiant. They were not complete in each strip — they told a story as they went along — so I wanted to read the funnies in sequence. I would start with the oldest paper and read the funnies in that and progress to the next date and so forth. Invariably it seemed that Joe Schapers would have a paper, reading it, and it would be somewhere right in the middle. He didn't pay much attention to the dates. He just liked to read the paper. Of course, I'd want to read that one next, when I came to it, so I'd patiently wait until he'd get finished with it and go on to another one. Once in awhile he'd fall asleep in his chair as he read the paper, but he never, ever let go of the paper when he fell asleep. It stayed right there in his hands. The only way you could tell he was not reading was to really look at him and you could see his eyes were closed and you could sometimes hear a gentle snore when he was sleeping. Several times I got very brave and I would go over and try to ease the paper out of his hands while he slept so that I could read that particular one next. It never, ever worked. He would immediately wake up and commence reading the paper again without even glancing my way. After trying that a couple times, I just patiently waited after that.

I can remember when he used to peel apples by the fire for Grandma if she was going to make applesauce or an apple pie, or when he would decide that he wanted applesauce or an apple pie. He'd go down to the apple house and come and sit by the heating stove in the living room and peel apples. When he would start, the apple peel came off all in one long stream. He never cut through it until he was at the very end of the apple. That used to sort of fascinate me when I'd watch him.

He never paid too much attention to me when I was a kid, but he did like my sister Pat pretty well. He seemed to look after her when she was out. He knew she had been sort of delicate when she was young and he

Laura and Joe Schapers

took quite an interest in watching her. I can recall him telling my grandma several times that "I was going to kill that little t'ing" if I wasn't a little bit more careful with her when I played with her.

My Aunt Jane had been his favorite among Grandma's children, when she was younger. She was one who was "tom-boyish" and liked all of the outdoor chores and so forth. Aunt Peg [Agnes] had been quite lady-like and very prim and proper when she was young. Aunt Jane had a lot more spirit, and I think that sort of appealed to Dad. She had been his favorite when they were younger.

Laura Schapers, My Grandmother

My grandmother was, of course, fairly old when I remember her. She had already raised four children, and then when my mother passed away she was faced with having a delicate infant to take care of and two more children to raise just when she should have been able to sit back and rest a little bit. Of course, there wasn't much rest on the ranch because there was always something for my grandmother to do: all the cooking for all the people who lived on the ranch, canning, mending, ironing. I can recall her ironing sometimes late at night. She had what we called flat irons that were heated on the kitchen wood stove, she would take a hot pad and lift the heavy iron off and iron on the ironing board. When that iron got cold she would put it back on the stove and take the next one. She always had about three of those flat irons on the stove when she was ironing. All of our dresses and that type of thing for school were always ironed. I don't think she ironed sheets and that sort of thing, like many people did in that day, because she simply didn't have the time.

As she got older she had problems. She had always had problems with her feet. She was very conscious of her big feet. I think she wore a number nine shoe.

157

When she was younger she had been very embarrassed by the size of her feet and tried to fit her feet into shoes that were too small and consequently suffered for it in later life. It was very hard for Grandma to walk along the county road that was dirt and gravel, and the bottoms of her feet were very tender. She had corns and bunions, so being on her feet and working all day was pretty hard on her, especially during the time when I was younger.

She was more of an inside person. She did not care too much for the outdoor chores and so forth, so she was glad to let me do those rather than the housework that I didn't like at all anyway. Although I did get stuck with the dishes a lot of times.

She was very religious. She talked about the Bible and her religion to almost anyone who would come. She just loved it if the preacher would come because then she could argue religion with him. She didn't belong to any denomination. She just believed what she read from the Bible. She did believe that Saturday, the seventh day, was the Sabbath, and she tried to observe that. On Fridays she cooked food ahead that could be warmed up on Saturday so that she didn't have to do any heavy cooking. She never planned on doing canning or any of the heavy chores, mopping the wood floors or anything like that on a Saturday — only doing what was necessary.

She was, I think, a good Christian lady all of the time that I knew her. Even though she didn't belong to a church, if anyone ever lived their religion, I believe she did. It used to get a little wearing to me and to my sister, what we thought of as "preached to," but she was doing it for the good of our souls, and raised us to the best of her ability. She always seemed like to me, even for her day, she was old fashioned. Rather than one or two generation gaps, there was about three generation gaps between our grandmother and us, but I don't think that hurt us either.

In those years when I was growing up I never thought of the sacrifices and the hard work that my grandmother had to go through. It was not until I was grown that I really appreciated what she had given up and what she had done for us. I don't think that anyone could have given us a better upbringing than what she tried to give us at all times.

One area of conflict was the fact that she wanted to treat us equally, and there is a five-and-a-half year gap between myself and my sister Pat. Quite often things that I wanted to do I couldn't do because Pat was not yet old enough to do them, and so therefore I couldn't do them.

A Trip to Lake Creek

I remember one time my dad had told me he would take me out on the trail with him when he went trapping out to Bear Creek. He had a cabin over on Lake Creek and then he also stayed in the Guerin cabin, which was up on a hill. It was left over from the time when there had been timber claims out in that area and people had moved out there and built cabins to satisfy the needs of the timber claim. They proved up on the timber claims and then moved back. Most of these people were from Myrtle Point and Coquille areas.

158

The Guerin cabin was still in good shape and was one of the better built cabins out there. When my daddy told Grandma that I would be going out with him next time, Grandma immediately objected because she knew that Pat could not make the trip. It was sixteen miles into the Guerin cabin. I believe I was about ten or eleven that summer.

Daddy told her, he said, "I have promised Alice that she can go, Mother, and so she's going. Yes, I realize that Pat can't go, but Alice is going." I was a very happy little girl and I did hike out there with my daddy. I wrapped up my valuables, which included some bubble gum and a comb and a few little things that were extraordinarily important to me. I tied them up in a bandanna, stuck a stick through the tied bandanna, and had it over my shoulder. I had seen pictures of people who took trips, and this is the way they went. So, this was the way I went.

We were about half way out to the first cabin and I had to answer the call of nature. I stepped off the trail and into the brush. When I had finished I had forgotten I had laid the bandanna with my treasures in it down beside the trail. I took off behind my daddy down the trail again, and it was not until we got down to Lake Creek and were ready to stop for the night at that cabin that I realized that my treasures were gone. I worried about them and mentioned them to Daddy, and he said, "Oh well, we'll pick them up on the way back."

Geo. H. Guerin homestead claim T 24S R 9W, 22. Jan. 29, 1911. Douglas County Museum photo #11465-2.

He had to leave and go on to the Guerin cabin because there were only blankets enough for one person at the cabin on Lake Creek. He asked me if I were afraid to stay by myself. I told him no, I would be glad to stay there by myself while he went up another four miles to get the blankets and bring them back.

In the meantime I went down to the creek to fish. I remember I caught one fish and it was just exactly the same length as the little finger on my hand. At that time my little finger was not very long. But I really wasn't afraid. I don't believe my sister and I ever were afraid of the woods, being by ourselves, because we were fairly used to both things. That was my big adventure of that summer that I got to do even though my sister was not old enough yet to join me in it.

Grandma did not spank us very often, but when she did spank, she spanked hard. She sometimes gave us lectures that I think probably went in one ear and out the other. I believe she suspected it at the time. Altogether it was a couple of lucky little girls who had a grandmother like her to raise them.

My Dad, Cleland Wilkinson

Then, of course, there was my dad, who lived at the ranch at that time. He trapped a lot, he picked ferns, he peeled chittam, he made a living off the woods whenever he could. When he couldn't make enough off of the woods or the ranch itself, he logged part of the time. He worked for Brady and Neal and got in some cash money by logging, which was hard work.

I don't believe his heart was really in the ranching part, but he loved to trap and hunt. Almost every winter when the cows were dry and there wasn't much milking to do, he would set a trap line. He had some cabins out in the woods that he would stay overnight in. He would check the trap lines and bring the furs home and stretch them on boards, then send them off, back East as a rule, to one of the fur houses,

Cle Wilkinson, hunter & trapper

and then wait and see what kind of a check he would get back. Most generally he was pleased with the results. Once in awhile he thought the furs had been a better grade than what the check came back for. I remember mainly he shipped to Lanstrom and Sons, because he felt they were the most fair.

My dad worked around the ranch and did chores. Generally, he was responsible for milking. I don't remember exactly what year it was but probably about 1937 or 8, or maybe even 1936, that he got a job as a government trapper with the WPA. Then he could run the trap line in the summertime too, and he trapped for predators like cougars, lynx, and bobcats. I think that was one of the favorite jobs that he had.

I don't remember whether he got cash, but he was able to get what they called commodities, groceries. Come into town at certain times and they would give things such as shortening and flour and a lot of repetitious things. Once in awhile he would get oranges, and that was a treat.

From the county he did get bounty money. I believe it was fifty dollars for a cougar and five dollars for a lynx or something like that. This money he was allowed to keep. He didn't have to turn that over to the government, but he did have to make reports on the numbers and types of animals that he caught and account for his time.

My dad didn't ever show any inclination to re-marry. He had thought an awful lot of my mother, and I think he was so busy during the depression years trying to scratch together a living for the family that he didn't think of re-marriage. Quite frankly, there weren't very many women who were the right age and state for him to look at. When I did finally get a stepmother I was in my forties, and that was long after everybody had left the ranch.

Fire Danger

One of the main worries at the ranch during the summertime was fire. It would get quite dry and there at the ranch we were aware of fire danger because each year the forest patrol would pack out the trail that went up Woodruff Creek and packed some of their men in to Ivers Peak and so forth. So, we were quite aware of fire danger. One morning we woke up and it was smokey all around us. The smoke had moved in during the night and we couldn't even see as far as the orchard. Daddy said, "There's a fire somewhere not too far away. It must be a big one but I have no idea which direction it is." At the ranch there were only two ways out. We could either go over the falls and out to Allegany or we could go up over the mountain and in to Loon Lake. That was the only roadway — the one that traversed the valley.

A few days later Uncle Bob came up from town and told us that Bandon had burned.[5] After several days finally the smoke cleared out but we spent a couple days wondering whether we should stay or try to run, and if so which direction to run. The only other access in and out of the ranch were the local trails in the area.

The Trails

About halfway between Mr. Howell's place and the Middleton place there was a trail that went three miles from the road up to Elk's Peak. Elk's Peak had been a lookout at one time. When I was young it was not manned, but it had been a lookout at one time. In later years the 3-C's built a road up to Elk's Peak that wasn't there in the early years. In about the 1940's Daddy and Baldy Crane made a trail from the saddle just before you got to Elk's Peak out to Elk Creek, where they had a trapping cabin. That was probably about four miles long and from there it joined up with the old trail network around the Elkhorn Ranch that the Goulds had pioneered.

There was a trail that led from the Elkhorn over to Scottsburg that I understand cattle were driven over. There was a trail that went from the Elkhorn over to the lower end of Gould's Lake. That was called the Salting Shed Trail. It was a trail that led from the Elkhorn to what they called the salting sheds, which was where they prepared the elk hides that had to be shipped out. The hides were salted down so that they wouldn't spoil and then taken out and shipped.

Another trail took off from almost directly across the road from the Middleton place and led over to Gould's Lake. It also connected with the network of trails that the Goulds had.

The trail that we knew most about was the trail that started out near the little house across the creek and went up Woodruff Creek. This went up over the ridge and dropped down into Lake Creek and Pheasant Creek and eventually went on up to

---

[5] This was the Bandon fire of September 26–7, 1936.

Guerin Cabin and then from there along High Ridge over to Ivers Peak and, I believe, eventually would come down in the South Fork of Coos River. There was also in the early days a branch that would take you to Roseburg. This is the trail that I went out with my dad when I went out to his trapping cabin in Lake Creek and on to Guerin Cabin. That was one of his main trapping territories; one of his earlier trapping territories.

Matson Creek

A little later on he [Cle] decided he might like to trap over in the Matson Creek area. Trappers in that day did not infringe on each other's territory. If someone was trapping in a particular area, then that was his territory for each season that he wanted it. If he abandoned it, maybe another trapper would move in the following season. My dad knew that no one was trapping over in the Matson Creek area.

There was a trail that went from just below the line fence between our place and Tybergs that went over the hill and then down Tyberg Creek and into Matson Creek. Up on the ridge there was an old cabin that had belonged to a trapper, and that was Lax's cabin. Most cabins were down in a creek bottom or along a creek valley so that there would be a water supply and of course mink, coon, and that type of thing were always found along creeks. Lax's cabin was a little bit different because, like Guerin Cabin, it was on top of a ridge. There was a spring that bubbled right out of the top of the mountain right close to the cabin and that was the water supply.

Daddy spent a couple of nights out there and scouted the territory and decided that Lax's cabin wouldn't work as a headquarters for him because he needed to be closer to the creeks where he trapped mink and that type of thing. So he moved on up Matson Creek until he came to a little fork that he named Paradise Creek. He built a cabin there that was called Paradise Cabin. Rather than going down to Tybergs and over the hill and down Tyberg Creek to get to Matson Creek, he went up the Woodruff Creek trail for a ways and then made his own trail from there over the ridge and hit Matson Creek closer to the mouth of Paradise Creek. He trapped out there for a number of years.

Lem Gray with lynx and other hides.

Elk Creek

It was only after that time that he and Baldy moved into the Elk Creek and Elkhorn territories of the West Fork. Frank Bremer had that territory and trapped it. It was vacant several years after Frank passed away. Frank had been out on the trap line and did not come in when he was supposed to, and his wife alerted people that he was overdue from his trap line.[6] Several of the trappers, including my father, went looking for him. They found that he had passed away while he was out by himself.

It was always a mystery as to what caused his death. They found where he had left his main trapping trail and headed straight down a mountainside towards a stream. My dad always theorized that possibly he had gotten a nosebleed, as he was known to have been subject to those. Knowing that he needed to get to water to stop the bleeding, he headed straight down the hill off the trail, and not been successful in getting it stopped. However, they couldn't tell for sure and there were no signs of violence or any signs of any other person being around. As I say, it always remained a mystery as to exactly what had caused his death. But it was several years after that before Daddy and Baldy Crane moved into that territory.

Top of Golden Falls

The Falls Road

The falls was quite an obstacle, of course, for vehicles to run. When Joe Schapers homesteaded up there, there were no fish in the creek because they couldn't get up over the falls. He and Jerd and some of the others got some cutthroat trout and put them in a five-gallon coal oil can and carried them up over the falls. In fact, they had two five-gallon coal oil cans. They would pour the fish from one can to the other every so often to keep the water aerated so that the fish wouldn't die.

It was also quite a job to get cattle up over the falls, even after the road was made. I remember Joe Schapers talking about bringing the first cattle up and they had to blindfold the animals and lead them up over the falls, blindfolded, so that they wouldn't panic and jump over the edge.

The falls also panicked a lot of people. Quite a few drivers wouldn't drive a vehicle up over the falls. One time after my husband and I were married, we were coming back down from the ranch and met a couple who had driven up the falls and the woman refused to ride back with her husband and asked if she could ride back with us when she found out we lived up there. My husband told her, "Sure." So, she jumped in our car and rode down to the bottom. My husband didn't tell her that at that particular time our car didn't have any brakes on it.

---

[6] Frank Bremer died while running his traplines on the upper West Fork in November 1938. His cabin was where Deer Creek enters the West Fork. Lem Gray also trapped the upper West Fork, but coming in from Glenn Creek.

163

Another time, as we started up the falls we met a car coming down just at the end of the Silver Falls bridge and the gentleman told us that we couldn't drive on up there. My husband asked him, "Why, did one of the lumber trucks break down in the middle of the road?" The man said, "Oh, no. It's just that the road is so bad."

CCC

I mentioned that the 3-C's had built the road up to Elk's Peak during the time that the 3-C camp was up above Mr. Howell's place. Most of the boys from the 3-C camp were young men, I would say probably between seventeen and twenty. Most of them were from states in the east and were not used to the hills and so forth that we had around there. I think most of them got quite a thrill their first ride up over the falls. They also did maintenance on the trails in the area, such as the Goulds Lake trail going over to the Elkhorn, and the Woodruff Creek trail, brushing out and so forth. They probably also helped maintain the telephone lines that ran along some of these trails.

There was a telephone line that went out to Guerin Cabin and on over to Ivers Peak. This operated mainly in the summertime so that there could be communication between the lookout on Ivers Peak and once in awhile there would be a warden stationed at Guerin Cabin. It also connected all of the neighbors up in the valley, from Tyberg's ranch on up to Mr. Howell's place. This was just a single telephone line that was hung on the trees and had the old round insulators that the wire ran through. Of course, each wintertime the line was inoperable because trees would fall across it and so forth. Normally, the Forest Service would come in to replace the lines, patch the broken places, clear the trees off, and haul the line up above the trail again so that it was operable during the summertime.

Each person on the line had a particular ring. Ours was a long and two shorts. The next neighbor would be three shorts, and so forth. If there were a series of little short rings on the line that meant there was some kind of news that everyone should hear, and so everybody ran and picked up their receiver. I think a lot of people picked up the receiver when any ring came, to see what was going on, but that was the signal that there was something of community interest that everyone should share in.

The 3-C boys often came down to the ranch. There was a swimming hole down by our orchards that they took advantage of. The water down at our ranch was a little warmer than it was up at the 3-C camp because we were farther down the river. They also got apples and produce that the ranch could provide, when we had an excess. Quite often when the boys came down they would bring bananas or oranges because they knew that type of fruit was a treat to us. It was furnished to them, a kind of trade-off.

The man who was in charge of the 3-C camp was a Mr. Hanrahan. The building up at the 3-C camp had living quarters for he and his family in the front of the building. The rear of the building was like a big kitchen and dining room. It had long tables with benches where the boys ate and all of their food was prepared there. There was a place where they bunked that was apart from the living quarters of the Hanrahan family.

I remember thinking how beautiful the fireplace was that was in their living quarters. There was also a small shed where tools were kept, and I think they referred to it as the fuel shed because the gasoline and oil and thinks like that were stored there. It was quite an event in the history of the valley when the 3-C camp moved in. We had never had that many young people in the area before.

Pinochle and Walnuts

They didn't take part in the regular social life of the valley, such as the visiting back and forth that the families did. Long winter evenings up there quite often we would walk down to Tybergs and a game of pinochle would be in progress among the adults. We children would sit on the floor and look at magazines or something like that. Mrs. Tyberg had a music box that we loved to listen to. You'd wind it up and then the little drum would pluck the little steel fingers and each little finger made a different tone. It played about three melodies and was very pretty music to my ear. Mrs. Tyberg often let us listen to that two or three times.

One night when all of the adults were playing pinochle and had forgotten more or less about us kids, I decided I would really get my fill of walnuts. We didn't have walnuts on the ranch. The Tybergs had a walnut tree and this is where the treat in the Christmas boxes came from each year. Mrs. Tyberg had a wooden bowl of walnuts with a nutcracker in it and of course the kids were free to help themselves. The pinochle game lasted so long that I ate too many walnuts. Before the evening was over I got deathly sick. It was quite awhile before I wanted any more walnuts, but I do still like them today.

Grandma never did take part in any of the pinochle games because she believed that cards were instruments of the devil and so she would have no part of them. Pinochle was never played at our house because Grandma did not allow any cards in the house. She even questioned whether or not she should let Pat and I keep a game of Old Maid that our uncle gave us one Christmas because it was played with cards. I guess she could not connect gambling with the game of Old Maid, so we were allowed to keep those. I think she was probably the most religious person in the valley.

Glenn Creek CCC Camp, main building.

165

The Missionary

I don't know whether most of the neighbors were Protestants or Catholics, but probably of Protestant persuasion, I guess, or if they were Catholics they probably kept it very quiet. Grandma made no bones about the fact that she thought the Catholic religion was not the right one and anyone who belonged to the Catholic Church was certainly doomed. So if they were Catholics, they probably never mentioned it after the first time.

There was no church services or anything like that available up in the valley, but one winter Grandma's friend, Amelia Noah, came and stayed for several months at the ranch. She had been a missionary in the hills of Kentucky and quite often we would all gather at one of the houses in the neighborhood, generally at the Tybergs or our place or Middletons.

She would tell us some of the adventures she had as a missionary in the hills of Kentucky. She had been there in the early 1930's and possibly even the late 1920's. At that time in the area where she was they were still actively feuding among some of the Kentucky hill families. She had firsthand seen some of the evidence of this.

She would hold Bible reading, and we would all sit around with a Bible on our lap and take turns reading verses from the Bible under her direction. Any stranger who came there would probably have been amazed to hear Jerd and Charlie and Joe Schapers reading, very haltingly, from the Bible. They were very serious when they did their verse reading. No one ever laughed at their halting reading. Most of them read fairly well to themselves. They could read a newspaper article and they knew what it said, but when it came to reading out loud, their pronunciation and so forth was a little strange. But as I say, they were very serious in their Bible reading and no one ever got impatient with them or anything like that.

We had a few hymn books that Amelia had brought with her and we would often sing some of the hymns out of the hymn books after we had our Bible reading. She also held some special classes at the ranch house for the children in the valley. We memorized certain Bible verses and received, I believe, gold stars on a piece of paper or something for the Bible verses we had learned. That was the closest thing to any type of church or religious services that we ever had up in the valley.

Amelia Noah had been the wife of Fred Noah from Allegany, who was a logger and high climber. She had known Grandma for quite a number of years. I don't know what the reason was for her coming up and staying with us for that period of time. She was hoping to be able to go back to the mission field again. I can remember a couple of times when she got together what she called a missionary barrel to send back to some of the people in Kentucky where she had been a missionary. The missionary barrel consisted of items of clothing that people had outgrown or could not use, household articles that were no longer needed; anything that could be used in a household or to clothe children mainly. Then they were shipped back to her people in Kentucky.

Mr. Elk Peak

To get back to Elk's Peak for a moment, I mentioned that it had had a lookout on it in former days. This was when my Aunt Jane and Aunt Agnes were younger. There was a building of sorts on top of Elk's Peak and it was connected to the phone line in the summertime. This phone line was the same one that ran between all of the ranches in the valley. Aunt Jane and Aunt Agnes, being young ladies who were quite spirited, along with Dora Brown, used to have quite a bit of fun together. One of the things they'd like to do (and I'm sure it broke the boredom for the gentleman who was stationed on Elk's Peak as a lookout), they would ring him up and have conversations with him. They had never met the man, and to this day I don't remember what his real name was, but they always referred to him as "Mr. Elk Peak."

Quite often when the Forest Patrol would come up to bring supplies they would pass by the ranch and possibly stop in for a meal on their way up to take supplies to Mr. Elk Peak. One time the girls were talking to him on the phone and they knew the Forest Patrol was coming up so they asked Mr. Elk Peak if there was anything he would like that they could send him. He said, "Yes." There really was something he needed really bad, and that was a haircut. They said sure, they would be glad to send him a haircut. What kind did he want? He said he would like to have a green, curly haircut. That was enough for the girls. They got busy and went out to the shave horse where Joe Schapers had been scraping some ax handles and things like that and they gathered up the curly shavings and took some green food coloring and dyed these shavings a bright green with the food coloring. Then they put all of the shavings in a box and wrapped it up real pretty and put a fancy ribbon on it and sent it up with the Forest Patrol to Mr. Elk Peak. That was his green, curly haircut.

They hadn't heard too much from him after that, and then one day Grandma decided that she was going to play her own trick, only she was going to play it on the girls. They were all out for a walk somewhere and a traveling salesman happened to come through. He was just a young man, so Grandma got him to one side and gave him a talking to and asked him if he would mind playing a part for her. He was to play the part of Mr. Elk Peak. Grandma clued him in on what the girls had sent him and some of the conversations that she had overheard on the telephone going on between the girls and Mr. Elk Peak.

When the girls came back from their walk the salesman was there for supper. When they walked in Grandma introduced him to them as Mr. Elk Peak. Well, they were rather taken aback because they never really thought they would ever meet the young man. Conversation was a little stilted during dinner time while the traveling salesman pretended to be Mr. Elk Peak. With the information Grandma had given him he was able to answer their questions and refer to some of the conversations they had had by telephone. It was not until after dinner time that Grandma finally told them who this gentleman really was. The girls were rather relieved and could see that the joke was on them that time.

167

Traveling Salesmen

Traveling salesmen were sort of a fact of life on the ranch. There were shoe salesmen that came through. There was a salesman who sold eye glasses. He would test the eyes and make the eye glasses before he left the place. The Raleigh man and the Watkins man, they came through even when I was still a child. I don't remember any salesmen other than them except for a cattle buyer who occasionally would come through. He was looking mainly for old, worn out milk cows and things of that nature. The animals he bought from the ranches generally went to the glue factory, the hides were sold, and that type of thing. They were not meat animals.

Most of these salesmen always got a meal and quite often they would stay overnight. Some other overnight customers that Grandma had in the early days were the people who came through on the stage from Scottsburg. They would stop either at the ranch or sometimes at Mrs. Tyberg's house. Mrs. Tyberg was a very good cook, and so one place or the other was generally the overnight stop for the stage that went through from Scottsburg to Marshfield.

World War I

The First World War affected the little valley up there somewhat. Aunt Jane's friend Walter Crane went to France and never returned. He was reported missing in action. I remember Grandma saying that his mother had never really given up hope that Walter would someday come home. Ray Stemmerman, the brother of George Stemmerman, was killed overseas in France. Alfred Leaton went to France, but got there just as the war was ending. As he was going to war my grandma had told him, "Now Alfred, if there's anything I can give you boys, you know all you have to do is ask." He told her, "Yes, there is something I want." She said, "What is it, Alfred?" He said, "I want Agnes!" That was the way he asked for my Aunt Agnes' hand in marriage.

Myself and My Sister

Then, of course, there was myself and my sister at the ranch. I recall her as kind of a pain because I was always having to look out for her. We did have some good times together. I think she probably thought of me as the one who got to do things that she couldn't. And she knew darned good and well that she could do them just as well as I could. A

The Raleigh Man, Bill Leaton (1888–1972). Bill lost his right arm in a sawmill accident when he was sixteen years old. He was the Raleigh Man off and on during the 1920's, 30's, and 40's. Here he is holding his daughter, Hattie.

gap of five and a half years is sort of a hard gap to get over when you're a small child. Once she grew up she turned out to be pretty good.

I recall one time we were having a picnic up on the county road. We had packed our sandwiches up there just above the old ranch house and were sitting there eating them and all of a sudden she gave a scream and started to cry. I couldn't figure what in the world was wrong with her. She started pointing down at her leg and I looked and there was a huge black ant that had fastened his pinchers right on the inside of her thigh, on the tender spot. I grabbed hold of the ant and pulled, and I pulled the ant in two, but the head and the pinchers remained in her leg. I got her back down to the ranch house and Grandma got the tweezers and finally got the pinchers out of her leg. She cried all the way down, and Grandma thought I had done something to make her cry.

While Pat may have been kind of delicate in health when she was small, she was pretty straight-forward in saying whatever it was she thought. I don't recall her being afraid of anything. Neither of us were ever afraid of the woods or of the dark or anything like that. We were on pretty good speaking terms with both. When Pat was small, Grandma had her crib in by her bed in the bedroom. Grandma's bedroom was downstairs and it got some of the heat from the big wood stove in the living room, so it was warm. She wanted to have Pat near her so if she woke in the night or had any problems, she'd be right there by her side. When Pat finally outgrew the crib she slept with Grandma.

Quite often Grandma would have nightmares. She had recurring nightmares and she would make really weird noises when she had these nightmares. She was evidently trying to scream or something and she would wake everyone else in the whole house up. But she would never wake up herself when she had these nightmares. My dad would run down from upstairs where he slept in the opposite end of the house from where Grandma's bedroom was, and he would go in and grab hold of Grandma's shoulders and shake her and wake her up to relieve her of what sounded like horrible pain of her nightmare.

Well, this didn't frighten Pat either. She was used to it. She knew what it was. I think a stranger in the house would probably have his hair stand straight on end when Grandma started one of her nightmares, but Pat sort of took it in stride.

One time when Daddy went downstairs to waken Grandma, just as he got to the bed, Pat sat straight up in the bed and she turned to Grandma and she said, "That's enough of that!" I guess she was tired of the noise.

The other noise that we used to have a lot of at nighttime was when Joe Schapers would sleep he was quite a loud snorer. It never took him long to go to sleep once he hit the bed. One time someone asked him, "How do you get to sleep so fast?" He says, "Oh, there's nothing to it. You just go to bed and think of nothing." Normally within five minutes you could hear him snoring after he went to bed.

Pat liked to puddle along the creek when she was little, and she still does. She played with the waterdogs and frogs and whatever else she found in the little pools in the creek. It wouldn't be anything uncommon at all for her to have a frog or a waterdog or some angle worms in her pocket. Sometimes Grandma found some of these things in sort of a sorry state when she went to wash her clothes. I recall one time when we went up to Middleton's, Pat was going around with her hands in her pockets. Aunt Frieda Middleton asked her what she had in her pocket. She pulled it out and showed her, and Aunt Frieda as rather sorry that she had asked, because she didn't expect something like a waterdog to be looking her in the face.

Pat wasn't as lucky as I in the way of playmates. When the Al Leaton family moved across the creek in the little house, my cousin Alfreda was just older than I and my cousin Clifford was just younger than I. Later, the Bill Leaton family moved in that little house. The two girls, Hattie and Wilma, were one on each side of me in age. Hattie was not quite a year older and Wilma was only a few months younger, so I was luckier to have playmates than Pat was. She often had to amuse herself and she did this with her little friends from the creek. Generally, the family dog was her companion too, especially Coony.

The Tyberg Place

On the place below us, which we refer to as the Tyberg place, one of the people who lived there was Mrs. Tyberg and when I knew her she had been widowed twice. I never knew Alfred Tyberg, but Mrs. Tyberg was a very energetic woman, not very large as I recall her, but very, very strong for her size. She could pick up a five gallon milk can and load it with no trouble at all. She often had to load sacks of produce such as apples or potatoes or something like that. She was a wonderful cook; she set a very good table.

Charlie Schapers getting into the Terraplane.
(frame from 8mm home movie by Harold Ott).

When school was in session, the school teachers normally boarded at her place, although at times we had the school teacher board with us. A couple of the married teachers like Mrs. Gray and Mrs. Diurks lived in a house up behind the Middleton house. But generally the Tyberg place was the residence of whoever happened to be the school teacher at that time.

Charlie and Jerd Schapers

Mrs. Tyberg's and Joe Schapers' brothers, Charlie and Jerd, also lived down with Mrs. Tyberg and helped to do the chores and that sort of thing. Charlie had at one time lived up at the ranch with us but later on moved down to the Tyberg place in

170

order to help his sister. When Daddy got the job as the government trapper, Charlie was sort of the "man on call" for our ranch. Most of Daddy's trapping was done in the wintertime when the cows were dry, except for one we had for a family milk cow, so it fell to me to take care of the cows: to put them in the barn, feed them, and milk the one family cow.

Daddy had told me that if I had any problems to call on Charlie. Often he would come up, a couple times a week, to see if there was anything that needed to be done that we couldn't handle by ourselves. One morning when I went out to feed the cows, very early in the morning — because the cows were left in the barn all night so that they wouldn't be out in the cold and the mud of the corral — I noticed that one of the cows was loose from the stanchion. When I looked I could see a calf's foot sticking out of the cow, so I knew that she was about to calf. I had absolutely no idea what to do. The fact that she was loose among the other cows disturbed me, so I hotfooted it down to the Tyberg place to get Charlie. By the time we got back the calf had arrived, the cow was cleaning it up and was perfectly happy, so we really didn't have a problem. But I had no way of knowing whether it was a problem or not, since I was not too experienced in that type of thing yet. I was about ten at that time.

Charlie always made a trip up to the ranch after he and Mrs. Tyberg had been to town because always there was a treat to be distributed among whatever kids happened to be up there. He would bring up the mail and quite often spend the evening there, after the chores were done. In the wintertime, the evenings were long because the chores had to be done before it got dark, and then there was the long evening to put in. We had a battery radio and listened to things such as "I Love a Mystery." Our lights were all kerosine lamps until late years when Daddy finally made a generator plant and we generated our own electricity. But during the time when I was a child all I remember is the kerosine lamps for light.

We always had coal oil around the house to fill the lights with, and it was also one of Joe Schaper's favorite remedies for a cold. He would tip up the kerosine can and let some of the kerosine trickle down his throat, and then he would go, "Ahhhhhh," just as if it tasted good. Then he would put the can down. He was a great believer that if a little bit of medicine was good, then quite a bit of medicine must be better. The kerosine, and sometimes quinine, were his remedies for a cold. I recall at least a couple of occasions when he overdosed himself on the quinine and passed out on the floor and scared everybody.

The kerosine, I knew, had to taste good just from the way he reacted when he would take it. One day I sneaked out on the back porch and decided that I would have a dose of that, too. I didn't necessarily feel a cold coming on, but I wanted to see how that tasted. Well, it tasted horrible, and I never tried that again!

Charlie was a very mild-mannered, gentle man and all of the kids just loved Charlie dearly. One of the favorite pastimes was to try and straighten out the fingers on his crippled hand. I spent many a happy evening being juggled on Charlie's knee along with another kid on the other knee because his knees were always filled to capacity with other kids waiting their turn to get up.

171

The other brother that lived down at the Tyberg place was Jerd. All of the Schapers brothers had big mustaches and all had nice heads of gray hair when I was a little girl. Jerd was kind of a putterer. He was a good man with an ax; he could carve a trough out of a log. A lot of the containers that held the food for the animals on the farm were of his handiwork, although all of the Schapers boys were fairly good with an ax. The pig's trough, the trough the chicken feed was put in, and all kinds of smaller troughs, like for the cat's milk and the dog's food, were all the handiwork of their axes, made out of logs.

Jerd also liked to putter around the creek, but unlike Pat, he wasn't looking for the small animals in the creek. He was looking for gold. He had various little bottles sitting on the windowsills in the house. All of them were filled with fine sand, some of one color and some of another. I think Jerd believed that there was what he called "color," meaning gold, in all of them. He could probably tell you just exactly which pothole in the creek he had gotten each little vial out of. I don't believe he ever sent any of his sand away to assay. He enjoyed looking at it too much to part with it, I think. Needless to say, he never did strike it rich, and I never did see any nuggets or anything of that type that he'd found, but he certainly had a lot of fun trying.

The Wonders of Modern Plumbing

When Mrs. Tyberg decided that she wanted running water down at her ranch house, my dad went down and helped put the water system in. He had been a plumber by trade. Jerd was very willing to help him with it. He didn't know anything about plumbing, but Daddy was able to use him as sort of a "gopher" man, and he'd bring Daddy any tools he needed or he would saw off a piece of pipe the length he needed to have — things like that to help Daddy get the water supply in. They had a bathroom with a bathtub and a washbowl and toilet in it. He also put water out to the kitchen sink.

When he was down visiting one time he noticed that Jerd went out to the kitchen and got a drinking glass, then he went through the dining room and into the bathroom and drew some water out of the bathtub and drank it. Daddy asked him, he said, "Jerd, why didn't you just get yourself a drink of water out there at the kitchen sink? It would be a lot easier." Jerd said, "Now Cle. You remember I helped you put that plumbin' system in. I know that kitchen sink is downstream from the toilet, and I'm not about to drink out of it."

Jerd Schapers at the Tyberg place.
(Frame from 8mm home movie by Harold Ott).

The Leatons

In the little house across the creek, various families lived after Daddy moved out. There was the Al Leaton family. That was my Aunt Agnes' husband, and so those Leatons were my cousins. There was Bob and Alfreda and Clifford. Bob was quite a bit older than I, probably five or six years. Alfreda was just older, and Clifford was just younger. We all went to the little schoolhouse there on Glenn Creek at various times. None of the Leatons completed their education there, as I did, but they were there off and on during most of the time.

The other Leaton family that lived in the little house across the creek was the Bill Leaton family. They had three children also. There were the two girls, Hattie, the oldest, and Wilma. Then they had a younger son, Eldon. All of them went to the little Glenn Creek School also at various times. Hattie Leaton did graduate from the little school the year before I did, but she did not spend all eight of her years there.

Joe Milton, Frieda's brother. Crippled from polio, he had no use of his legs.

Bernice Leaton was the daughter of Mr. Howell who had what we called the upper place, which was the one farthest up Glenn Creek. They lived not only in the little house across the creek, but they also had lived on the Middleton place at one time, and in between, I believe, they were in town and moved back and forth to the valley several times.

The Middletons

What we call the Middleton place had a family on it. We were never allowed to call adults by their first name. Some people disliked being called Mr. or Mrs., as did Mr. and Mrs. Middleton, so we addressed them as Aunt Frieda and Uncle Slim. It was all right to use their first name if we gave the title of Aunt and Uncle or something like that to them, which in my grandmother's estimation gave respect to our elders. They were almost as dear to us as an aunt and uncle, and they lived there for quite a number of years because Freddie went through all eight grades with me.

Uncle Slim was just that. He was a tall, slim man, a very friendly, outgoing person, always ready to help a neighbor when it came time to make hay or any other thing that took some extra hands. Aunt Frieda was a little bit heavy set, a good cook, and also a very happy, outgoing person.

They had a son, Freddie, who was about six months older than I. He and I were in the same grade all through school, sometimes friends and sometimes enemies. Freddie at one time saved my life. We were down fishing, about four of us kids, down fishing along the creek one time during a freshet, which means high water in the creek. Now, fish don't bite during a freshet, but you know, kids fish whether they think they're going to catch fish or not. Maybe we weren't aware at that time that fish didn't bite during a freshet.

Anyway, I waded out and something happened and my feet were swept out from under me and I was swept into the swollen creek. We were only a few hundred feet above the line fence between our place and the Tyberg place. This was a fence stretched across the river to keep the two herds of cattle separated and it was made out of barbed wire. The first strand or so of barbed wire was underneath of the the high water at this time and I was being swept down to the fence. Freddie ran along the gravel bank and handed me the end of his fish pole, which I grabbed and he pulled me ashore. If he hadn't done this I'm sure I would have been swept underneath the fence and probably caught on the barbed wire and held under until I had drowned.

Really, I don't imagine we were supposed to be around the creek at all during that time. Grandma had a sort of a fear of the creek. She was afraid that some child would drown or something like that, and most sections of the creek were not visible from any of the ranch houses, but us kids loved to play along there.

The Middletons also had Joe Milton staying with them. He was Frieda Middleton's younger brother. He'd had infantile paralysis when he was young and his legs were absolutely useless. He dragged himself around on his hands and he could do almost anything that most other people could do. He was very, very strong in his upper body, which came from pulling his body around. I don't think any of us really thought of Joe as being a cripple. We knew he was different; his mode of locomotion was different than ours. But we never thought of him as being disabled. We accepted him as he was. He made no excuses for the way he was and none of us ever even thought of him as being inferior in any way to us. He was probably in his early twenties when the Middletons lived there.

Mr. Howell

On above the Middleton place, with quite a space in between the two places, was Mr. Howell's ranch. The area in between had never been homesteaded to the best of my knowledge. There were quite a few old-growth trees along the road going up to his house. He didn't have as much bottomland, or pasture land as the other places, but he didn't keep any herd of cows or anything like that. He did have a little black horse that he rode quite often. When he would come down to our place or to visit the other neighbors he often rode his horse rather than bringing his automobile. Compared to our big old work horses, Dick and Prince, he was nothing but a pony. He was not an old work horse like we were used to. He was a riding horse and Mr. Howell was very proud of him.

One time Mr. Howell also had some mules. Once when my cousins and I made a trip over into Ash Valley after Middletons had moved over there, we walked as far as Mr. Howell's place, which was about three miles from the ranch, and from there we rode his mule on over into Ash Valley. That was quite an adventure. I think probably I was around twelve that year and my cousins Alfreda and Bob Leaton were the other two who went on this adventurous trip over to Ash Valley to visit the Middletons. We came back the same day, which was about an eighteen mile trip altogether.

Mr. Howell also wore a mustache. He was not a large man. He was rather thin and wiry. He lived by himself on the Howell place. He had been married at one time but all of the years he was up there he was an old bachelor and lived by himself except for a period of time when his daughter Bernice and her three children made their home with him while Bill Leaton was away somewhere. I remember going up and staying overnight with Hattie and Wilma at the old Howell place. Mr. Howell was an early riser and when Mr. Howell got up he made sure that everybody else in the household was up. It was a novelty with me to get up as early as he did. Normally, daylight was getting-up time at the ranch because that was time to go and do the chores. As soon as it was daylight: fairly early in the summer but fairly late in the winter.

Road Work

It was about twelve miles from the ranch down to Allegany. Almost every winter, and in the fall when we had windstorms and a lot of rain, the road would be closed between the ranch and Allegany by fallen trees and sometimes slides would come down across the road. All of the neighbors up above the falls would get together and the men would go down with their shovels and axes and saws and clear out the road. They left it up to the residents. The residents would keep track of the time they spent on the road and then later on turn it in to the county for so many hours of work.

The county at that time had no money to pay the men, but they would issue warrants for the amount of so much per hour. These looked like a check but they were not. You couldn't take them to the bank and cash them. The county would have to redeem them within seven years, so many of the doctors and lawyers in town and some of the merchants would buy these warrants, not at face value, but sometimes as low as fifty percent. If you had a warrant for ten dollars you might be able to sell it to one of these people for five dollars. They would hold it until it came due and the county paid about three percent interest after seven years. Even the teachers were paid this way by the county and by the school boards. Taxes weren't being paid at that time during the depression so the county had no cash. A warrant was a sort of a promissory note.

The Mills

It was during the depression that the taxes on the ranch didn't get paid for lack of cash flow. It was probably this that prompted my uncle Bob to sell the timber on the ranch to George Youst in about 1939 or 1940. The Yousts moved up to the valley and they lived in the little cabin across the creek for awhile. There was George and Doris Youst and their three children. Carol was about my age, probably a few months younger, and Lionel was somewhere closer to Pat's age, and then there was Lorry, or Laurence, the youngest boy.

Mr. Youst built a mill up on the hill first, up above the lower field where our orchard was. After the lumber was sawed, they had built a chute and it came down onto a loading platform below the orchard and the slabs and waste products came down another chute into the field above the orchard. It got to be quite a pile after awhile and one winter day we all went down into the field and they set the slab pile on fire. It made quite a spectacle down there. I don't think today you could tell where the slab pile had been, it's all so overgrown.

Later on Mr. Youst built another mill between the ranch house and the little house across the creek. A dam was put in the creek to put the logs into. Mrs. Youst was one of his best lumber truck drivers. The falls were not easy to negotiate with any kind of vehicle, let alone a truck. I know that Daddy had quite a bit of admiration for Mrs. Youst when she would pilot one of those lumber trucks down over the falls and back up again.

There were various men who came into the valley and left the valley during the time that the lumber mills were there. A lot of this was during the war and a lot of younger, able-bodied men were gone. So many of the men who were up there were older people. I remember George Baker, who was the sawyer. Then there was Pete Lousignont and his brother Gus Johnson. Pete liked to hunt so he and Daddy often went elk hunting together. They seemed to enjoy each other's company quite a bit. There were a few married people. Once in awhile one of them would move into the little house across the creek after the Yousts had moved out.

Others had built little cabins down below the orchard, little shacks that they would live in during the week and maybe go home to town on the weekend. There was much more activity in the valley during that time than what we were used to. Later on there was another mill down on the old Tyberg place. But most of that was after I had left the valley to go to school, so I don't know too many of the people who were down there.

By the time that the mill came into the valley, the Tyberg place had changed hands, more or less. Mrs.

Part of the Youst sawmill crew: Bobby ?, Al Moser, George Youst (on truck), George Morin, Pete Lousignont, Laurence Youst (boy), MacFarlin.

Tyberg had cancer and was finally bedridden and Molly Stokes and her husband came up to be there at the ranch and take care of Mrs. Tyberg. After she passed away they were on the place for several years. After they left, there was Joe and Daisy Morris who lived on the Tyberg place. Joe and Daisy were fern pickers and more or less made their living off the woods the same as my dad liked to do. It seems like the area up above the falls was a good place for people who liked to pick ferns. My uncle Al and some of my cousins also picked ferns. When Daddy couldn't trap he also picked ferns, a way of making a living.

When I was old enough to go to high school I left the ranch and came down Coos River to live with my Aunt Jane and Uncle George so that I could go to high school. Pat continued to go to the little school up above the Golden and Silver Falls until I believe she was in the third grade. Then she also came down to stay with Aunt Jane and Uncle George and go to grade school down at Coos River.

After I came out to go to school it was only summertimes that I was on the ranch. A lot of people who came and went that were connected with the mill I only had summertime contact with.

Another family I remember that lived in the little house across the creek were the Bergers. I don't believe that they were connected with the mill in any way. They lived up there for a year or possibly two years. There was a Chuck Berger, who was about the age of my sister. He and she, I think, did quite a bit of fishing together and that type of thing. The thing that seemed the most unusual to me about the Bergers was the fact that they ate elderberry blossoms. They'd make a batter of some kind and dip the elderberry blossoms in the batter and deep fry them. We had not thought of using the elderberry blossoms in that way but they were pretty good the way they fixed them.

In later years while I was still in high school, I believe about my senior year, Grandma got so she was not in very good health so Daddy decided to move her into town. That way both Pat and I could stay with her and I could go to high school and Pat could go to grade school.

177

Chapter Twenty-two

Marvin Stemmerman Remembers Hunting Stories[7]

This story was related to me by my uncle and it had to do with three of the Schapers boys, Jerd, Charlie, and Joe. Joe was the man who later became my step-grandfather, the only grandfather that we knew. We always called him Dad.

It seems that in the very early days up there things were kind of tight and groceries were real thin and winter was on and the boys were out hunting for meat, and they were down in the vicinity of the Golden Falls. As the story goes, Joe was off kind of by himself and Jerd and Charlie were over a ways from him when suddenly they heard him begin to holler at them. He says, "Oh boys, boys, come quick. Oh boys, come quick. Oh, he's a big one, boys!" They started over for him real suddenly and they got over there and looked across the canyon just in time to see this great, magnificent elk turnin' and walkin' up the hill into the brush. He was a huge old monarch bull. Joe says, "Isn't he a beauty, boys. Isn't he a beauty, boys." Jerd says to him, "Yes, he's a beauty, but why you don't shoot him?" Joe thought for a minute and he said, "Well, I guess that be all right too, but I hadn't thought of it!"

This is [another] hunting story Uncle Cle told me about himself and Al Leaton. It was during the depression, and it was raining. It was a real wet night and they were out about ten o'clock at night. They'd gone up the creek, clear up by Middletons, past the schoolhouse, up through that way. They'd crossed the creek and coming back down the other side. They'd just got across the creek and Alfred was carrying the gun and Uncle Cle was carrying the spotlight. Alfred said, "Hold up a minute." So, he stopped. Cle said he had to have a smoke there and waited a few mintues and Al

Baldy Crane, lft, Cle Wilkinson, rt. With a string of racoons; deer hanging in loft. At "Peaceful Valley Manor," the Elk Creek cabin.

---

[7] Tape recorded by Alice Wilkinson; transcribed and edited by Lionel Youst.

come back around the bush and he said, "OK, let's go." So they go on down the creek and boy, they're spotlightin', spotlightin', spotlightin', and not seein' nothing and they get clear down to the other side of the creek somewhere above where the old mill used to be and Cle seen something. Cle says, "I held the light like this and a nice three-point buck lifts his head up out of the berry patch. I just stood there, like this, and I say, 'Shoot! SHOOT! Why in the hell don't you shoot?"

"I can't shoot."

"What do you mean you can't shoot?"

"I left the gun back where I took a shit!"

Cle and Baldy [Crane]. Do you remember the year that they had the agreement? Cle was gonna fix the roof on the house. He was gonna get in the wood for the winter, and there was one other thing he was gonna do. Baldy spent the whole summer widening the trail from the [Elk] Peak end to the cabin and by hand. I got up to the ranch. Joe Morris come up. We were visiting there for quite awhile and finally Joe took off and went back below. Cle said, "What do you say we get in the truck and drive up to the peak and walk in and see how Baldy's doing?" This was probably just before school starts, in September. We drive up to the peak, and hike in. We get in about, I don't know, two or three miles, something like that, pretty quick we hear chopping. And there's old Baldy. The sweat is just rolling off him. He's whackin' on a log. He's trying to widen it where an old growth is across the trail and they just had a piece sawed out of it, you know. But he had been sawing and widening on it, and the sweat just rolling off him. We hailed him so we wouldn't scare him to death and hiked on in there. I think we packed in a little sack of sandwiches or something. They hadn't seen each other in probably three or four weeks. Baldy's living in the cabin and he'd hike out and work on the trail and Cle was, of course, at the ranch with his thing. So we sat down, eating lunch there. They lit up their cigarettes, of course, and I don't think I ever seen Baldy any madder. Pretty quick Baldy — we was just talking, you know — and he says, "You got the wood in for winter?" Cle says, "No." Baldy says, "You get the roof on the house?" "No." "Well, what you been doing?" Cle says, "Well, Joe's been helping me!" Baldy just absolutely turned livid. He'd been working his fanny off, you know. You know how old Joe was. He'd come up and visit and you could just while away day after day with him, you know, or Daisy. And that's exactly what had been going on. No, the wood wasn't in, and no, the roof wasn't fixed. They had this big agreement: you're gonna do "this" and I'm gonna do "that." But "this" got done, and "that" didn't get done! Baldy just come unglued. But Uncle Cle, nothing ever really got to him, you know, or phased him, or riled him. But Baldy, he could get pretty riled.

I never forget the time [young Bob Wilkinson] and I was up there pigeon huntin'. You know, Bob had never done very much stuff like that. We went pigeon huntin' and we killed some birds. He wanted to learn how to cut up and butcher the pigeons. He said, "You just do it and I'll do everything you do." We got 'em all done and I put mine in the stew pot, and run some water in there. He was finishing up on his, I didn't think nothin' of it. He put his in the pot and went on in the living room. They were simmering away out there on the stove and before long I guess

Uncle Cle went out to see how they were doing. He pulled the lid off the pot and he says, "Hey, boys. Come out here a minute." He says, "Look in this pot." We looked in the pot and here's this big pair of yellow feet stickin' up to the top! He hadn't seen me cut the feet off. He was gonna do everything I did! We really razzed him over that.

Peaceful Valley Manor, Cle and Baldy's cabin on Elk Creek

A Letter from Robert Wilkinson III

Dear Mr. Youst:

I wish I had known you were writing your book "Above the Falls" before it was printed. I have some information that you were not aware of at the time.

My father Robert Wales Wilkinson the 2nd was born Aug 2, 1897. My mother Anna Mary Weber taught school at the little school on the ranch about 1928–30 and that is where my dad met her. After they were married they moved to Klamath Falls where my dad worked for Weyerhaeuser as a logger. This is where I was born 1-12-31. About 6 months after I was born, the depression caused my dad to be layed off so we came back to the ranch. My earliest memories are when we lived there. I was 2 ½ years old. In the summer of 33 we went to Loon Lake and lived in a tent while my dad worked for a Mr. Cardell in a little 2 man saw mill. After that we moved to Marshfield where my dad got work at Coos Bay Lumber Co (The Big Mill).

In 1939 or early 40 my dad bought a mill and had it setting in our front yard. It sat there until your dad bought it from him and moved it to the ranch.

Joe Schapers went to Marshfield in 1925 and bought a 1925 Chevrolet pickup. The salesman showed him how to drive it and he drove it to the ranch. He never drove it again. It was different than most pickups because the top went all the way to the back. It had curtains on the sides to keep out the rain. After the old truck was no longer driven, Cle used the engine to run a wood saw.

My dad died of a heart attack on Nov 1, 1945.

In 1938 Joe Schapers got sick and came to Marshfield to see the Doctor. He staid with us while in town and my dad took him to see a Dr. McKeown. The Dr examined Joe and called my dad to another room and said, "Get him out of here before he dies in my office." My dad took him to another Dr (Dr. Johnson I think) who said he could help him and they put him in the hospital. Within a few days he died.

I don't know just when it happened but Joe Schapers gave my dad the homestead certificate to the ranch. I found it in my mother's things when she died.

I have enclosed a copy. As you can see it is not signed by Pres. McKinley, but for him by a secretary.

If you ever have another reunion I would like to come.

Very Truly Yours,

Robert Wales Wilkinson
Black Butte Ranch, OR

Logs in the East Fork at Allegany, 1900. Picture taken from behind the Allegany store. Cabin at left is home of George Stemmerman. There were logs in the river near this location for more than 110 years – from 1877 until the Weyerhaeuser log terminal was closed after the last raft of logs went down the Millicoma River on January 4, 1989.

PART SEVEN

THE TIMBER

Weyerhaeuser truck on private road, with about 18,000 board feet of logs. Driver: Roger Ott.

Business history, however, is no simple subject.
--Joseph A. Amato, *Rethinking Home*

Upper Glenn Creek Timber Chronology

Forest fires

Solid stands of Douglas fir naturally re-seed themselves following forest fires. My thanks to Jerry Phillips for sharing with me his knowledge of the fire history of the area.

1440 – Presumed fire on Upper Glenn Creek. There were a few living trees and many old snags dating from that time.

1770 – A large fire from the east of Glenn Creek, burned most of the timber that was standing at that time on what became the homesteads of Upper Glenn Creek.

1840 – A fire from the north of Glenn Creek, burned most of the timber on the Glenn Creek side of the ridge, except the re-growth from the fire of 1770, which was not burned. This fire did not go into the West Fork side of the ridge.

1868 – The Coos Bay Fire burned the West Fork side of the ridge, but stopped before it got into Upper Glenn Creek. Therefore, the youngest timber at the time of first logging was regrowth from the fire of 1840, but most of the timber was re-growth from the fire of 1770.

Logging

1940 to 1948: George Youst and Vic Dimmick sawmills logged the timber from the Joe Schapers and Elizabeth Ott homesteads.

1950 to 1991 – Weyerhaeuser Timber Company began to log in the Glenn Creek drainage during the mid-fifties. By 1978 they were logging in the Frog Creek drainage, adjacent to the Elizabeth Ott homestead. They were logging various sites within the Glenn Creek drainage off and on until 1991. The Weyerhaeuser lands were all re-planted by hand soon after they were logged, in compliance with state law.

2000 – The very young timber from the Joe Schapers homestead, logged by George Youst during 1940 to 1945, was logged in 2000 and re-planted. The first of the lands logged by Weyerhaeuser during the 1950's will be logged again during the next decade , and the cycle can be expected to repeat itself indefinitely.

Chapter Twenty-three

The Timber and the Land

The great Coos Bay fire of 1868 had evidently started near Scottsburg. It was a dry year and somebody's slash fire got away from them. It burned 300,000 acres of the finest old-growth fir in the world. Douglas fir and the land it grew on was so unimportant in Coos County in 1868, however, that it is barely mentioned in contemporary records. Within a few years settlers and hunters were counting that fire as a blessing. It provided a large pasture for the elk herds and it made hunting much easier.

Elhorn Ranch in the Big Burn, about 1890

There was a pack trail into the "big burn," as it was called. It ran from Elkton and Scottsburg past the south end of Loon Lake and up to Elk's Peak, following what was probably the old Coos Indian trail from Marlow Creek to the Umpqua. At Elk's Peak it branched north into the center of the burn. George Gould built a home for his family there in 1868. He derived a good bit of his cash income from elk products: hides, dried meat, antlers, and teeth.

In those days elk were just another resource to be exploited. Among the "market hunter," in addition to the Goulds, were Kentuck Thomas and James Jordan (b. 1816). In 1931 Jordan's son Peter (b. 1874) testified at the U. S. Court of Claims hearings in North Bend and told a little of the market for elk. The hearings were to determine whether the Indians of Coos County had any money coming in payment for the land and resources that were taken from them seventy years earlier. Among the lines of testimony were attempts to answer questions relating to "what became of the resources?" Peter Jordan testified as follows:

> Well, I know that sailing vessels used to come in here and take stuff out. Often when they was here they used to get elk meat for their meat, to make their voyages, in place of beef. My father used to hunt. He was a hunter and he used to take orders and go out and kill elk and fetched it to them. And they would take as high as five or six elk to each sailing ship. Then there was a time here when they used to run those logging camps along the bay and they used the tallow from the elk to grease the skids with so the logs would slide along.[1]

---

[1] Harrington, reel 24, frame 833.

An interesting sidelight was the market for elk's teeth. Elk have two canine teeth, which had sometimes been used as money among certain Indian tribes. According to Don Taxay in his *Money of the American Indians* (p. 106), they were used especially among the Shoshone, Bannock, and Crow of Idaho, Montana, and Wyoming. In the 1890's they were valued at about 25 cents each. These teeth later became very valuable — about $5 each — to be used on watch fobs and tie clasps for members of the Benevolent and Protective Order of Elks. There was a time when virtually every member of the Elks would like to have had one of those elk's teeth. The result was that by 1910, the Millicoma River elk herd was nearly extinct. The state placed a moratorium on the hunting of elk, and the Goulds moved out of the big burn.

The extent of the depletion of the elk herds was reported in 1912 by George H. Cecil, supervisor of forest reserves for Oregon. Twenty-five years earlier there had been tens of thousands of elk in the state. Following is a summary of elk remaining in 1912.[2]

Cascade National Forest	30
Malheur National Forest	20
Oregon National Forest	75
Siskiyou National Forest	50
Siuslaw National Forest	200
Umatilla National Forest	13
Whitman National Forest	125
Crater Lake Forests	15

Tributaries of the East Fork of the Millicoma River were not part of the big burn. The last time most of it had burned was in 1770, and by 1912 the timber was about 140 years old. Because this was commercially valuable timber, it had been selected by the Southern Pacific and Northern Pacific Railroads as part of their federal grants to be resold to timber interests. It was thus in private ownership and the elk census, above, would not have included estimates of the elk within it. Hunting elk in this forest was quite a different thing from hunting in the big burn. Herds exceeding 100 could easily hide, and I doubt that anyone knew the extent of their numbers.

To help build up these seriously depleted herds, the state imported elk from Jackson's Hole, Wyoming, and introduced them into upper Matson Creek. Above Matson Creek Falls there is a valley somewhat similar to the Upper Glenn Creek valley. It is called Horseshoe Bottoms, owing to its horseshoe shape, and was the location of the Dan Matson homestead between 1898 and 1906. It is only a three-mile walk from there, up Tyberg Creek and over the ridge to get to the homesteads on Upper Glenn Creek.

The moratorium on hunting continued until 1940, and by that time the elk herds on the Millicoma drainage had increased from a few hundred to many thousands. It remains one of the major elk herds in the state.

---

[2] Gaston, vol. 1, page 478.

State Lands in Township 24-10

In my analysis of the ownership of the land within Township 24-10, I noted that by 1940 it was virtually all in the hands of the Weyerhaeuser Timber Company except for the old Joe Schapers and the old Elizabeth Ott homesteads, and a "few forties belonging to the state." The state forties in this township are in Sections 6 and 18. The Section 18 state lands are within the Golden and Silver Falls State Park, and are discussed separately. The state lands within Section 6 is in the Elliott State Forest.

I wasn't too sure how the Elliott State Forest came into these few forties in the extreme northwest corner of the township. Jerry Phillips, with the help of a title company, came up with the story. It is both interesting and instructive, and it is another example of ways in which our timber ownerships came to be the way they are.

As mentioned earlier, a standard section of one square mile contains 640 acres. Section 6 of T 24-10 has 935.92 acres. These odd-shaped sections come up because the world is round and the survey is rectangular. Also, surveyors sometimes make mistakes. Adjustments have to be made and this was one of those adjustments.

This section is on both sides of the ridge separating the West Fork from Glenn Creek. The Coos Bay fire of 1868 didn't go over that ridge. At the turn of the century, when the Northern Pacific Railroad had its locators and timber cruisers out, they must have looked very carefully at the limits of that old fire. As it turns out, Section 6 is the only place within Township 24-10 which had been touched at all by the fire of 1868. Northern Pacific wanted only the big timber, and they certainly didn't want the thirty-year-old regrowth that was then coming up following the fire. As a result, when they were selecting good timberland in lieu of the commercially unproductive lands they had owned within the newly established Mr. Rainier National Park and Timber Reserve, they were fairly careful not to include anything but the best.

The best of the timber within Section 6 was on some 292.76 acres on the east half of it. In so selecting, Northern Pacific left a little old growth in the public domain, but they didn't take any land that was not old growth. The limit of the fire had more or less followed the ridges. Surveyors follow straight lines for their rectangular survey. The locators for the Northern Pacific took the straight line that most closely fit the meanders of the fire.

I don't know anything about Jennie and Esther U'Ren, two sisters who in 1909 purchased eight of the odd-shaped forties in the west half of Section 6. There was a total of 316 acres involved. The sisters purchased them directly from the United States government under provisions of the Land Act of 1820. This act permitted "cash entry" to certain lands within the Public Domain, at a cost of $1.25 per acre. I'll discuss this act below, under the section on "The Lake Creekers."

In July 1926, these two sisters, now married, sold their lands to Adlesbury, Conrad, and Harrington. The deeds were notarized in Portland and in Canada. In 1931 and 1932, interests were shifted among family members of the new owners, and in 1936 Coos County foreclosed for failure to pay taxes. In 1940 the county deeded these lands to the state. In 1960 this old growth became some of the first timber in the Elliott State Forest to be logged.

Weyerhaeuser Timber Company[3]

Because of its immense implications for the history of Coos County, it is worthwhile to review how it was that Weyerhaeuser Timber Company ended up owning so much land here. It was almost entirely the result of decisions made and pressures applied thousands of miles from Southwestern Oregon. No one here had much to do with it, with the possible exception of Binger Hermann, originally from Myrtle Point.

Binger Hermann had been a congressman for several terms and was President William McKinley's Commissioner of Lands at the time that most of the Coos County timberland came into the hands of the big timber companies from Minnesota. Federal land policy was essentially to transfer as much as possible of the public domain into private hands, and to do it as quickly as possible. Binger Hermann, as Commissioner of Lands, with the help of his land office in Roseburg, sometimes went overboard in carrying out that policy.

In their eagerness to carry out the federal land policies by ignoring the letter of the law, and in some cases to enrich themselves with bribes and kickbacks, some of the land office personnel ended up in prison. Binger Hermann himself was indicted on several charges relating to land fraud, but was not convicted. The upshot of years of scandal, lost fortunes, tarnished reputations, and court cases reaching to the Supreme Court, was that the big timber companies from Minnesota were able to retain clear title to the hundreds of thousands of acres of timberland involved. Only a few of the speculators and crooked officials were punished for their crimes.[4]

By looking at the land transactions only within Township 24-10, we can see in miniature some of the ways in which such huge concentrations of timber ended up in so few hands. In the case of Township 24-10, the action was in motion before the first survey in 1896. The results became apparent not long after the survey was complete.

Northern Pacific Railroad

Weyerhaeuser came into Coos County through the Northern Pacific Railroad by an act of congress approved March 2, 1899. The original Northern Pacific grant, from the Act of July 7, 1864, was to aid in construction of a railroad and telegraph line from Lake Superior to Puget Sound. The railroad was to choose from alternate sections of a strip of land along the right of way. The Northern Pacific, however, didn't like some of the land it was to choose from. For example, some of it was on the slopes of Mt. Rainier and the higher elevations of the Cascade Range. These lands were commercially unproductive.

---

[3] Data is from deed records filed with the Coos County Clerk.

[4] *Looters of the Public Domain* (1912), written by S. A. D. Puter while serving time in prison for land fraud, is the best inside account of the practices that resulted in transfer of title of the timberlands from the federal government to the timber companies.

Through powerful lobbying efforts the Northern Pacific, on behalf of itself and its business associates in the timber industry, managed to have Congress establish the Mt. Rainier National Park and the Mt. Rainier National Forest Reserve. The timber industry associate was primarily Frederick Weyerhaeuser of St. Paul, Minnesota. Mr. Weyerhaeuser's next-door neighbor was Jim Hill, Chairman of the Board of the Northern Pacific Railroad.

The environmental and conservationist groups who naturally lobby for national parks and forest reserves probably never knew that they were playing directly into the hands of the timber industry. It happens time and time again, and is really amusing if one can maintain some perspective on it. Neither the timber industry nor the environmentalists have much of a sense of humor, however, either then or now.

The establishment of Mt. Rainier National Park and Timber Reserve removed those unproductive lands from the selection pool. Very cleverly written into the act establishing the park, the Act of March 2, 1899, was a provision allowing Northern Pacific to select "in lieu thereof" an equal quantity of public lands "lying within any state into, or through which the railroad runs." It just so happened that the Northern Pacific Railroad had thirty miles of track in Oregon.

Among the public lands they selected was one block of 61,860 acres, which included among other lands most of the previously unselected even-numbered sections within Township 24-10. This included all of Sections 12, 14, 22, 24 and 26 and parts of Sections 2, 4, 5, 6, 7, 8, 17, 18, 19, 20, 30, 31, and 32. The patent on this land was signed in the name of President William McKinley and was dated January 29, 1902.

Nine months later, on October 2, 1902, the Weyerhaeuser Timber Company received title to 24,584.14 acres of those lands from the Northern Pacific for $5.00 per acre. This purchase included all of the previously listed Northern Pacific lands within Township 24-10.

There were a few other small and miscellaneous parcels remaining. For example, in 1927 Weyerhaeuser picked up forty acres from the Aztec Land and Cattle Company of Arizona. Aztec had got the land in trade to the government for thirty-seven acres in the San Francisco Mountain Reserve, Arizona. By then there wasn't much left unaccounted for in Township 24-10, except for the Oregon and California Railroad lands.

Oregon & California Railroad (O & C)

The Oregon and California Railroad had a grant from the U.S. Government to build a railroad from Portland to the California line, down the central valleys. The railroad was to choose twenty square miles of land for every one mile of track that it built. The twenty square miles could come from anywhere within a sixty mile swath. From Roseburg, for example, that meant that most of the unclaimed land in Coos County was susceptible. The railroad, which was integrated into the Southern Pacific Railroad system in 1887,[5] received title to lands as the road continued south, and as surveys were completed. The total amount of land claimed by O & C was 3,187,215 acres.

On February 2, 1899, the Oregon and California Railroad received the patent to 14,082 acres in Coos County; 6,400 of these acres were in Township 24-10. As stipulated in the grant, these were all from odd numbered sections: 9, 11, 13, 15, 17, 23, 25, 27, 29, 33, and 35. President William McKinley signed the patent to the land, as he had a few months earlier for the homesteads of Elizabeth Ott and Joseph Schapers.

One of the conditions of this very liberal grant of twenty square miles of land for each mile of railroad constructed was that the land must be sold to "actual settlers" in tracts of not more than 160 acres each, and at not more than $2.50 per acre. Much of the land, probably most of it that had been selected in Coos County, was timbered, remote, and steep. The fastest market for that kind of land was the big timber companies from the Great Lakes, companies such as Weyerhaeuser, C. A. Smith, and Pillsbury for example.

Beginning about 1894 O & C had begun selling the land they had already gained patents on. There is no evidence they had tried to market any of the Coos County land to small buyers, as required by the grant. They sold to speculators and timber companies, not actual settlers, and they sold in tracts larger than 160 acres, and at prices in excess of $2.50 per acre.

They had sold a total of 819,928 acres before they got caught. Of this, only 295,727 acres were sold in lots of 160 acres or less. 372,399 acres were sold in lots exceeding 2,000 acres. The average sale price of all sales was $8.04 per acre.[6]

The Oregon and California Railroad stopped sales of timberlands just a few months after Weyerhaeuser had obtained the Northern Pacific lands in Coos County. O & C decided to hold its lands for speculation, as the price of timberland was on the increase. This was in 1903.

In 1907 the Oregon Legislature asked Congress to take action against O & C for violating the grant conditions. As a result, the U.S. Attorney General brought suit against them, and after several years it ended up in the Supreme Court. In 1915 the Supreme Court decided that indeed the O & C had violated the grant conditions, but it didn't even slap their hands. Instead, it decided that the government would "bail them out" and buy the disputed 2,890,833 acres from them for $2.50 per acre.

None of this would have anything to do with our story except that some of these lands were in Township 24-10. An act of May 31, 1918, allowed the government to trade former O & C lands in exchange for private lands. In 1927 the Weyerhaeuser Timber Company obtained 3,200 acres in Township 24-10 under the terms of this act. By that time there was only a few forties belonging to the state and the three 160-acre homesteads that were not owned by Weyerhaeuser in 24-10. By 1958, two of those three homesteads would be owned by Weyerhaeuser.

[5] Gaston, *The Centennial History of Oregon, V. 1*, p. 524.

[6] Ibid, p. 534.

The Pillsbury Tract

Weyerhaeuser's last major acquisition of Coos County timberland was in 1944 when it obtained 47,000 acres from the Pillsbury Lumber Company of Minneapolis, Minnesota. Pillsbury had acquired its original holdings here from the Oregon and California Railroad around the turn of the century and some of it was in litigation for years. Pillsbury obtained clear title to some of it in 1907, and in 1914 obtained clear title from the courts to another large block. In 1923 it completed its holdings with acquisition of 21,512 acres of former O & C land. Most of it was on the South Fork of the Coos River and the upper Coquille River. It was contiguous with the Weyerhaeuser holdings in Township 24-10 and adjacent townships.

Acquisition of the Pillsbury lands brought the Weyerhaeuser holdings in Coos County up to 100,000 acres according to the May 25, 1944, edition of the *Coos Bay Times*. Subsequent purchases, trades, and adjustments have brought the Weyerhaeuser timberlands in Coos County up to 106,000 acres. There are another 108,000 acres contiguously in Douglas County, bringing the "Millicoma Tree Farm" total to about 214,000 acres at this time.[7] The stories of how each of those individual parcels were added to the Weyerhaeuser empire would fill a book with very interesting reading. It is, however, beyond the scope of what I'm doing here.

I did talk to Howard Henderson, who was a Weyerhaeuser timber cruiser and land buyer from 1943 until he retired in 1967. He had been working for Weyerhaeuser about a year when the Pillsbury deal went through. Howard was born at Gardner in 1902 and spent his entire life in these woods. He was ninety when he told me he had been instrumental in buying more timber than any other person and had experiences "that would stop a clock!" I asked him about the Pillsbury deal. He said, "The Pillsbury deal was too big for me. It just happened, Bingo! It was done by the big shots." Then he remembered that he did have something to do with it. He said he was with Weyerhaeuser's head cruiser, Ted Gilbert, and "the two Kelly boys," Jim and Joe.

> We were cruisers, so we stayed in the best hotels. We had suits and neckties for the evening, you know. We were staying at the Umpqua Hotel in Roseburg and we were introduced to two other cruisers. They were working for Menasha and they said they were cruising the Pillsbury tract. They said Menasha was going to buy it.
>
> I called the company headquarters in Tacoma at 6 pm and mentioned this. At 7 pm we got a call back from a big shot — the man right under Weyerhaeuser himself — and he said, "Whatever you're doing, stop it and get on the Pillsbury tract!" We had the Metsker maps, and we each took part of it. I went up to a lookout to figure where the corners were. It only took three days for us to cruise 47,000 acres!

---

[7] Telephone conversation with Tim Slater, Weyerhaeuser Company, Coos Bay, January 9, 1992.

It was fast, but a pretty accurate guess. We reported it to head-quarters and somebody from there went to St. Paul [where Pillsbury headquarters was] and the deal was made.

It was after that deal came out in the papers that Weyerhaeuser began introducing to the public the concept of "sustained yield." They said that after the war they would build a mill at Coos Bay and that it would run forever. The timber they owned here would be cut on a 100-year cycle. When it was cut off the first time, they would start over, keeping a stable work force employed indefinitely. Virtually the entire holding was actually cut off in forty years, however. This was more than twice as fast as their publicized plans had indicated that it would be cut.

The Lake Creekers

Upper Lake Creek lies over the ridge to the east of Glenn Creek, in Douglas County. From the Joe Schapers place it was about twelve miles by trail. The history of that area is enmeshed closely with upper Glenn Creek, and so I will tell what I know about it.

We are talking about Township 24, Range 9, Douglas County. It was almost too remote for homesteads. There was no practical route up Lake Creek from Ash Valley. The trail from Joe Schapers place was how you got in and out. Most of the odd numbered sections of the township had been selected by the Oregon and California Railroad immediately following the surveys in the late 1890's. In 1902 the Northern Pacific Railroad picked most of the even-numbered sections and sold them immediately to Weyerhaeuser, as they had in Township 24-10. There were five sections (sections 10, 15, 22, 27, and 34) right in the middle of Township 24-9 that weren't selected by the railroad locators. These sections contained timber which was considerably younger than the rest, and so it remained in the public domain.

After the railroads were finished with their selection of timberlands, some important administrative decisions were made by President Theodore Roosevelt and the newly created Forest Service. These decisions have had profound effect, down to the present day. In March 1907, virtually all this land not previously claimed by the railroads was withdrawn from the public domain and incorporated into the newly created Umpqua National Forest. In addition to the main block of the forest, these lands included scattered parcels here and there throughout the Coast Range. It included those five sections in the middle of Township 24-9, on the upper Lake Creek drainage.

In 1908 most of those lands within the Coast Range were incorporated into a newly created Siuslaw National Forest while the lands within the Cascade Range became the Umpqua National Forest. The Umpqua NF, however, kept administrative control of those isolated parcels which were in the Coast Range but generally south of Township 23. Isolated parcels within Township 24-10 and 24-9 were thus within the Umpqua NF, but the Umpqua NF didn't want them.

Because the administrators decided that they didn't need it, the land was opened to entry by settlers and speculators for purchase or for forest homesteading. The speculators may have come from anywhere. I don't really know anything about them. They bought some of the last $1.25 per acre timberland in the world, in the hope of making a profit on it. Some did and some didn't. It's possible to lose money even on a deal like that! There were several laws in effect which permitted the Forest Service to divest itself of these lands. One was the Forest Homestead Act of 1906. This act permitted homesteads on "agricultural land" within the national forests. Amazingly, the old Land Law of 1820 was still on the books as well. It permitted outright purchase of certain public lands at $1.25 per acre in lots not to exceed 320 acres. These were the laws that applied to the "Lake Creekers."

The settlers who took advantage of this opportunity for the upper Lake Creek lands were not from Douglas County. They were from around the Honorable Binger Herm- ann's hometown of Myrtle Point, Coos County. They moved in after enactment of the Forest Homestead Law of 1906 and built cabins, planted orchards, and tried to clear some ground. This was not the good bottomland of Lake Creek, however. It was west of Lake Creek, along Bear Camp Creek and on the ridges. It is not at all what one would have selected for a homesteading claim.

During the years between about 1910 and 1920 these "Lake Creekers," as they were known to the Glenn Creek people, would assemble from time to time on the Joe Schapers place and "pack in" to their claims on Lake Creek. They are said to have been frequent boarders at the Tyberg place during that time. They built some fine cabins and in some cases planted orchards. They lived in these cabins for several years, and their objective seems to have been to improve the property for subsequent resale.

Most conspicuous among the Myrtle Point folks was the Guerin family. Eckley, George and George Jr. each had a claim. A daughter of George Guerin may have been born there in 1912. Fred B. Garrett, David McNair, Ben McMullien, George W. Laingor, Thomas W. McCloskey, and Dora Berry, all of Myrtle Point, had claims. It was quite a settlement. At one place four of the claims intersected and four cabins were built adjacent to each other, each one on its own 160-acre lot. This place was called "The Town." Upper Lake Creek had a history which is completely lost now. No one living remembers any of it.

There were actually around thirty individual claims on Upper Lake Creek. Most, perhaps all of them, were purchased from the U. S. Government by a "cash entry" of $1.25 per acre under the Land Law of 1820. Only a few of the purchasers ever saw the land. The Myrtle Point people were the exception. For several years they were quite serious about improving their claims. The Guerins obtained patents to their land in 1918 and sold to Weyerhaeuser in 1923. Five other Myrtle Point "Lake Creekers" sold to Weyerhaeuser at the same time.

The following year, in August 1924, Joseph W. Fordnay of Saginaw, Michigan, under the name of Fordnay Yellow Fir Timber Company purchased eleven more of the claims. These were all subsequently sold to Weyerhaeuser. We must give the Weyerhaeuser timber cruisers and land buyers credit for a lot of creative work in consolidating virtually all of the timberlands within 216,000 acres under one ownership.

Geo. H. Guerin claim, T24SR9W, S22

The cabins remained on Upper Lake Creek for years. During the 1930s Cle Wilkinson ran his trapline from one of the Guerin cabins. It was a bit too far from the creeks where the traps were, however, and so he built his own cabin on Bear Camp Creek. Later trappers used these cabins until the late 1940's.

The Guerin cabin was used for years by the Fire Patrol as a fire lookout. In November 1945, an Army aircraft crashed on Pheasant Creek, and some of the survivors took refuge in one of the cabins. In the 1960's Weyerhaeuser began logging that country and the cabins were bulldozed out of the way, the apple orchards destroyed, and all trace of the "Lake Creekers" was obliterated.

The Joe Schapers Sawmill

During the homesteading period, the timber above the falls was just something to get rid of. To clear the fields, the trees were burnt. A hole was bored through the trunk of the tree and a fire built which, when it got its draft through the hole, would ultimately burn down the tree. This was done one tree at a time, one acre at a time, until after a lifetime of backbreaking work the Glenn Creek valley was cleared.

Only a few of these old-growth trees were used. The fine, straight grains of this 200-year-old timber was perfect for split stock. Logs were bucked into eighteen inch bolts and shakes were split from them. Sometimes they were bucked into ten or sixteen foot lengths for fence rails. Shakes were the main building material for the roofs and siding of most of the houses, sheds and barns of the valley. Split rails were the main material used in the fences.

It's hard to build everything needed around a homestead if all you have is shakes, poles and rails. Sawed lumber is a great help, and nowadays no one would think of building a house or barn without it. In those early days of Upper Glenn Creek, however, lumber was an unobtainable luxury. If it was to be used, it had to be manufactured on the premises.

Joe Schapers built a primitive sawmill at the west end of his place. The boards which were used in the many buildings of the three homesteads may all have been cut in that mill. No one living today remembers the time that Joe Schapers' mill was running, and we don't know what kind of mill it was. I suspect that it was most likely an old-fashioned sash mill, using a reciprocating saw and powered by a waterwheel. This is the type most often used at wilderness homesteads and George Gould had one over on the West Fork, at Elkhorn Ranch. Alice Allen told me that she believes the last lumber cut at Joe Schapers' mill was used to build the Golden Falls schoolhouse in about 1918. During her time — the 1930's — the gate to the west of the barn was still called the "Sawmill Gate."

For the next twenty years or so hardly any timber was used because the buildings had been built. Split shakes to repair roofs and siding, and split rails for fences didn't take many trees. I remember watching old Jerd Schapers splitting shakes as late as 1942, not long before he died. He only needed a few, for repairs.

The problem with deriving any economic gain from the timber on the homesteads was that there was no way to get it to market. Logs could not be hauled over the Golden and Silver Falls road, and the price of timber was so low until after World War II that it wasn't worth thinking about anyhow. In 1939, however, Joe Schapers died at the age of 82. Now there was the problem of inheritance.

In his will Joe left the 160-acre homestead, valued at about $1,000, to his two stepsons, Robert and Cleland Wilkinson. To their sisters, Jane Stemmerman and Agnes Leaton, he willed $500 each. In 1939 the effects of the depression were still with us, and there were delinquent taxes on the place. Cash was needed to clear title to the property and to give the girls their inheritance. The only possible source of cash was from the sale of timber, but where, in 1939, could a buyer be found?

The Economics of Gyppo Sawmills

1939 is actually the year that ended the depression, because the war in Europe began that year. There were more orders for lumber. In fact, there were more orders than the big mills could fill. The remainder could be "brokered" out to small, gyppo sawmills. The problem was that there were very few small gyppo sawmills in Coos County in 1939 and there was very little timber available to them that would meet the strict grading specifications of the time.

Bob Wilkinson was working as a lumber grader for Herbert Busterud's lumber company. Busterud was a timber broker — the only one in southwestern Oregon. He encouraged and helped the small gyppo sawmill operators to get started and to stay in business. He needed them to fill his orders for lumber.

I don't know the specifics on lumber grades at that time, but I do know that there was no market for the coarse grained, knotty limber produced from the "third growth" Douglas fir that was available to the gyppos. The third growth was the sixty-to eighty-year-old timber that had grown out of the earlier bull team logging around the bay, and from the great fire of 1868 and subsequent fires. Virtually all of the old growth, and better grade second growth in Coos County was either owned or controlled by the large timber companies, or it was otherwise inaccessible. It was a hard time for gyppo operators. That's why there weren't many of them.

George Youst's Mill

My dad, George Youst, had started gyppo sawmilling in southwestern Washington in 1925. Before that he was a logger in the railroad logging camps in Washington. When he began sawmilling, most of his orders were for railroad ties and bridge plank. The timber broker for western Washington was Fairhurst of Tacoma. During the 1930's Fairhurst had 125 sawmills that he was trying to give business to, but orders were few and far between. My dad had a half-section of good second-growth timber on the Little Kalama River, Cowlitz County, which he had bought from the Northern Pacific Railroad. He had the timber, he had the sawmill set up right in the middle of it, but there were very few orders for lumber.

In 1936 he heard that timber around Coos Bay was opening up for gyppos. He came down and met with Herb Busterud, the broker, and looked at some timber he had. From that, Dad decided to move his mill to Oregon. His first setting was at Hauser, across the highway from where Sunny Hill School now stands. That mill burned in 1938, and all he saved was the yarder. He then contracted to do some logging — first with John Aason and later with Dave Levison at Cherry Creek, near McKinley. All this time he was looking for timber that would be suitable for another mill.

That is where Bob Wilkinson came in. My dad had got acquainted with Bob because Bob was a lumber grader. Bob needed to get some cash out of the timber on the Old Ranch above the falls. He took Dad up there, introduced him to his brother, Cle, and showed him the timber. My God! It was perfect. Two hundred years old, fine grained, and 150 feet to the first limb. It was so straight and tapered so slightly that on a twenty-four foot log it was impossible to tell which was the small end. It was a gyppo's dream as far as quality was concerned. He made the deal, paying the Wilkinsons $1.25 per thousand for the first forty acres. It then went up to $2.00 per thousand, about the going rate at that time.

The problem was getting it out to market, but he thought he could do it. This was against the advice of everyone in the business. They all told him he'd go broke trying to get lumber down over those Golden and Silver Falls. Well, it wasn't easy, but he did it. The mill cut about 20,000 board feet per day and was the first commercial sawmill on the drainage of the North Fork of Coos River, and maybe the first one on the entire Coos River drainage. Hundreds of millions of board feet of logs had gone down those streams to the big mills in town, but this was the first time a commercial mill was set up in those woods to cut the timber, in situ.

Geo. Youst sawmill, 1944.
Laurence Youst, George
Baker, George Youst.

196

The mill was set up to handle comparatively large logs. The head rig had two sixty-inch circle saws, top and bottom. The carriage would handle a six-foot log. Quite often larger logs would end up on the carriage, however. The mill would then have to stop while the crew chopped the log down to size so that it would pass the husk of the saws.

For the record, George Youst had four more gyppo sawmills in Coos County following World War II. These were at Hollow Stump; Willanch Inlet; Gravelford; and Allegany, West Fork. These were the years of a great boom in gyppo sawmills. During 1947–1950 there were over 200 gyppo mills in the county. Obviously, the lumber specifications had been relaxed due to the incredible postwar demand for lumber. There was a ready market for even the coarse-grained, knotty third growth!

Vic Dimmick's Mill

In 1943, after both Jerd and Charlie Schapers had passed on, the timber from the Tyberg place was sold to Vic Dimmick. My dad had the road in reasonably good shape by then and had demonstrated that it was possible to haul lumber over it. Vic Dimmick, from a pioneer Coos County family, was getting in on the gyppo sawmilling a little ahead of the postwar boom. He set up his mill in the meadow below the Tyberg house.

He had the dam for his millpond built in Glenn Creek and the timber from the hill south of the creek was logged directly into it. The dam washed out a few months before they finished cutting and some of the logs went all the way down over the Golden Falls. Some of them can still be seen there, in the park at the bottom of the falls.

When Weyerhaeuser built the fire access road up Woodruff Creek toward Lake Creek, the timber from the right-of-way was sold to Dimmick. There was a big "snag patch" on Lake Creek which Weyerhaeuser wanted to sell to Dimmick as well. Roy Mast hiked in to look at it but the snags were 500-year-old trees, eight to ten feet on the stump. Roy reported to Dimmick that they were too big for the mill.

Hap Culver (b. 1900) told me that he was sawyer there for the first two years. Roy Spires was the high climber and timber faller. Roy Mast did the logging at the end. Roy Mast told me that Dimmick wanted the yarder moved out, with the forty-foot sled. It wasn't possible to haul it down over the Golden and Silver Falls road, but Roy said, "I'll get it out for you." He moved it, on its own power, over the ridge and down through the timber of the Golden and Silver Falls State Park, loading it out at the park parking lot and picnic area below the falls. Pretty audacious, even for those days!

197

Chapter Twenty-four

Gyppo Sawmilling Above the Falls
By George Youst[8]

I guess I got connected with Bob Wilkinson through Busterud. [This was Herbert Busterud, of Busterud Lumber Company, a timber broker.] Bob was trying to get some money out of that timber, and he had been to Busterud's.

Bob took me up, and I'm telling you she was a pretty rough show. That road was *bad*. I came back and started telling Doris [Youst, his wife] and Bud [Huff, his nephew] how bad it was. I says, "It's up to you guys, if you want to go up there." I took them up the next day, and when I got over the falls they said, "Where's that bad place?" I had made it sound so bad they were expecting worse! So I made a deal with Bob for that. I got the timber for a dollar and a half a thousand for the first forty.

I had to leave the sled. Had to take the donkey off the sled because we couldn't take it over that hill [the Golden and Silver Falls road was too steep, narrow, and crooked]. Bud and I had to build a new sled up there. Had to fall some trees. Got the donkey up there, and unloaded it on the ground. We tied it to a stump and yarded in a couple sticks to make sled runners. We got the sled built — a good sled, too. Then we moved it up the hill.

George Youst (1899–1975) at Wilkinson place, 1942.

The mill we got had been at Tenmile Lake. A real estate guy had bought the mill from out of there — had it in his back yard. Bob Wilkinson had made him a deal for it. It had a long carriage — twenty-four feet long. I cut it down, made it shorter, lightened it up a quite a bit. The feed works was no good at all. We used it on the first setting. The flywheel turned, then there was a paper wheel you shoved in between two wheels. If the carriage didn't start just as soon as you hit it, you'd wear a flat spot on the paper. Many times I'd have to take it

---

[8] I tape recorded this narrative in Coos Bay during August, 1967. The transcription is verbatim. My explanatory notes are in brackets.

Youst mill under construction. Mill and track set on hewed timbers.

to town to get new paper put in it or get it turned down with the lathe to get it evened up again.

When we moved down below [to the second setting] I went to Portland at Alaska Junk Company and bought big frictions that had a stationary wheel in between. It had two paper frictions that went against one side or the other side, and that made a good feed works. It had power enough to move [the carriage].

We set the mill up after we got our donkey sled built. We set it up on top of the hill, then we shot the slabs down into the field so we could burn them away from the slash. That worked out pretty good. We let the slabs pile up in the field. There must have been a hundred, hundred and fifty foot jump — for the slabs to jump off the end of the chute out into the field. They covered quite an area. Then, Christmas Eve, they set it afire and it lit up the whole valley. For a long time it burned.

I figured I'd have to chute the lumber down the hill. I didn't know just how it was going to work. I had Bud [Huff] and Vik [Graham] and Fred Debuque dig a hole by the county road to make a landing for the lumber. When we got the mill running, and started chuting the lumber down, heck, it wouldn't even slow down when it hit that little platform. I had to build the chute clear across the field. Then had to make a flat place for it, must have been a hundred feet long, to slow it down. Then we put a big log at the end with a piece of plate steel to keep from beating the log to pieces. And it did beat two pieces of steel to pieces. We had tires, too, to cushion it. The hemlock would go down so fast they would just accordion for three or four feet of the end of them when they hit.

I tried to cut orders when we started, but those big timbers, when they went down, they split that big log in two. Drove right through the big log! So then I got down to where I just cut two-by-fours, that's all. We could handle them. They were all the same size. But even those sap pieces of two-by-fours, they'd go down and jump all over the place!

Then the donkey engine quit. We had to take it out and take it to town, get it fixed up, and bring it back. Bud and I had to pack that motor back up the hill. I'm telling you! We had a pole on each side — one in front and one behind, packing that motor up the hill. Just the two of us packed it up there and put it back in. It worked all right after that.

The "Above the Falls" Road

But then, to get somebody to haul [the lumber], that was the next thing. The first three or four guys that we got to come up to haul— just one load and they wouldn't come back. Finally Sedgy, he had a truck. He took two loads out. He said, "You just as well get out of there." John Aason told me so too. He said, "You just as well get out of there. You'll never be able to get any timber down over that road." That's when I said, "I think I know a guy who can get it out."

Reloading lost lumber at Frog Creek. Note planked road.

I just sent a "mental telepathy" to Dude [Ogle], up at Stevenson [Washington]. I never wrote him a letter, or nothing. Sent him a "mental telepathy" and in three days Dude was down here. He says, "What do you need?" I says, "I need somebody to haul this lumber out of here." He says, "You got anything to haul it on?" I said, "No." He says, "You get me something to haul it on, I'll haul it."[9]

Landers [Kenny and Lionel Landers, of Allegany] had an old V-8 Ford truck that had hauled logs for Sjogren and Whittick until they had wore it out. Then Landers bought it, then I bought it from Landers! I think I paid Landers $600 for that old truck and trailer.

Dude started in on that. He was staying with us. The first day we loaded him up a load of lumber. He started out and didn't get a hundred feet from the dock till he was stuck. We worked on the road that day. We went and cut a bunch of planks to plank the road. So Dude came in that night and he wrote on the calendar, "Stuck."

We got the road planked out to the county road. The next day he got about 300 feet down the road, and stuck again. So that night he came in and wrote on the calendar, "Still stuck!" The third day, he got to town with it, and back. Every day after that, one day he'd get one load and the next day he'd get two loads. You bet!

Roy Strickland, down at the store [at Allegany] called him "Perpetual Motion." Couldn't stop old Dude! Down at the dock, they called him "Old Dirty." Those guys told me that everybody else, when they took their chains off, they'd hold them out away from them when they loaded them into the jockybox, but not Dude! He'd grab them in his arms, right against him [the muddy load chains].

The tires weren't good on that old truck. Dude had a flat tire one night. He didn't get home till pretty late. The only tools he had to change that tire was a bolt and a railroad spike, to take that tire off and fix the tube, and put it back on. A truck tire at that. Yeh! You couldn't stop that fellow. No way of it.

One time up at Stevenson, before he came down here, he had lots of trouble with his teeth. He went down to the "bone cruncher," he called him. Painless Parker, in Portland. Got all his teeth pulled out that time. It had been freezing, one of those silver-thaws. And he started back up by the summit on the Washington side. There

---

[9] Dude Ogle was George Youst's sawmill partner in Washington, before he moved to Oregon in 1937.

was cars off on the ditch on both sides of the road. He went up with his car as far as he could go, then he started back, and slid off the road. Right behind there was a bunch of boulders. He lifted up the trunk and filled it with boulders, and took off. Right over the top. Couldn't even stick him with a silver-thaw.

Dude fixed the road up a little bit all the time he was there. He'd see some rocks along the road and he'd pick them up and throw them in the jockey box behind the cab. He carried a sledge hammer with him. Anything he could lift, he put in there. When he'd get down to one of those big mud holes, he'd pack those rocks around to the front of the truck and throw them in the hole and take his sledge hammer and beat them up. Hard sandstone is what the rocks was. Be golly, by the time the snow got

Doris Youst and her GMC with 4000 ft. of lumber, on the road to town.

off up at Stevenson, where he was at, we got to where we could hire some truckers.

That's how he happened to come down — the snow was on and he couldn't work up there at Stevenson anyhow. In March the snow was off up on the Columbia River, so he went back up there.

We got to producing too much lumber for one truck to handle. There wasn't quite enough for two. We had an extra truck, and Doris started taking one load a day.

She said if I'd take the load down the hill [over the Golden and Silver Falls road], she'd take it to town. So for several days I'd take a load down and she'd take it on into town and bring the truck back. Finally one day she said she would take it all the way down that day. I said, "I'll follow you." I followed her, and she made it all right. She took it every day after that. And that was that tough show nobody could get out of there with! Yeh!

The Landers started hauling again. The Landers' was hauling when they broke that bridge down. Two of Landers trucks — one was Lionel's truck — he had another young fellow driving it, and Kenny was driving the other one. Kenny would make one load and the other guy would make two loads. Three loads a day we was getting out of there. Then, they'd haul over the weekend too, when the mill was shut down.

Anyhow, Kenny was coming back, empty, and the other truck was coming down with a load. He drove out on the old bridge, rotten. He came back to talk to Kenny, and while he was talking to Kenny, two bents of that bridge went down, with the truck. He got in with Kenny and came up to the mill and told me what was the matter. I loaded a bunch of rigging and blocks and line in the pickup and drove on down. I got down there and seen what was the "diffugulty." The first two bents had gone down. The front wheels of the truck was still on the third bent. It

Kenny Landers hauling logs for George Youst at Hauser, 1938.

Silver Creek Bridge at base of Silver Falls, 1913.
The two bents at fall right were rotten and collapsed
with a load of lumber in 1941.

was steep — the trailer and truck was down like that. I got up on the hind wheel of the truck and took my ax and, whang! I took that chain, and bang! The whole load went clear to the bottom of the canyon just that quick. Just one lick. There was an awful strain on that chain, the way it was laying. Then we pulled the trailer up on the road. I rigged a tightline across to lift the back of the truck up with Kenny's truck. He'd jerk it, and lift the back end up, and we had chain binders and chain on the front and we'd pull that truck ahead what we could till the frame would hit the bent again. Then Kenny would back up, give it another jerk, and that would raise her up a little bit more and we'd pull it ahead and that's how we brought that truck right back up on the bridge. Just bent the running boards a little bit.

Then we went up on the hill and fell a couple trees, drug them down with Kenny's truck. We rolled them to one side and bucked them in the lengths we wanted for posts. Then Kenny would back up, we would roll them back in the road, and he would push them ahead with the truck. Then we'd stand them up, put the bunks and planks on them, braced her up, and there we put in those two bents. We put stringers on top of them, and we were in business again!

That load of lumber was down in the bottom. I took the tightline and put it over there, and Kenny run his truck. We tightlined the lumber over and put it on the other truck. That worked out pretty good. We didn't lose any.

We had the one truck of our own. I always made it a point if I could hire it hauled cheaper than I could do it ourselves, I'd hire it. If I couldn't, I'd haul it ourselves. A while after that, I had two guys driving. They would take turn about. They would run that truck about around the clock, trying to keep the lumber out. Couldn't hardly do it, though. So I got another truck from Pat Rooney. Got it inspected and sent it up. The next morning I was taking the crew up the hill. Below the big hairpin turn [between the Golden and Silver Falls] I met the old truck coming down. Harry [Abel, the driver] says, "Where'd you meet Rex?" I said, "I didn't meet Rex." He says, "He was just ahead of me." I said, "He didn't get down this far." So we started walking back up around the curve, and here come Rex up out of the brush from below that hairpin curve. He just had a little scratch on his forehead, and lost his cap.

This rig had a Brownie [two-speed axle] in it and evidently he got it out of one of the gears when he went to shift and the brakes wouldn't hold it. He said he tried to run it into the bank but it was raining and the rocks were slick and it would just slide along. When he came to the curve it had enough speed by that time she just went straight over. There was a log there [a guard log, along the curve] and it went over the log. When the trailer went over the log it knocked the bark off of a tree, way

Jim Moore topping spar tree, 1940. Note one of the 500-year-old snags, left.

up high. It twisted loose. Rex said the truck turned over. He got under the cowl and it slid way down the hill, three or four hundred feet. The lumber was clear to the bottom of the hill. The trailer was way down further than the truck.

So then Hosking and Gething was just getting started. They just had one old truck. They didn't know nothing about using a block or how to get that stuff out of there. So I went up and helped them get it out. We got the trailer back up on the road. Then we got the truck up. They hauled it to town, and totaled it out. I bought the tires off it for another truck.

They charged the same insurance — it was half what the insurance on the truck was, for the trailer. I didn't put any insurance on the trailer. The truck was totaled and only the tail light was broke on the trailer! Cost $5.00. That's all it cost. I beat the insurance company that time. I lost my down payment on the truck. All it was insured for was what I owed Pat. Then he let me have another truck — that GMC. Had to sign a note for the down payment on that. I didn't have money enough for another down payment. That's how we got down out of that outfit.

The Dam

When we got through with that setting, there was some timber too far to get, and too big for us to saw. I decided to haul some of it to town — put it in the river and splash them on down. Sell them as logs. So we rigged a tree and hauled some of them down. The logs the size we could saw, we hauled them over and dumped them in our pond. We built a splash dam there in the creek [Glenn Creek], and set the mill up in the field, in the potato patch there.

We had built the dam [for the mill-pond] with what you call a dead-head, which held about four feet of water, all the time. That gave us water enough to float the logs so we could get them up in the mill. Then we had eight or ten feet above that. We had logs across the top, and we put plank that [laid against the top log and rested on the lower log. We could open that dam up and let the water through for high water. [The upper eight feet of impounded water could be released.]

George Youst dumping peeler logs from above the falls into the East Fork, 1941.

203

I had a guy living in a shack right by the dam. He had instructions that if the creek started rising, like it was going to go over the top of the dam, to open it up and let the water go through. But we had a big rainstorm. We just got to saw one day, in this new mill, and next morning we went down there and the water had washed out around the end of the dam, and the top log had dropped down, and there she was.

She was a pretty sad looking deal around then. I told the crew, "I've got money to pay you what you've got coming as of today. If you want to stay and help fix this dam up, and wait till we get sawing to get the rest of your money, well, OK. If you don't, well, just go on home and we'll fix 'er up ourselves." Nobody went home. They all stayed.

We rigged up. We had a spar tree across the creek and we put a tail hold on the other hill, so the rigging came right over the dam. Slacked the mainline down and put a choker on the top log, tightlined it up in the air — put the haulback on to hold it so it wouldn't slide endo. We lifted it up and cut a couple posts to set underneath of it, let it down on the posts, and that held it up. There was about twenty feet or so had washed out around the end of the dam. We put in braces back to the bank. Had to put two more logs in, cut planks, and put them in. You could tell when you hit bedrock, going down through that soft muck and stuff. Bud and Dave Browning were in the water up to their chins getting those planks in. We got'er together; finally got'er fixed up.

We sawed out plank, to plank the road 1000 or 1500 feet through Cle's [Wilkinson's] field to get to the county road again. We done pretty good on that setting.

When we got through with our first spar tree we moved up on a hill. We yarded and tightlined the logs into the water from there. A big fat guy came up to unhook in the pond. He was so awkward, he was in the water all the time. The only way for him to unhook was to stand in the water up about to his tits and unhook 'em! He couldn't work in the water at all. In a few days, I said, "No, I can't use you."

When we got through with that setting, I gave Roy Mast the contract to log, and he logged the rest of it. We built another splash dam above. We tightlined the logs into the pond that was above the dam. When they'd get the pond full they would send a guy down to the mill to tell me to open the dam below so the water wouldn't run over the top of that one.

When I opened the dam, I'd just let those planks go that I opened to let the water on through. I'd pick up just any old scrap plank to fill in the gap. [This gave the dam a ragged appearance, with planks of random length sticking up along the top.]

One day the bucker — the one they'd send down to tell me — he'd got mad and quit. So when he got down to tell me, the water was already going over the top of the dam. He says, "You better get the dam open." I looked out and there it was, going over the top.

George and Doris Youst at the Middleton place, 1941.

The mill in its second setting, in Cle Wilkinson's potato patch. Mill pond, left. Loading docks, right. Photo taken from the county road.

I dashed out to open up some hole to let the water through, but there was so much weight against it I couldn't move the planks. There was one plank sticking up above, quite a little ways. I worked on that one, and couldn't get it to raise enough to slip out. Then, like a fool, I put my arm around in front of that plank. And when I raised it up, whang! She took me right over into the water and I came right back through the hole where the plank went out. How I went through where a foot board came out, but I did.

I just curled up like a spider when I went through. I'd seen spiders fall, and they curl up like that. I hit that water — lots of water coming through, at least eight feet of it deep, and a foot long. It made an eddy, and was washed out pretty deep. I remember coming around underneath of that water — it forced me down a third time before I got to the rocks and could pull myself out in water I could stand up in. The whole crew was out there. They thought I was done for by that time. Funny thing, never hurt me a particle. Didn't even get cold, and in the wintertime too. That was quite an experience right there.

The Crew: Larry

Men kept getting more scarce. They took the men for the war. It got down so about all I could get to work was old winos and some of those fishermen, and the likes of that. They couldn't pass the examinations.

One day I was at Koontz's Machine Shop. There was a big Irishman there. I don't know where he'd come from. I found out afterward he was an ex-convict, and that's the reason they didn't have him in the army.

He said he'd come out and work and he'd bring me out a crew. He got hold of some of them fishermen and brought them out. They was about the dirtiest bunch of people I ever had work for me.

The mill in its first setting, on the hill above the Wilkinson ranch. There was no road to it. A chute was used to get the lumber down into the field where it was loaded onto the trucks.

This big guy, I put him on the carriage [setting ratchets]. He was pretty slow, but it gave me a man, anyhow. He worked there for a while, and Cle was picking ferns. Cle was making pretty good on the ferns. They was paying I think

205

Youst mill, planked dock area with loading jacks. Earl Gray with truck. May 7, 1945.

seventeen cents a bunch. This Larry thought he could make as much or more picking ferns as he could working in the mill, and he wouldn't have to work as many hours. So he quite, and went to work picking ferns. I put one of the other fellows working there on the carriage. He was better than Larry, but Larry was living in the house across the creek.

Larry tried this picking ferns a few days, and found out he couldn't pick many ferns. One day at noon, time to go to work, this guy I had on the carriage didn't get on the carriage. I says, "What's the matter? Ain't you gonna work this afternoon?" "I'm not getting back on that carriage," he says, "until something's done about Larry." I says, "What's the matter?" He says, "He was over here and got in an argument with us and we got in a fight, and I hit him with a club and he said if I got on that carriage this afternoon he'd shoot me off of it. You'll have to get that gun away from him." He was over there with a .22, Larry was.

I went over, and Larry was so mad he was shaking. He had this .22. What the argument was, he wanted his job back on the carriage. I got him calmed down a bit, and finally got him to let me see the gun. I looked it over, then asked him what he'd take for it. Ten or twelve dollars he wanted for this .22, so I gave him a check for whatever he wanted. I took it over and one of the other kids said he'd like to have that gun, so I sold it to him.

So, I got the gun away from Larry and talked him into catching the next truck to town. He left. But he had his wife in the family way, and she was ready to have a kid within two weeks, and now I'm stuck with her. She didn't have no, no nothing, see.

Come the weekend, I took the pickup and loaded up her stuff to take her to town. She was living in an apartment when I had hauled her stuff up there. I went back down to that house and the woman there wouldn't let me unload. No. I asked if there was anyplace else she could go. She said she knew some people over at North Bend. I took her over there, and they wouldn't let me unload either. I brought her back to the first place, and gave that woman a big sob story, so she let me unload, and I got rid of her.

Quite a while after that the FBI came out to the ranch, looking for Larry. I had inquired around town. The last anybody had seen of him, he had caught a truck and was heading towards Portland. That's all I knew about him.

Lionel, Carol, and Laurence Youst: the scrap rubber drive of 1942. Roy Strickland at Allegany store paid 1 cent/lb for these tires. They had been used as bumpers on the lumber chute.

Pete, Gus, and Mac

We went on running the mill. I got a rupture and went to get operated on in November. I left Pete Luisignot and his brother Gus [Johnson] up there to fall timber while I was in the hospital. They came down Thanksgiving time, and I asked how much money they needed. "Oh, we don't need much." Pete rattled the money in his pocket. I think I gave them $75. Not very long after that, they picked 'em up and put them in jail. Pete and another old guy. They called up the Allegany Store [the closest telephone, about twelve miles from the mill]. They wanted me to come down and bail them out again. I went over to Coquille. They were in jail over there and wanted $600 to get them out. This old guy, I'd never seen him before. I asked them how much they had coming for the falling. Pete said, "That's all right. That's all right!" I'd sent a bucker out to buck up them logs they'd fell. He came back the same day and said, "What do you want me to do now?" I said, "Buck them logs those fellows fell." Twenty-two trees is all they'd fell. They'd been moonshining all this time!

They was driving through town in that old car of Al Stokes. They was going between Marshfield and North Bend and the tail light wasn't working, so the cop stopped to check on the tail light, and they had a couple gallons of whiskey setting in the back seat. That's how they arrested them.

The next morning the revenuers went up and old Jerd Schapers and Gus was playing cards. They had a pitcher of moonshine setting on the table. When the revenuers came in, they offered them a drink. They took Gus into town, but they didn't bother old Jerd. Jerd was way up in his 70's anyway, so they didn't take him.

I got Pete and Gus out of jail and left the other guy in there, till I was ready to go sawing. Then I got the other guy out. Gus and Pete stayed till they paid their fines off, and then they quit. But the old guy, Mac, [MacFarland], he stayed with me till I got through up there, and then came over to the ranch and worked. He pulled the old woodshed down and cleaned things up at the ranch, and got so full of fleas his wife was going to divorce him, packing all those fleas home out of the old woodshed.

The revenuers came up after that — after Pete and Gus quit. They had a bill against them for bonds on the whiskey they'd made. So Pete and Gus, they was gone, but old Mac was still there. You know, Mac had $55 coming and they insisted I had to give them that $55 to go on the bill. And Mac didn't have a thing to do about that moonshining. He was just riding in the car. The revenuers wanted $180. They just estimated, and came up with a figure. I gave those revenuers a cussing out. I said, "Why don't you get the guys that was doing the moonshining? Don't pick on this poor old guy. He didn't have nothing to do about it. He was man enough to stay and work. The other guys left, soon as they got their fines paid off." I thought it was pretty good of 'em to stay that long!

207

Vic Graham

We had a young feller come to work for me when I was logging for Levison, getting those logs down off the hill [at Cherry Creek, near McKinley]. He was just a kid then, maybe around eighteen. He just took up with me, I guess. Stayed with me just like my boy!

When we went above the falls I couldn't use him until I got the sled built and was ready to set up the mill. He went someplace else and worked for a while, then came up above the falls with us. We didn't have room for him in the little cabin we were living in, so he set up a little pup tent by the creek, and he stayed in that.

Vic Graham, in the Navy through the war.

We went up there in May [1940]. It must have been November or December when there was a carload of Indians came up. They started to drive across the creek to the shack where we was at. Vic seen them coming. He had his deer rifle, and he took the rifle and went over to talk to these Indians. He knew them, well.

The thing of it was, this Indian's daughter was in the family way and she claimed Vic was the daddy. The old guy insisted that Vic marry the girl. Vic told the old guy he'd be down tomorrow. He left tomorrow, all right. He left, quit, and took off, and we never seen him again until January.

He came back January 1st and said, "Just like coming home!" He told us he had heard that somebody else had married this Indian girl. She was a cousin of John Van Pelt, that Vic ran around with from Brookings.

Van Pelt worked for me a while too. He was telling me that where he lived down there, "The more dogs you got, the higher standing you got in society," and, he says, "We had the most!" He was pretty lazy. He wouldn't overdo himself. I think he was the laziest guy I ever had work for me, and the poorest, but I couldn't get anybody else at that time. I finally canned him, though.

John DeHart

Then I had one of those Alaska Indians work there. He was a pretty good man. He'd taken up with a white woman here in town. When I got him to go up, they was living in the apartment across from Koontz's Machine Shop. She wanted to go up with him. He said, "No, they don't have no place for you up there." She says, "What am I going to do? I haven't got any money." He says, "Go to the Salvation Army!" I felt sorry for her. She was a good-looking woman. In fact, she was beautiful.

We was building more shacks all the time. After a while we got shacks enough that he brought her up. Once in a while she'd get to go to town. He'd go too, but I'd take him back to work [on Sunday night], but she'd be drunk or something, and wouldn't come back. One night she caught me downtown. I was coming back in the pickup. About every bush along the road, she'd want to stop. Got to find a bush.

208

I got as far as the store at Allegany, and I went in to get the mail. Our truck came along, and I said, "Take Mrs. DeHart up to the mill." When I got up there, he [the driver] was pretty mad at me. "Christ, I thought I'd never got up here. She had to stop behind every tree to take a leak."

John DeHart, he finally quit. He used to talk about how much money the government spent on educating him. He had pretty good education, John did. He liked to drink, but he died of the quick TB, not long after he quit.

George Baker

Then I had the old sawyer, George Baker. He was half Indian. He was a real good man, that fellow. I guess he weighed about 220 or 230 pounds, and stout as a bull. He knew his sawing job, too. I think he was sixty-three years old when he went to work for me. He worked five years. He was sixty-eight when he finally quit.

I went to making ties [at the Hollow Stump mill, on Haines Inlet]. He was too slow for that, and he also didn't understand that you get the fine grain at the edge of the tie — the fine grain out — in the sap. He'd make a tie up, all right, but he wouldn't pay no attention to the sap. When you're cutting third growth and trying to get the grain, just the little slack in the rack — the top end is ahead on your log. You pull it out about where you want it, then pull that slack out of it and you've got it out there. Just about the bark is all you're taking off of the edges of it. What few fine grains there is, you've got in your tie.

George didn't understand that, and I jumped in one day to show him. I fought the tie over, and showed him how to do that. He just stepped back. "This mill ain't going to be no good, anyhow," he said. That's what he thought. That mill made more money than all the rest of the mills I ever had! That's when he quit.

Above the falls, sometimes we'd yard a bunch of logs in. We couldn't get crew enough to run the woods and mill too. We'd go out and log, and get a bunch of logs in the pond. Then we'd saw them up. Old George, I'd let him punk whistle. He was kind of a bull-headed old fellow, not too good out in the brush.

There was a broken chunk laying with the slivers sticking out on it, and George put his hand on it, going to walk by. I said, "Lay off of that, it'll roll." Just about that time he gave it a little shake and away it went. One of those slivers caught

A unit of 24' 2 x 12's delivered to Al Pierce dock at Bunker Hill.

his pants and turned him end over end and throwed him down the hill and into the brush. He was ashamed and astonished too. He wouldn't make out like he was hurt, but I know he was stove up pretty good. It was quite a flip. He didn't realize that it didn't take anything to start things rolling on a steep hillside.

He showed us plenty of stuff, too, old George did. About rolling those big logs down the skids to get them onto the carriage. The big end travels too fast, and the little end is way back here and your log is going on endways! George — first time I saw him do this he took a 2 x 4 — we was rolling one down and the big end was going ahead. There were five or six skids. George picked up a piece of 2 x 4 and laid it on this little skid. I thought, "What the heck's he doing that for? It's hard enough to roll it without the 2 x 4 in the way." He wanted to roll it back so he could shove the 2 x 4 in closer to it. Then he tipped it a little bit, and that raised the small end, and he had it in balance. Just cut that end around, put the little end ahead, rolled it down, and she came on just right! Yeh! That's the way. He savvied how to do those things. I learned a lot of things from George.

And those big logs. We had to roll them with a peavy. George Baker knew an old mill on the south end of town that had an overhead camming gear. So George said, "I think you can get that for any price you want to pay for it." So we went over and saw the guy. I got the equipment for $25, and we had to take it out of the mill.

He'd be sawing away, and get hold of a log where the saw wouldn't be cutting perfect enough. I'd tell hem, "By God, George, we'd better take that saw off and get it pounded." "Naw," he'd say. He'd turn a little more water on the saw, back up, fill his pipe, and let her run. Puffing his pipe, he says, "She'll be all right when we get through with this log. This is a bad log." When he'd get through with that log, he might change his guide, to hold her into the wood a little bit more. Then when he got through with that log and got another, he'd set his guide back where it should be for an ordinary log. He didn't have much trouble.

Cle Wilkinson at the mill.

Old Herman, down at the dock [in town], used to come over to the loads of lumber with his calipers and rule. He'd go down the boards like that. "How do you get 'em so even?" he'd say. I'd say, "That old sawyer I got, and that farmer I got on the carriage." That's when Cle was setting ratchets.

Cle Wilkinson

Cle worked for me a while setting chokers, when I first started. He jumped over a log and he had one of those trick knees. Put him on the bum. He didn't work any more then — well, pretty near forever. Till we got down to where — well, I had to have five men or I couldn't operate. That's all there was to it. That's the least I could get by with.

Once I got down to where I only had four men. I went to see if I could get Cle to come over. He said, "Now, you know I can't do that. What do you want me to do, anyhow?" I said, "I want you to set ratchets." He said, "No, I can't do that. Besides, I just bought a team of mules to pack ferns on. I gotta use them." I said,

"Those Japs are sinking our ships right off the coast. If we don't all get our shoulders to the wheel and start rolling, those Japs is going to have control of this country." So, Cle came over to set ratchets.

Charlie Schapers at back of mill.

Old George, you know, he liked to no more than stop and he was right back into the cut. But Cle, he wasn't that fast. George would come back and Cle would start jacking'er out. George would start ahead and get 'er into the saw, and Cle would just keep jacking. Push it right into the saw! George would have to back it out quick, and let Cle get it where he wanted it. It had to be on the mark before Cle would stop jacking.

Well, it didn't take George long to learn that he'd have to wait till Cle got it out where he wanted it. That worked pretty good. Finally, I told Cle, "You're the best ratchet setter we've ever had." They was even. George couldn't hurry him up.

Cle raised a bunch of cattle, and there was an old fellow used to come up and buy the cattle. He'd kill them wherever they was at. They was pretty wild. One day he came up, he had bought a steer that Cle had. He shot him with a .30/.30, but didn't kill him. That steer took off, and ran — he had to go half sideways to keep from flying. He ran across the bridge we had across the pond — I thought surely, running sideways and bucking like he was, he'd go in the water, but he didn't. He made it across, and on the hill and way up the creek he went. About six weeks later he came back down. Cle notified old Steve that he'd come back down. So Steve came back and shot him again. This time he killed him. But that first time he'd shot one eye out. That's probably the reason he was going sideways. Kind of a funny thing.

Cle's kid had a dog there. Called it Coony. Jerd [Schapers] had a big hound. Them dogs would get running deer. One day the fellows were falling, way up the creek, and they heard the dogs barking and they could hear this deer bawling. So they went down and the dogs had the deer hamstrung. They was just about to kill him. One of the fallers knocked Coony in the head — he could get close enough to Coony — and killed him. The hound got away. They dug a hole and buried the deer and Coony together.

Cle got hold of it that they'd killed Coony, and he was going to have this guy arrested for killing his dog. There was quite a commotion about it. Finally it looked like we was going to lose our fallers over this deal so I got hold of Cle. The war was on then. I told Cle, "Having those guys arrested isn't going to get Coony back. And, if you have them arrested, I'm apt to have to shut this outfit down. Your income and our income will stop if we can't get men enough to operate this thing." So, Cle decided he wouldn't push it any further.

Blackie

We had another guy up there — Blackie [Lem Thorpe]. He was another ex-convict. He'd served four years in the pen in California. Him and another guy was in a robbery and a police got killed. Blackie's partner got killed too, so Blackie claimed his partner was the one who shot the cop. So that's how he got by serving four years. But he was a little off in the head, you know. He used to come up and shoot around in the night. He said he just did it to worry the game wardens.

One weekend it was raining terrible hard. Wasn't fit for a grindstone to be out. But three of them went out, and they killed three deer. They was living in a shack up at the old CCC camp then. They hung the deer up in a tree. They were going up to get them the next night, after work. They brought the liver down to have some fresh meat to eat. The next morning the game warden was up there, while they were getting breakfast.

The game warden over the hill, on the Loon Lake side [Douglas County], had heard the shooting. He'd come up and found the deer, then called the guys in Coquille [Coos County] to tell them to come up. That's how they knew about it so quick. They arrested Blackie and Pete [Luisignot]. Took them down and throwed them in jail. They stopped to tell me to come down and bail them out.

I went down to bail them out. Blackie said he was going to fight the case. Pete was tickled to get out. $50 was all it cost to get him out. I left Blackie in there. When he came up for trial, it cost him $150! He was guilty, all right. That didn't pay very good.

Blackie came up to the house one night — we was just ready to eat supper. I told him to come on in and have supper. "No, no," he said. I took hold of his arm, to take him to the table, and Jesus, he reached out and took me by the throat. I jumped up and put a scissors hold around the middle of him, and cinched up on him. He fell on the floor with me — still had a chokehold on me. You probably saw it. Blackie was trying to choke me, and I was giving him the scissors. Finally he reached around to get hold of my foot. He let go of my neck. When he went to reach for my foot, I cut loose and grabbed his arm and bent it over my leg and just about broke his arm on him. He took a lot of punishment before he gave up. I told him I didn't want to break it. He only worked a few more days for us after that. He worked with that hand in his hip pocket, he couldn't use that arm. Then he quit and went to town.

He got a job running edger out at Empire. Finally he got hurt and they put him in the hospital in North Bend. He got up out of the hospital, and got hold of a gun and held up one of the taxi drivers. They arrested him then. They took him to jail and they examined him and then sent him to Salem, to the nut house. We heard about that, but that's the last we heard of him for a long time.

Before we got through there, we bought the ranch. We had got a contract with Al Pierce for 1100 acres of timber [at Hollow Stump, Haines Inlet]. We had to go through this ranch to get it, so I bought these two ranches to get the right of way. We done pretty good on that setting.

212

One night we came home from the mill, Doris said, "Who do you suppose called me up today?" I wouldn't know. "Blackie called and insisted we go down to the Chandler Hotel." Doris was afraid of him because he was nuts the last we'd seen of him. So she got Zara [Devereux] to go down with her. Blackie was sitting in the lobby. He was making fish nets in the lobby of the hotel. He insisted that he come out for supper that night. She couldn't refuse him.

We had just bought that six-wheel GI truck. Laurence and I were putting the licenses on it, when Blackie drove up to the house in a Buick — pretty good-looking car. He was all dressed up, had a little short mustache. He looked pretty good, but I didn't give him any encouragement at all. Doris was frying steak and pretty soon hollered out that supper was ready. Laurence and I walked right in and paid no more attention to Blackie, but Blackie followed us in anyhow.

We sat him down at the table. I hadn't talked to him enough to know whether he was still nuts or what. He started in telling us about what had happened to him when he was running that edger. He said they had taken the guards off it to straighten them out. They get bent, you know. Some of the slabs that go through there are shaped like a salmon, and they're too short to reach the next roll to feed them on out. He had a stick to poke them on through. They'd be dancing up and down.

He was poking a 4 x 4 through, and he didn't know nothing until he woke up in the hospital. It had come back and hit him in the head. They put him in the Keiser Hospital. He said they put him to bed and put an ice pack on his head. He said his head would hurt something terrible when he'd lay down. He'd set up and when the nurse came in she'd say he was supposed to stay down. She'd grab him by the feet and jerk his feet down and flop that bag of ice on his head. He got tired of that. They had put his clothes in a little cupboard, so he put them on and went downtown.

He didn't know just what was going on. He didn't remember much about getting the gun. Maybe he didn't want to remember! They took him to the nut house. One of the doctors took a liking to him and took him to his house and let him stay in the basement and work around, taking care of the flowers.

They had an insanity hearing on him before they sent him up there. Old Dr. Horsfall here, voted against him — that he wasn't nuts. Between Horsfall and the other doctor they got him back on compensation over the accident. They made a deal to take him back to Mayo's Clinic. When they took him back there they found he had a blood clot on his brain, so they operated on him.

Blackie told us how they done it. They shaved off his head, then they cut the skin this way, then they cut it that way, and peeled it back. They had an auger like they use to get a core out of a tree. They cut a core out of the skull. Then there's a grey padding under that for the brain. They skinned that off, and there was a blood clot in the brain. They had a sucking rig that sucked that blood clot off. Moved the grey padding back, put the plug back in and put two screws to hold it in. They put the skin back on and sewed it up, and that brought him out of it.

Laurence was butting in while Blackie was talking, and I told Laurence what I was going to do to him if he didn't shut up. Blackie says, "And nobody knows better than I do what he can do to you, too. My arm is still sore, yet!"

213

That night we was going to the wrestling match. Blackie went too. He had a seat on the other side. He kept looking over, but we didn't pay any attention to him. We'd had about all of Blackie we wanted, before that time. We probably hadn't ought to have been so bad with him, but a nut like that, I tell you, the less you can have to do with them, the better. That was the last we saw of Blackie.

Some of the crew from above the falls:

George Baker, head sawyer	Earl Wasson
George Morin, dam builder	Al Moser
Elvin Hess, faller	John Moser
Cle Wilkinson, ratchet setter	Pete Luisignot
Blanche Mast, trim saw operator	Gus Johnson
Roy Mast, contract logger	Mac Macfarland
Percy Calhoun, donkey puncher	Dwayne Johns
Charlie Strack	Ray Henderson
Bud Huff	Dude Ogle, driver
Vic Graham	Sam Spearbeck, driver
Warren Browning	Kenny Landers, driver
Dave Browning	Lionel Landers, driver
Hank Gosney	Harry Able, driver
Gene Gosney	Rex ?, driver
Lem Thorpe (Blackie)	Doris Youst, driver
John DeHart	Earl Gray, driver
John Van Pelt	and many others
Fred DeBuque	

Blanche Mast, trimsaw operator.

Doris Youst (1906–1982)
Mill partner and truck driver.

214

An Exchange of Letters with Cliff Leaton

Dolan Springs, AZ
August 6, '91

Dear Lionel,

Were you the one who was run over with a logging truck? My Uncle Cle was telling me about it years ago. He is dead now, but years ago he told me that one of you Youst kids got run over with a logging truck. Seems as though your mother was driving it up the Falls and she had you kids get out and walk cause it was so dangerous and you kids were walking along behind it when the motor stalled and when you lose power you also lose your brakes so the truck rolled back and she could not stop it and it rolled right over one of you kids. Was that you it ran over?

Uncle Cle said the tire track of the dual wheels was left right across your body — whoever it was of you, and that it just squashed the shit out of you like when you squash a toothpaste tube. He said he and some of the guys from the mill walked down and took a look and he said there was a turd about 3 feet long that the truck had mashed out of you. He said it never seemed to do no permanent damage but I bet it sure scared heck out of your mother.

Yours sincerely

Cliff Leaton

*** *** *** *** *** *** *** *** *** *** ***

Allegany, OR
August 8, 1991

Dear Cliff:

I really got a kick out of your retelling about me getting run over with the truck. Yes, it was me. The story is better the way you told it than the way I remember it, but for the record, here is what happened:

It was the last day of school, 1945. Mom was driving one of the trucks. I don't know if you remember, but from Dad's mill the lumber was 24 feet long, and to get it over the falls road they had to use logging trucks and trailers to get around the turns. Mom was coming back empty, with the trailer loaded [on the truck] and us kids were at the store, having got out of school early because it was the last day. I asked if we could ride up to the mill. She just said sure, get on. So Albert Lundberg, Roger Ott, my brother Laurence, and myself got on the back, with the trailer. We were living 4 miles above the store, in what had been Lem Morin's place (and I live there now). Mom stopped at the house and took a picture of us on the truck. I've still got that picture [bottom]. Then we headed up to the falls. When we were on the very top of the cliff above the Golden Falls, I was telling the kids some cock and bull story about an elk that got stuck on the ledge of the falls and insisted they look down there. I was hanging onto the cab-guard and leaning over, trying to get the others to do the same, but they wouldn't do it. Must have hit a little bump or something — my hand slipped, and I went down. The truck couldn't have been going more than 3 or 4 miles an hour, but I was under the wheels, on my back. I saw the duals coming, right onto my chest. As they got on top of me, I blacked out. You are absolutely right. It squashed the shit out of me. I woke up when the kids all ran back to me, then my mom came back. I asked what happened. She said the truck ran over me. I asked why wasn't I dead, then. She went on up to the mill and got my dad and they came back in the pickup to take me down the hill. The two of them were in the front with me crossways on top of them. When they got to the house they stopped to get the car. Dad said, "We'd better wipe his ass." Mom said no, they'd do that at the hospital. So I know that if Cle and the others found a turd three feet long, it's not likely it was mine. Mine was still with me when we got to the McAuley Hospital. Doc [Dr. Robert] Dixon pulled my eyelid back and took my pulse and said, "We'll have you out of here in a few days, Sonny.' I was there 15 days. It had broken two ribs, and cracked my chest bone and left leg, and squashed all my innards. I was on crutches 2 or 3 weeks, then limped for about a year. That was it. Cle is right that it "didn't seem to do no permanent damage." I'm OK as far as I know, and it's been 48 years now.

Sincerely,

Lionel Youst

Note: It's been sixty years now, and I'm still OK, as of 2003!

Last day of school, 1945. Albert Lundberg, Lionel Youst & Roger Ott on cab guard of truck. Laurence Youst (back to camera). My mother stopped the truck and took this picture in front of our house on the way up to the mill. About 20 minutes later we were on top of Golden Falls and I had fallen under the truck and was run over by the right dual wheels.

Chapter Twenty-five

[In this narrative of Warren Browning's I have retained his account of his four years in the Army during the war. His wartime experience was neither more nor less significant than that of any of the others, but I think his experience was certainly representative. In its way it is part of the history of Upper Glenn Creek.]

WW II — Before and After
by Warren Browning[10]

Pre-War

I went to work for the Coos Bay Logging Company. They was operating right there at Allegany back up, well, they call it Woodruff Creek now. That was William Vaughn, George Vaughn's father. The woods boss was a man by the name of Leauthald, Bill Leauthald. The camp was right there where the Weyerhaeuser terminal is now. But the camp was maintained by Kruse Brothers, who were gyppo logging for the Coos Bay Logging Company. They had established the camp before Vaughn moved in there.

Vaughn had been over here at Sumner and had logged off this old Blue [Ridge] country. When they wound that up they had those holdings at Allegany and they moved over there. Kruse Brothers had a camp already established so Vaughn's crews just stayed there, the ones that stayed in camp. An awful lot of us never stayed at the camp. I lived up at the West Fork.

When Vaughn finished up there at Allegany — let's see, what year was that? I think it was about in '38. They moved over to the South Fork, right up above Dellwood. I didn't want to get up and drive that far to work so I stayed at Allegany and went to work for a short while for Brady and Neal — right where your folks lived at Glenn Creek. There was the camp there, but I never stayed in camp there either. I drove back and forth, but it wasn't near as much of a drive as it was over to the South Fork.

When I was working for Coos Bay Logging, Percy Calhoun was running yarder for Kruse Brothers. Kruse Brothers machine was diesel but Coos Bay Logging was still steam. The steam they had was real fine machines. Damn, they had power. Awful nice power too, when you got your steam up good. All you got to do is keep cracking it a little bit. I'll tell you, those steam yarders will walk right through a choker, or a mainline too, if you're not careful. The line would go, "ping

---

[10] From taped interview at Sumner, OR, Feb 11, 1992. Recorded and transcribed by Lionel Youst.

ping ping ping" and the riggin' slinger would holler, and we'd be all ready to duck! Them was the days. Nothin' like that again.

Roy Strickland was running the two-speed there. The hook tender would tell him, "Now, goddamn it Roy, be careful." Roy would say, "I'll give you two fair and square pulls. If you don't stop me, I'm going ahead on 'er!"

Beautiful old-growth cedars and hemlock would get knocked flat. Vaughn did get an order from the Japanese for some hemlock. One summer they logged about four million feet of it. They had a patch that was damn near all hemlock. I worked on the rig-up crew quite a bit. We went down and rigged up a crotchline loading system there, and then logged into it with a cat.

Brady and Neal had some steam. I worked with Roy Mast there. Roy must be getting along — he's quite a bit older than I am. They had a little bit of everything. They had gas and diesel and steam. They had a Humbolt [steam donkey].

I worked on that Humbolt when Percy Calhoun was running it. Percy was real meticulous. He'd keep track of the wraps on the drum on the mainline especially, and he always knew when he was just about back to the riggin' crew. He'd slow down, and them chokers would float in there so nice. I never had any other operator do that. He was a good hook tender too. Percy was a real knowledgeable logger. He knew his business.

I know they rigged up a Tyler system at Brady and Neal one time. I'd never seen one of them before, but it's a gravity system. Percy was running the yarder and he knew more about setting it up than the hook tender did. We was dropping the logs into the East Fork above the dam. That was a long time ago.

I worked the rest of the summer and into the fall there and got laid off. The machine I worked on, they didn't have any more work for it and they shut the machine down. I was off all that winter I think. I think it was in the spring, spring of '40 I think, because it was in '39 that Vaughn moved over to the South Fork. I remember now it was '40 because that was the year they reopened elk season. God, everybody went mad, hunting. The state must have made a billion dollars sellin' elk tags! It hadn't been open for years, you know. Lots of elk.

Left to right: Jerd Schapers, Charlie Schapers, Allen Stokes, Nettie Dagget, Pete Michelbrink. At the Tyberg place, 1940.

I was sayin' I had to get back to work and Al and Molly [Stokes] said, "You can stay with me and Molly," he said. "You can go to work for George Youst. He needs men, I know he does." I didn't go up and see him. I think Allen just told George, and George said, "Well, tell him to come on up." So I went on up and stayed with Molly and Allen there on the Tyberg place, and went to work for your dad.

Molly and Al had lived up on the West Fork when we moved up there, and I had known them ever since. It was 1934 when we moved up on the West Fork and they had just moved in there themselves. We'd been friends and neighbors ever since. Molly had gone up to the Tyberg place to look after Mrs. Tyberg. She was pretty frail by then, you know. Molly nursed her, and was doing that when Mrs. Tyberg died. I don't know what arrangements they had with Jesse Ott, but they just stayed there on the place. Old Jerd and Charlie [Schapers] lived there too, you know. Jerd and Charlie just stayed there, and Allen and Molly did too. Allen worked at the mill. In fact, the first job I had with your dad was down there on that lumber dock loading the dang loading jacks.

Vic [Graham] and Bud [Huff] was logging, then Vic got a wild hair and took off for Brookings, where he'd come from, and left. Then I went up and worked with Bud, logging. Bud ran the yarder and I was out in the brush.

My brother, Dave, was in and out, from time to time. Your dad would get so put out. One time Dave pestered your dad until he let him drive the truck, to haul the lumber for a while. As soon as Dave mastered the job, got to where he could do it real good, he quit. Another time he came back and worked for a while — he set ratchets for George Baker. He got so he could do that real good, then he went off somewhere else. The last time, he went back to college.

I stayed in the brush, working with Bud. You know, even back in those days up above the falls, that was quite remote. It was hard for your dad to keep a good solid crew there all the time. Especially the cutting crew. Sometimes all you could get was those damned old winos. They'd be there until they got enough money to get some more wine, and they'd be gone. That's when Bud and I had to fill in on the falling and bucking. I remember one weekend we fell all day Saturday, then bucked it all day Sunday. We had enough logs left over Friday to get the mill started Monday, then Bud and I had to get in real early, your dad helped us, made a new layout and started logging. We just got pulling in some logs just in time to keep the mill going. We was cussin' the old winos all the time!

Bud and I went into Matson Creek on a Saturday and fished. We ate all the fish we caught for supper that night, and camped. Then we caught some more fish and brought them back out Sunday morning. Matson Creek had a lot of those eastern brook trout. That's what old Jerd and George Schapers took in there and planted.

In Glenn Creek it was cutthroat. Bud and I used to fish in Glenn Creek all the time. Especially right after a big rain. The water would be up good, then it would start dropping off to where it wasn't so riley, but still a little dirty yet, then cast in there and let the hook sink right to the bottom, 'cause that's where the fish would be. Man, we used to catch some of the prettiest cutthroat trout you ever saw like that. Had to have a kind of a "bopper" on the line. Seventeen-or eighteen-inch trout, you know. Sometimes twenty inches or a little better.

We'd go up to Gould's Lake. There was a part of a raft up there. We'd get on it and shove it out with a stick. Used to catch some nice trout there, too. They were mostly cutthroat, and some rainbow.

What I remember most about Jerd [Schapers] was his mining operations on Glenn Creek. He had kind of a sluice box deal rigged up there. He had water running down the flume, with baffles all up and down. He shoveled there day after day. He had something — and he got lots of garnets. They was pretty. He swore up and down he had platinum. He had little bottles, just full of stuff. He showed me a whole mess of them one evening, after work.

He sent some samples off to the school of mines in Butte, Montana. When the assay came back, they told him what it really was, you know. I don't know what they called it, it might have been iron pyrites or something like that. He said, "Ya see dat!" He'd talk so broken. "Da dirty t'ieves!" I guess he figured they was going to rob him, by telling him that it wasn't any good, and then as soon as he quit they'd come in and mine it themselves! "Dirty t'ieves. They're trying to rob me."

The sluice box was just up the creek a little ways, from the house. On the same side. There was kind of a sandbar, and gravel bar there. He really did shovel the stuff through there, I'll tell you. He had lots of bottles of garnets, too. Looks to me that if he'd hung onto them and took 'em to some jeweler somewhere, he might have got some money out of them. They use those garnets lots of times with diamond settings and such. They'll put in a garnet or two. At least that's what I've heard.

I remember the first day or two I was there with Molly and them, he took me to the barn and under some hay he pulled out a jug. It was whiskey he'd made out of potato peelings. I took a snort of that and I thought the top of my head was going to go right off. Whoooee! It just burned all the way down. "Have another." "No," I says, "that's plenty, Jerd!" He'd get the potato peelings from Molly, but he never showed me just how he made it. Must have fermented the potato peelings some way. It didn't hardly have any color to it at all. I couldn't tell, because the jug he had was brown. I just took a snort of it, and I never will forget that. Charlie [Schapers], he wasn't much to drink, but old Jerd always seemed to have about half a snoot full. They were funny old guys.

The Middletons all lived there at Eastside, and I went to school with Charlie Middleton. He was a good friend of mine. He was quite an athlete. He was a cracker-jack catcher. He was a year ahead of me in high school, and as soon as he graduated they moved up over the falls. I think the family had already moved. I never did see him again, until I saw him up at that picnic. I didn't think he'd remember me, but he did. We was neighbors there at Eastside and we'd play baseball and went to school together. He always liked a good time.

WW II

I worked there all through 1940 and 1941, up until I got drafted. I was drafted in October 1941. I got the draft notice the latter part of September. The war started in December while I was at training camp at Callan, about 30 miles this side of San Diego. I was taking my basic training there on the coast defense guns, those one-five-fives [155mm].

When the war broke out they realized they didn't have much anti aircraft artillery, so I was hastily shoved into an anti-aircraft battalion. For a while they was under the Coast Artillery Corp. When we "detached" from them and "attached" to the 7th Division, we went to Fort Ord. I was with the 7th all through the war. I was just a few days over four years in the army.

We was attached to the 7th Division, and the 7th Division went up to the Aleutians and that's when they had the battle for the island of Attu. We was with them. There was Japs occupying Kiska, and there was Japs occupying Attu. We went into about a month's real intensive amphibious training.

During the battle of Midway, in 1942, part of the Jap task force went up into the North Pacific. That's when they bombed Dutch Harbor. Then they dropped back. I think they bombed Dutch Harbor just to throw a scare into people, mostly. They didn't attack it outside of just bombing it. And their bombs didn't do much damage, either. Then they dropped back and one force occupied Kiska and another one occupied Attu.

You see, the United States wanted to put in a real advanced naval base up there, at Attu. You see, Attu is the last island on the Aleutian chain. It just sticks right out westward into the Pacific. That put the Japanese islands within bombing range. Well, they decided not to take Kiska at that time, for some reason or another. I don't know why. They didn't consult me, you know! Kiska had a nice harbor, and so did Attu. But the Japanese fouled up that harbor with ships and stuff. They had a way in and out, but they were the only ones that knew how to navigate it.

When the 7th left San Francisco, the convoy rendezvoused out there a ways, and that's when we found out where in the hell we was going. We was going to take the island of Attu. Of course, everybody wondered why they didn't just let the Japs have it. It served them right! We stopped at Dutch Harbor on the way up and got to see the bomb damage. We also stopped at Kodiak, and from there we went to the island of Adak. The navy already had somewhat of a base there at Adak.

Being in the anti-aircraft artillery we wasn't on the initial landings on Attu. Just the infantry went in. In fact, we didn't think we was going to have to land until the battle was over. We thought that when they went to take that island it would be all over in three days. Well, in three days, they came back and got the anti-aircraft artillery — our regiment was the 78th — and took us up there and we landed in Massacre Bay too.

The day we landed, the field artillery had a battery set up right in the middle of the bay there, and they was lambasting the hell out of something. Our battery was the only one (of the anti-aircraft) that even took their guns off the boat. We set our battery up in case the Japs sent bombers or they tried to come in from Kiska. They had some planes there. We got a little bit of activity from them, but the thing of it was they couldn't do anything because the navy was out there with a carrier, and that took care of anything they tried to do. We didn't worry about Kiska much.

One evening a Zero [Japanese fighter plane] got through, it came right on top of the ocean. The weather wasn't so bad. It had

Fort Ord, March '43. T-5 Brogan, T-4 Blatner, & Corporal Warren Browning.

221

pontoons on it. It dropped a bomb or two in Massacre Bay but it didn't do any damage. They never even hit the ground. He got shot down before he even made one pass.

Anyway, as soon as we got set up we started helping the infantry. We'd pack in ammunition; we'd carry in rations. Sometimes if a line got a little thin, they'd shove us into the lines. We was in and out of it. The navy and their "three days!" Good god, it was three weeks before that island was completely secure. And the last twenty-four hours we wound up in a hell of a battle.

The thing of it is, the Japanese force that was there wasn't able to get supply. They didn't have no food; their ammunition was running out. So, they made one of those banzai charges. They had I think between 800 and 1000 men that was left, and a lot of them were wounded. They broke through the infantry lines on what was called Fishhook Ridge. Above Massacre Bay, a ways there, was a bench in there. It was kind of flat and they called it Engineer Hill. Our engineers had a supply dump up there. That's where we were moving the supplies up.

When they made that banzai charge, there was a battery of field artillery there, 105's, and then this engineer detachment. That's what they aimed for. There was a forward dressing station there too, and they overrun that — they just gunnysacked that, and the engineers. They hit those engineers in the real early hours of the morning, those Japanese just screaming at the top of their lungs.

We was back on the beach at that time. Hell, they rattled us out and each one of our batteries had to send fifty men. I had a regular cartridge belt full of ammunition and two bandoliers and about six grenades hanging on me, and away we went. We rendezvoused just below the supply dump, and picked out a spot.

The thing of it is, they was just scattered all over hell, and so was the engineers. They told us not to fix bayonets because the Japanese had fixed bayonets. They realized that they was probably real low on ammunition. They told us not to fix our bayonets because if we did we might get taken for Japs. So, the American forces took their bayonets off. Anybody with a bayonet out there was fair game.

We finally got organized and figured out where most of the Japs were, and just attacked them. We stayed with it all one night and about half the day the next day. They wouldn't give up. I seen about six of them that had committed suicide. They took a grenade and pulled the pin and held it on their guts. The Japs didn't have a big grenade. It was just a little round black ball, it looked like to me. Hell, if it had been one of our grenades there wouldn't have been anything left of them. But it would just blow out their guts is what they done.

Along about two o'clock in the afternoon we linked up with the Alaskan Scouts and finished 'em off. We checked all the foxholes in the whole damn country. Whenever we'd find some, we'd toss a grenade in. I think before that banzai thing, there was about 3,000 men there. Out of that, I think there was twenty-three prisoners taken altogether. They just surrendered, give up. The rest of them wouldn't give up. One hell of a mess. I guess the body count was about 800 dead Japs on that last hillside.

We lost about fifteen men out of the 78th, fifteen or sixteen. I don't know how many boys were lost altogether, about 600 Americans. There were 200 and some buried on the Holtz Bay side and 400 and some on the Massacre Bay side.

We stayed there. Actually, that's what the 78th was brought there for, to have a high-altitude defense. If the Japanese bombers came in, we wouldn't have had anything there. My battery, I was in C Battery, they moved us over to the island of Shemya, which was about forty miles back toward the mainland from Attu. When we got over there they were building a base for the heavy bombers. In fact there were two squadrons of B-24's moved in there. We helped the engineers build the runways.

That's still an active base. It's also kind of an emergency for the airlines—Anchorage Alaska to Korea and Japan. That Korean airliner that was shot down? Shemya was the last contact they had. Of course, those steel mats that we laid for the runways, they're not there anymore. It's all concrete runways now, I understand.

We came back to the States in '45, in January of '45. I got a twenty-one day "delay en route." We came back to Fort Lawton in Seattle, and the battalion went down to Fort Bliss, Texas. That was the headquarters for anti-aircraft artillery. When we left for Attu we were taken out from under the Coast Artillery altogether. They put the anti-aircraft artillery under one head. Anyway, the headquarters was at Fort Bliss and I got a twenty-one day delay en route from Seattle and got to go home. When the time was up, I went down to Fort Bliss.

We were there a little over a month, around the first of March they moved us. Well, the whole regiment didn't go to Seattle. C and B Batteries went to Seattle, and I think one battery went to Biloxi, Mississippi, and one was sent to San Francisco. Wherever they figured they might need them. I don't think they needed to worry about being bombed by the Japanese by then. What they were afraid of, I read later, was that the Japanese still had some great big flying boats, four-motor buggers, great big old crates. They thought they might try some suicide deal, you know, run them in there and try to hit San Francisco or Seattle.

We took over two batteries on Puget Sound, in south Seattle. We was there till July, then they moved us back to Fort Bliss again. About the hottest time of the year, we came out of Seattle. Oh, my god! We got off the train there outside Fort Bliss, waiting for some transportation, and the heat just set on you. There was some guys passed out from the heat. They sent the medics out, and most of them passed out before they got to where these guys were. God, it was hot. And it was so dry around there, we learned later they hadn't had any rain there for three years.

Anyway, we was at Fort Bliss till the end of the war. By that time, they were preparing for the invasion of Japan. While we was there they tested the bomb out there at White Sands, New Mexico. We heard about it after it was set off. We was getting ready to go to the Philippine Islands.

When they dropped that atomic bomb, the first one, you know, we was about a week away from going to San Diego. You see, the Philippine Islands was the staging area for the battle of Japan. Just what the hell we'd have been doing after we got there, I really don't know. The Japanese Air Force was kaput. There wouldn't have been no use for us. I figured they would take us, we had the ninety millimeter [anti-aircraft artillery] by then, and turn us into another field artillery outfit, or something like that. We didn't have any idea. That's where we was going, anyway. If that atomic bomb hadn't gone off, I'd have been in the invasion of Japan. I was glad of that. Yeh. Hiroshima was the first one, and Nagasaki was the second one, and the war was over.

A bunch of us was in Fort Bliss when the news hit. I'll tell you, that fort went wild, and so did the city of El Paso. Man, what a wild time!

The battery wasn't right in Fort Bliss, it was about fifty miles north. It was right over the New Mexico line at a place called, what was the name of that place? The boys always referred to it as the Buzzard's Roost. Just a store and a post office. They sold beer and whatnot.

Where we were was kind of a proving ground. They had a lot of barracks and stuff there. We'd been trying automatic rammers on the guns. They had a bunch of ancient tanks spotted out in the desert here and there and we'd open up on them and blow the hell out of them. By that time too, we didn't have the old range directors for fire control. We had a computer. A forerunner of these computers they have now! It was a great big bugger, you know.

We trained on them for a while, too, so we could be proficient if we ever got to use them. In fact, our first computer, we got before we ever left Attu. You know, the old range director was itself kind of a forerunner of the computer. What it done was, if you had your target up here, and your battery down here, you'd track that target across and you'd get your line of sight and the radar would give you the altitude, and you'd have your range to solve and that's what it would do. It allowed for the speed of the aircraft, the wind resistance, and all that. That's what the old range director done.

The computer, we had a tracking head with it. All it done was track the target, and send that line of sight into the computer, and it computed the whole works. The radar would send the altitude. We had all the literature, and one book was just the problems you could put into it to check it and make sure it was within tolerance. Anyway, that's where I got discharged and went home.

Back Home

Me and my brother-in-law, Fred Huppi, tried our hand at running a sawmill. The mill was on our place, on the West Fork. We got to where we might start doing pretty good, and the damned longshoremen struck. We had got us a new edger and we had got us a new motor and we had all those payments to make and they struck and they stayed out and tied the harbor up until we finally had to give up.

Besides, there had been not too far before then — you remember that French ship? There was a labor dispute on that, but we was able to hang tough on it because we was able to ship by rail. I forget now who we was selling to, but we did a lot of shipping by rail. Anyway, we cut a lot of ties and that kept us solvent. We sold to Al Pierce and also to Cape Arago. But that longshoreman strike put the quietus on us.

So, we gave up. 1949 was the last year we was able to work. That damned strike started in '48. We thought we was going to be setting pretty. John Reiher was loggin' for us. We had one logger who finally left us and I'm glad he did. He wasn't worth a damn. He had a good crew, but he was kind of a flaky bugger. You couldn't trust him.

Anyway, I run into Bob Gould one day at Allegany. I'd heard that he'd gone to work for Weyerhaeuser. You see, Morrison-Knutson had just about finished up. They had put in that road for Weyerhaeuser from Allegany clear to the top of the falls at Matson Creek. Mark Defreese had taken over as boss for the road work, construction superintendent. Bob, I think, was running the rock crusher. So, I ran into Bob on the Allegany store porch and I asked, "Are they hiring anybody up there, Bob?" "Every day," he says! "Come on! Go see Gaines."

Bill Gaines was the superintendent. They had some houses built across from Allegany by that time, so I went over there and asked Bill if he needed any men. "Yep!" Bill was always abrupt, you know. He told me to come to work in the morning.

I showed up in the morning and he said, "Did you have your physical?" I said, "No. I didn't know you had to get one." "Well," he said, "get you a physical and be back here in the morning." I went and got my physical, and came back and went to work up there with old Mark Defreese. He needed somebody that knew something about powder, so I went to work for him. I did powder work in the quarry for Bob, and also worked out on the road with Mark. That was June 15, 1950, and I worked for them for twenty-seven and one half years. I never had any idea I was gonna stay.

I had a friend of mine that had been in the Alaskan Scouts up there when I was up there, and I was thinking seriously about going to Alaska. He had mining claims. "If you run out of something to do down there," he says, "write me a letter." I kind of wish I had of, because I guess he done real well after the war. Got him a gold dredge. He was doing it for about $35 an ounce. Later, it once got up to $900 an ounce. He'd have done real good at prices like that! He was somewhere above Fairbanks. Anyway, I never did get up there.

I met Doris [Crooks]. Of course I had known Doris ever since she — knew her folks and one thing and another [Paul and Bertha Crooks]. When I came home from the army she had grown up to be a very beautiful young woman, and I lost my heart! Doris, she had married another guy, but the marriage didn't work worth a darn. She wasn't too awful keen on men about that time. But I persevered! Anyway, we've had a very happy life. She's been a wonderful person.

Warren and Doris Browning with a steelhead from the West Fork, January, 1953.

I went to work for Weyerhaeuser. The first day I was up there I helped old Mark build a bridge on Matson Creek, just above the 'Y' there. We'd

225

build a thousand or two feet of road, or sometimes just 500 feet, where they had a setting all laid out. Then they'd leave it, and later on they'd decide to take more timber out of there, we'd built some more road. That's the way the 1060 and 1040 and 1080 and them got built. Eventually, they ended up down in Glenn Creek.

The first tree that they logged was right there at the 'Y'. [Where Tyberg (Conklin) Creek runs into Matson Creek.] That's where the logging started, in the early summer of '51. I'd been damn near a year there. But roads had been built. I know the 1040, quite a bit of it was built. I think by the time they started logging they had started the 1060, but I don't know how far it went because I didn't work on the initial part of it. I built some of it later on. There's one place on the 1040, I was down there to build some landing spurs. One place there I could look right down on the Tyberg house. By that time, Dimmick had that mill down there.

I built some of the 1080. The 1080 is the one that goes down into the west arm of Lake Creek. It heads right there on that divide between Glenn Creek and Lake Creek. Glenn Creek goes down on one side, and the West Fork of Lake Creek goes down the other. 1080 comes down the West Fork of Lake Creek right to Lake Creek itself. I built a lot of that. I built more of that than I did on the 1060 or 1040.

There were some cabins on Lake Creek. Part of one was still there. In fact, I built a spur that went right through the old yard. The rusty old cook stove was laying out there, and tin cans and bottles and stuff all over the place, and some apple trees too. Whoever had that homestead had put in apple trees. It was on Bear Camp Creek, just before you get to Lake Creek. Every once in a while you'd run into an old homestead on Lake Creek, quite a bit. The 2170 went right down into Bear Camp Creek.

I built a lot of road up on Pheasant Creek, too. It was on Pheasant Creek where that airplane went down. We 'dozed the fuselage out of the way in order to start that spur. Some outfit came in and got the fuselage, but somebody had already got the motors.

That one spur, off of Bear Camp Creek, when they removed the timber out of that area, one of the fallers found the shroud and strings out of a parachute hanging in one of the trees they fell. You know, they never did find anything of that one young fellow. That happened in '45, just after I got out of the army. It was pretty well over with before I even heard about it. I didn't come down out of the West Fork.

Come to think of it, I did hear about it. My sister Margaret [Bremer] was principal of the Allegany School. They used that gymnasium for kind of a headquarters for the navy and the air force and what not. They had radios and stuff there. She used to come home every night just full of news about it. The kids was all excited, you know. Army and air force and navy personnel coming in there! They'd give the kids all kinds of candy and stuff.

The 2170 comes down Bear Camp Creek, a little above Lake Creek. We had a quarry up Bear Camp Creek. Sandstone. That's all there was. If a man could have found some good basalt up in there he could probably have made his fortune. They needed it so bad. They used to haul in a lot of hard rock, but god, it was expensive. Spurs that was only gonna be used one summer, they didn't put any hard rock on them. They mostly just put the hard rock on the main roads. The 2170, they used it an awful lot because it was way out there on Lake Creek, and it was a lot shorter to come that way.

I built just about all of the 3580, all the way up to Blue Mountain, and built a spur off of it down to the property line on the other side.

They're still logging some of the original timber, yet [in 1992]. At first, before they started clear cutting so much, they left patches of timber. Seed strips, they called them. They left 'em here and there. I think they're still getting some of them. I imagine they've got most of them by now. But the original timber, what's left, is in Douglas County, way up Williams River. Bear Mountain. I had a crusher on top of that. It's about thirty-two or thirty-three hundred feet. Even in the summertime we'd be a little bit chilly up there.

I've been hearing for the last ten years that they only had five years logging left. But Bob [Gould] tells me that they've bought some more yarders, and a loader, and apparently they're gonna keep on logging. Of course, they don't have the plywood mill here. They've got their pulp mill. I think they buy a lot of alder and stuff for that, don't they? They sell fir [logs] — to Roseburg, and to Bandon, to Rogge. Weyerhaeuser quit exporting [logs, in 1990]. I hear they're doing real well with the little CBX mill at Bunker Hill [Coos Bay Export mill, opened 1990, closed in January, 1998]. They're sawing some pretty big timber in it. It's all automated, you know.

Anyway, that's what I had to do with it. I built some of the roads.

Off-highway logging truck crossing Bridge 2, Weyerhaeuser private road.

227

Weyerhaeuser Road System T 24S R 10 WWM
(Coos County)

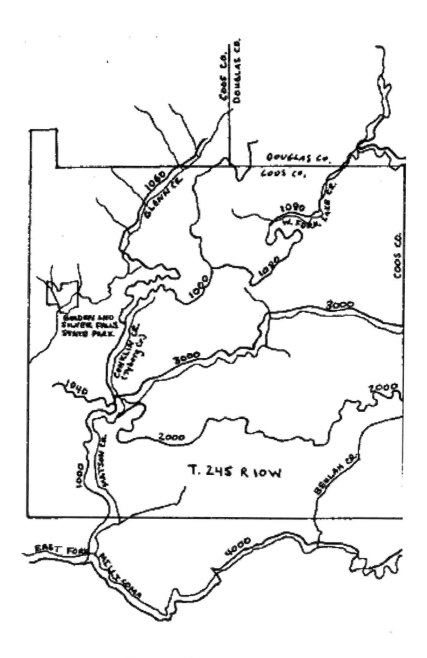

(Note: township is 6 miles square)

Weyerhaeuser Road System, T 24S R9 WWM (Douglas County)

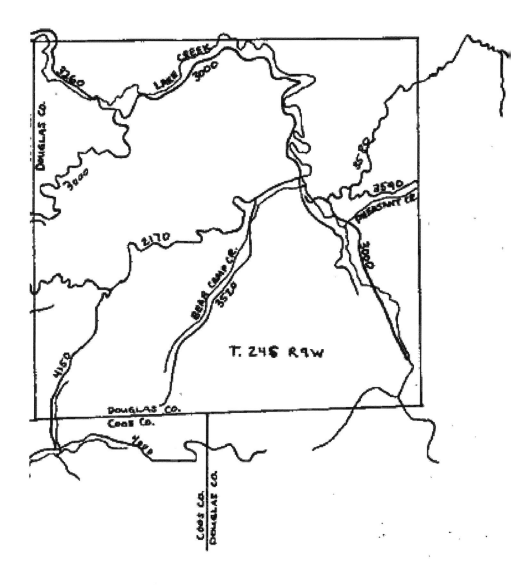

(Note: township is 6 miles square)

PART EIGHT

EPILOGUE

Lower Coos River filled with logs awaiting export to Japan, 1967.

Local historians . . . must describe agencies and effects unequaled since settlement itself.

--Joseph A. Amato, *Rethinking Home*

Chapter Twenty-six

An Airplane Crash and Rescue

It was the last week of November 1945, and off the Oregon coast another storm was approaching. This would be the first big one of the season, and it would be a doozy! It would last six days and its gale winds would drive eighteen inches of rain into the woods above the falls. Because of it, the general public for the first time would become conscious of how large, how wild, and how remote these woods really were.

The great Douglas fir forests of the Coast Range have succeeded themselves for perhaps sixty generation – 10,000 years or more. They are sustained by an annual 60 to 100 inches of rain. Most of this rain comes from the southwest, off the Pacific Ocean from which it arrives by a succession of storm fronts during the six months between October and April. It rains during the other months as well, but the big storms and the large rainfall occur during that time. The result is a temperate rain forest with a prodigious vegetation of mosses, ferns, fungi, shrubs, and trees of amazing variety, linked together in an ecology no one has ever yet figured out.

Before the days of weather satellites, the storms often came by surprise. The barometer would fall and sometimes within a few hours a hurricane-type storm would be on us. Nowadays, the nightly TV keeps us informed of the progress of these fronts across the Pacific. Not so in 1945.

World War II had ended three months earlier, when the Army Air Force dropped the atomic bombs on Hiroshima and Nagasaki. The business of reorganizing for the post-war era was just starting. Tens of thousands of men were being discharged and equipment was being transferred for sale, scrap, or storage. It was an unsettling experience, for peace to break out after four years of war.

At McChord Field, near Tacoma, Washington, there were six L-5 aircraft that someone in the Air Force had decided should be moved to Eagle Field, California. The L-5's were single-engine liaison planes built by Stinson-Vultee during the war years. They had a 185-hp O-435 Lycoming engine and they were used for ambulance, cargo, aerial photography, and general transportation. They were good utility planes, and the Air Force did not declare them surplus at the end of the war. They were still using some of them in the 1960's.

To fly those six L-5's to California, some-one else in the Air Force had decided to use six pilots who were at Sedalia, Missouri, and Denver, Colorado. On Saturday morning, November 24,

C-46D Commando

1945, a Curtis C-46D "Commando" departed Sedalia on the first leg of a mission to deliver those pilots to McChord. The C-46 had two 2000-hp Pratt and Whitney R-2800 engines and a 48,000 pound gross weight. They were good cargo aircraft and the Air Force had received 1,410 of them during 1943 and 1944. It was not a small plane by any means. It was, in fact, the largest twin-engine aircraft in production during its time. It had an 1800-mile range with 8.5-hour endurance with full fuel load.[1]

During the very early morning hours of that fateful Saturday the crew chief, Pfc Walter Smoyer, ran his pre-flight check list. The aircraft could not have been more than two years old and was no doubt in excellent condition. Smoyer, like many good crew chiefs before and after him, would have taken great pride in the excellent condition of his "bird." He would have cranked up the two Pratt and Whitney "Double Wasp" engines and they no doubt "purred like a tom cat!" These were fine engines, well cared for. All they needed now was fuel.

At the terminal there were two men who were looking for a ride to the West Coast. Corporal Everette Bailey was on leave and looking for a ride home. Major Frank Gaunt had been discharged from the Army and was on terminal leave, also on the way home. There was plenty of room. The C-46 could carry twenty-eight passengers and a crew of four.

Probably an hour or so after Pfc Smoyer arrived, the other three crew members would have shown up. They had already filed their flight plan, which called for them to fly to Denver to refuel, then to Ogden where they would remain overnight. When the crew showed up, each member had his own pre-flight check list to run. The pilot, Captain Hugh B. McMillan, the co-pilot, Captain Harlow A. Marsh, and the radio operator, Sergeant Robert T. Neal, each had their individual responsibilities. Everything checked OK. Things were looking good for this mission.

In those days, as soon as the passengers were manifested, they were fitted and issued parachutes. Nowadays this would only be done for flights on combat aircraft, but back then the Army thought the passengers needed a way out. While the crew was running its pre-flight inspection, the passengers would wait in the terminal with baggage and gear.

It was a routine flight, but a long one. At Denver they refueled and picked up four more passengers, then proceeded to Ogden where they stayed overnight. The next morning (Sunday, November 25), they flew over the Sierra Nevada Mountains at 16,000 feet, without oxygen or pressurization, to Fresno, California, and then on to Oakland. Smoyer felt "pretty sick" after about two hours at that altitude, but that evening he and Sergeant Neal went to San Francisco where they had a great time. Sergeant Neal called his fiancee in Los Angeles and told her they were leaving for the north in the morning. He had been to San Francisco once before and was able to show Smoyer around. They rode the cable cars and took a ferry ride across the bay. Smoyer said the whole evening only cost him $1.05, and he had a great time.

---

[1] I am grateful to Melissa Huppi, an aircraft pilot from Allegany, for giving me specifications and insights into the C-46D.

In the morning (November 26) the four crew members loaded their two hitchhikers, Corporal Bailey and Major Gaunt, and the six flight officers who were scheduled to fly the L-5's back from McChord: Robert T. Kennett, Dave Reid, Floyd C. Waddill, Ralph Foster, Theodore Hartsong, and Second Lieutenant Jonathan D. Clark. At about eleven o'clock they took off for a routine flight to Portland.

Back up above the falls at Allegany it started to rain during the evening before, and this morning it was obvious that a good one was coming. Cle Wilkinson normally rose at daylight, and when he got up he could see what they were in for. He was baching these days. His brother-in-law, Alfred Leaton, was staying with him at the time. His mother, Laura, quite elderly now, was living with her daughter in town. Cle's daughters were both away at school. Pat was staying with her aunt and uncle in Coos Bay, and Alice was at college in Monmouth. Cle got up and cooked breakfast.

Vic Dimmick's mill on the Tyberg place was still running. George Youst's mill had been shut down for several months. Weyerhaeuser had started building a fire access road up Woodruff Creek from Cle's place, along the old trail to Lake Creek. Logs from the right-of-way had been sold to Dimmick and cut in his mill. The road had been punched through about eight miles and there was a small trailer house at the end of that road, where dynamite was stored. The Weyerhaeuser presence was not obtrusive, yet, but everyone knew that now the war was over, they would be building a big mill at Coos Bay. Big changes were due in the land above the falls.

Below, the old Tyberg place was now owned by Roy Grant. Vic Dimmick's sawmill was in the field with a dam in Glenn Creek, which backed up water for the mill pond. Roy Spires was the timber faller and high climber for Dimmick. It would be too windy for him to work today, so he would take care of things around camp and at the mill. Most things were going as usual that Monday morning in November 1945, but it was clear that we were already in the middle of a very big storm. Offshore, seas were extremely high. There was a *big* blow behind them.

At Oakland, California, there was no indication that such a storm was hitting the Northwest Coast. California was in sunshine. It was only about three hours flying time from Oakland to McChord, and so the C-46 probably took off with enough fuel for six hours endurance. As they flew north, they were east of the Coast Range and the worst of the storm did not affect them. But before they got to McChord, they knew they were in trouble, and by the time they arrived, no aircraft was allowed to land. This was probably a little before 2 p. m.

The control tower at McChord ordered them to Pendleton, according to first reports released by the Army. Pendleton was clear. Later, the surviving passengers said they had been ordered to Portland. Radio reception was bad, and the crew may have understood the tower to have said "Portland" when in fact it said "Pendleton." We'll never know for sure, but it was fatal.

Arriving over Portland thirty minutes later, they could not land there either. The control tower at Portland ordered the plane to return to Oakland, and the crew accepted the order and continued south. They had enough fuel left for two more hours. Oakland was almost three hours away, even had there been no headwind. But there was a headwind, and as it turned out there was only two hours of fuel left.

234

The storm had increased and promised to be perhaps the biggest of the decade. Slides had closed the roads from the valley to the coast. The Coos Bay — North Bend water system had washed out. Highway 101 was flooded between Coos Bay and Coquille. A barge had broken loose from its tug and was adrift offshore of the Umpqua River. No ships could cross the Coos Bay bar. Coos River was at flood stage, and the Enegren Ferry could not cross. Allegany residents who were in town were stranded there. Schools at North Bend and Coos Bay would be closed for the rest of the week.

Radio communications on board the aircraft failed. One can only imagine the attempts that Sergeant Neal, the radio operator, was making. Their radio compass must have been faulty as well. The last transmission received by the ground indicated that the plane was about thirty-five miles offshore from Florence. This was at 3:15 p.m. How they could have been so far off course remains a mystery, but it seems they were flying right into the storm all the way from Portland. I'm told that with the radio navigation aids of that time, it would have been quite easy to get on the wrong side of the beacon and not be able to find it again. That may have been what happened.

By that time there was only fifteen minutes fuel left. The two Pratt and Whitney dual-wasp R-2800 engines continued to purr along, but they couldn't keep it up much longer. A heading correction was made, and they continued southeasterly. Passengers and crew had their parachutes on and were ready to jump when ordered. Major Gaunt, on terminal leave after four years of war, had already bailed out of two disabled aircraft, and this would be his third. The war was over and he was so close to home.

The point at which the C-46D finally ran out of fuel and the engines quit was about fifty-five miles southeast of their location over the ocean off Florence. It was over the Lake Creek area where Cle Wilkinson had his trapping cabin and where the Guerin's and other Lake Creekers had homesteaded thirty-five years earlier. It had been a remote wilderness then, and it was still a remote wilderness.

This was just a few minutes before 4 p.m. The engines quit and the aircraft descended below the clouds. At a little over 1000 feet there was a brief clearing in the weather. Passengers and crew saw a small meadow below them, in the midst of a forest which stretched to the horizon. That meadow must have been the site of Guerin's cabin, above Bear Camp Creek. Captain McMillan, the pilot, turned toward the meadow and gave the order to bail out. Major Gaunt acted as "jump master," and was the ninth man out. The tenth and last man out was the crew chief, Pfc Walter Smoyer. Smoyer said that Sgt Neal, the radio operator, was very scared, and asked if he should count to four before pulling the rip chord. "I told him to pull it right away as we were very low."

Smoyer said, "I went out last and my chute opened and I started to sail on to the ground. My chute caught on the top of a giant fir tree that must have been 250 feet high. I looked at my watch and I landed in the tree at 4 p. m. I heard the plane crash and then everything went silent. There I was all alone just hanging in my chute and scared to death that my chute would blow off the tree. The wind blew me into the trunk of the tree. I tied myself to the trunk of the tree that night. I don't think I slept but I did doze off a little."

Major Gaunt's chute opened just before he hit the ground, and he heard the crash of the aircraft at the same time. Sunset that day was at 4:27 p.m. When the sun

235

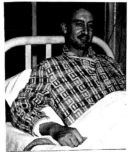

Major Frank Gaunt

goes down in those woods, it is dark. It is especially dark during a storm. The flyers had less than thirty minutes of light. It was fourteen miles by trail, if they could find the trail, to the closest human being — Cle Wilkinson. The flyers didn't even know what state they were in. The Coast Guard and Air Force thought the plane went down at sea. The worst storm in memory was closing in on them.

At Brookings there was 6.28 inches of rain that night. At North Bend there was 4.07 inches. The hills above the falls typically receive almost double the rainfall of the coast, so the full extent of this downpour can only be imagined. The creeks and rivers were raging torrents.

If I were capable of writing a full account of the amazing rescue of these flyers, it would fill a book. I would give the account of how, twenty-four hours later, Flight Officers Waddill and Hartsog stumbled onto the Cle Wilkinson ranch, telling Cle that David Reid was stuck in the top of an old-growth fir tree fourteen miles to the east. I would tell how Cle went down to the Dimmick sawmill at the old Tyberg place and got Roy Spires, the highclimber. Hartsog then led Cle, Cle's brother-in-law Alfred Leaton, and Roy, back through the woods, in the dark and storm, to Major Gaunt and Flight

Officer Foster, who were waiting at the Weyerhaeuser "dynamite" trailer. I would then tell how Major Gaunt led the rescue party another three miles in the dark to the exact tree that Reid was in.

Reid had been hanging 150 feet up in the crown of a 200-year-old Douglas fir for thirty-six hours. During that time the rain and wind had hardly let up for a moment. At this point it would be necessary for me to describe one of the most astonishing rescue feats on record. Still in the dark and the storm, Roy Spires, a fifty-year-old logger, put on his belt and spurs and climbed the 150 feet to the first limbs of the tree. Once there, he sat on a limb, took off his climbing gear and put it on Captain Reid, who by then was paralyzed

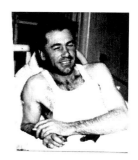

Flight Officer David Reid of Altus, Oklahoma.

with cold and exposure. I would then describe how, miraculously, Reid had somehow made it safely to the ground. Spires pulled his belt and spurs back up with his pass rope, donned the equipment, and himself climbed down, the seven of them returning the fourteen miles through the woods to Cle's house – still in the rain.

Waddill had, I believe, suffered a mild concussion when he landed. He was taken to town by someone from the Dimmick mill. When he got to the Enegren Ferry, which crossed the lower Coos River, they couldn't get across because of the high water. Telephone lines were still working, however, and they contacted the John Milton ranch. Milton relayed the information to town. A tug boat was pressed into service to help the ferry cross the river.

This was the first anyone knew that the plane hadn't gone down in the ocean thirty-five miles west of Florence. It was now reported on the radio that the plane crash had been somewhere "about fifty miles east of Coos Bay," and that there were survivors.

236

My brother-in-law, Jerry Baughman, heard about it on the radio. He decided to drive out to the Enegren Ferry to see what was going on. There were several Army officers and an ambulance waiting there. Word had it that there were three more flyers at Cle Wilkinson's place. Did anyone know where that was? Jerry said he did, so they asked him to guide the ambulance. It was after dark, now fortyt-eight hours since the crash. Jerry told the driver to be carful as they climbed, through the darkness, over the cliff road of Golden and Silver Falls. The rain was turning to sleet that almost stuck to the windshield as they crossed the Silver Creek bridge.

At Cle's place there were a number of loggers ready to go into the Lake Creek country to find any other survivors. No one knew whether there were any. Among the loggers there were several who knew quite a bit about the area, even though it would be several years before any logging would take place there.

At daylight, now sixty hours since the crash, Jerry Baughman returned in the ambulance with the three flyers who were at Cle's — Foster, Reid, and Major Gaunt. When Jerry told them that the Coast Guard had reported them lost at sea, the flyers were shocked. It was the first they knew that they had been thirty-five miles over the ocean only fifteen minutes before they ran out of fuel. After they got to the ferry, Jerry returned to join the search party, which by this time was growing. Fifty Army and Air Force personnel from Camp Adair and Portland Air Force Base were on the way.

State Game Warden Harold Stromquist was among the searchers. He was in charge of a contingent of men from the Coast Guard. With the possible exception of Hitler and Tojo, Stromquist was probably the most hated man any of the loggers and ranchers knew of. He was hated not so much because he arrested those he caught violating game laws. Any game warden would do that, and all poachers understood it.

Flight Officer Ted Hatsog of Greenwood, South Carolina.

Stromquist had earned a special degree of contempt because of his practice of enticing children to talk about their home life and thus unwittingly incriminate their parents. I remember that he once grilled me about our diet at home, with special emphasis on how often we ate venison.

Flight Office Floyd Waddill of Laplata, Missouri.

Children in the Allegany area were taught never to use the words "deer meat," "venison," "elk meat," etc. We could take the Lord's name in vain, but we couldn't use words relating to game lest we inadvertently use the same word in front of Officer Stromquist. My parents didn't even hunt, but there was the danger that we might cause a neighbor to come under suspicion. Stromquist was feared and hated.

Jerry Baughman was in the group with Stromquist. He told me that the first night they were out, everyone was freezing cold and wet. The loggers had all brought extra socks along with them, but Officer Stromquist hadn't. Stromquist, with his wet and cold feet, looked longingly at

237

Flight Officer Ralph Foster
of Witchita, Kansas.

those spare, dry socks the loggers had brought and said that he would "sure like to have a dry pair of socks." The loggers wouldn't give him any. He begged. The loggers teased him, asking if he would let them go if he caught them with illegal meat. He said, "Of course not. I can't do that." "Sorry," said the loggers. "No dry socks!" And Stomquist went through the search with wet, cold feet. Afterwards, Cle Wilkinson observed that Stromquist did a very good job on the search. He was knowledgeable of the area, and he knew what he was doing. Cle had as much reason as anyone to dislike Stromquist on principle, so praise from Cle carries special weight. Actually, everyone who was on that search acquitted themselves well. We can't fault any of them.

Corporal Charles Bailey of West Palm Beach, Florida.

By this time the newspapers were picking up pieces of the story. Knowledge of the geography of this great forest was slight indeed. It was one vast *terra incognita*, as far as the outside world was concerned. Reporter Leroy Inman, who covered the story for the *Coos Bay Times*, gave the following description on November 29 (page 1):

> Whereabouts of the remaining passengers were not determined, but it is believed at least some of the men are alive and trying to reach civilization. It is believed they may have landed on the opposite side of a ridge and may be following the course of Bear Creek, which makes a wide circle, finally coming out to a road at Stolls Falls. The round-about journey would take a man an estimated two weeks, unless they can be contacted earlier.

It is hard to imagine a more distorted view of the lay of the land, but it is an excellent example of how little was known by anyone other than the few trappers and woodsmen who had actually been there. Stolls Falls are on the West Fork, which flows ultimately into Coos Bay. Bear Creek (Bear Camp Creek on the maps) runs into Lake Creek, which flows into Loon Lake, which in turn empties into the Umpqua River between Reedsport and Scottsburg.

Cle Wilkinson's old trapping cabin was on Bear Camp Creek, not far from its confluence with Lake Creek. It was the swollen waters of Bear Camp Creek that Floyd Waddill had parachuted into, almost drowning before he got out. Waddill's experience was a close call, but so were the others. Three of the four remaining flyers who had successfully bailed out landed in the top of the old-growth Douglas fir. Their stories are as interesting as adventure stories can get. They are each different.

Flight Officer Richard T. Kennett landed in an open space about twenty feet square, between the trees. He turned his ankle, but was otherwise uninjured. Kennett was the only one of the group who had ever previously seen Douglas fir. Neither he nor any of the others could believe, however, that trees could be this large. Some of the men thought they had landed in the California redwoods.

Corporal Charles E. Bailey landed high in one of the trees, hanging in mid air, suspended by his shroud lines. It took him about twenty minutes to unhook his leg harness. Still hanging by his shoulder harness, he swung himself to the top of a smaller tree. Once in the smaller tree he unfastened his shoulder harness, leaving his chute in the first tree as he climbed down the second, limb by limb. When he reached the lowest limbs, still too high to jump, he was able to catch hold of the top of a tall sapling, on which he swung, unhurt, to the ground. He had been within earshot of Kennett during much of this time and after about twenty-five minutes — well after dark — they found each other.

Lt. Jonathan D. Clark, of Rogerville, Tennessee, must have been a cool character. He landed in the very top of a very large old-growth fir. Not knowing exactly what his next best move might be, he filled his pipe, lit it, and casually had a smoke in

2/Lt Jonathan Clark
of Rogerville, Tennessee.

the rain and storm, 250 feet off the ground and fourteen miles from the nearest road. Finishing his smoke, he got out of his parachute harness and started climbing down through the crown of the tree.

Below the crown this was an unusual Douglas fir. As an even-aged Douglas fir forest matures, the trees tend to prune themselves. The limbs below the crown die, break off, and ultimately disappear. The tree trunk grows out around the wounds of the old limbs, and it is typically 100 feet or more of smooth tree trunk to the first limb. All signs of the knot are normally gone. Sometimes a tree might be standing a bit more to itself, and pruning would come later. In this case, pin knots — knots that were dead but still adhering to the trunk of the tree — would stick out from the trunk. The pin knots may be as short as three inches, and up to several feet long. Some of them would fall off if they were touched. No one who knew the Douglas fir forests would think a man could use the pin knots to climb to the ground.

The tree that Lt. Clark landed in had pin knots all the way to the ground. He threw down his parachute, shoes, socks, and camera and started down on the pin knots. An hour and a half later — well after dark — he was safely in the ground in the company of Kennett and Bailey. He was only able to find one of his shoes.

That first night the three men huddled next to a tree, covered with the parachute. The rain and storm increased, and after a few hours the three men began uncontrolled shivering, which didn't stop for six days. Their matches were wet and their cigarette lighters were dry. They could build no fire.

Pfc Walter A. Smoyer, the crew chief, had the hardest time of all the survivors. He landed in the crown of a tree evidently some distance from any of the others. Alone

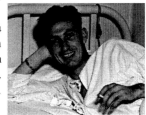

Flight Officer Richard
Kennett of Chicago, Illinois.

239

and in the dark and storm, he tied himself to the branches, where he swayed in the wind, soaked to the skin, until daylight. At that time he recognized that he was strictly on his own. He cut himself loose and used part of a shroud line as a safety rope, climbing down to the last limb, which was about fifty feet above the ground. His "safety rope" was too short to reach around the tree at that point, and it seemed his only chance was to let himself go. He cut the safety rope and went down, feet first, being knocked unconscious for awhile upon hitting the ground. It had taken him four hours to get down.

He wasn't too far from the raging waters of Lake Creek. Smoyer followed it through almost impenetrable brush as best he could. Freezing with wet and cold, he made about two or three miles per day. About six miles north of his starting place and still in the rain, he crawled out from under a log eighty-four hours later and he could go no further.

Kennett, Clark, and Bailey had better luck. They stumbled onto an abandoned trapper's cabin Tuesday morning, where they found a can of carbide. Not many people would know what to do with carbide, but Lt. Clark — the Tennessean who smoked his

Army jeeps waiting at the *Enegren Ferry.*

pipe in the top of the tree — knew what to do with it. He punched a hole in the top and poured a little water in it. As the gas escaped, he lit it with the flint from his cigarette lighter, and they had a bit of fire. That night they rested a little better.

The next day, Wednesday, they came upon Cle Wilkinson's old trapping cabin near the junction of Bear Camp Creek and Lake Creek. In the cabin they found matches, three potatoes, a half gallon of meal, half a cup of bear tallow, and some syrup. They converted this into french fries and hotcakes, of which Bailey said later, "This was the best meal I'd ever eaten!"

Meanwhile, the search party was growing larger. Most important among the guides was Cle Wilkinson and his brother-in-law Alfred Leaton. They had run traplines in the Lake Creek area for much of their lives and it is unlikely that anyone knew it better than they. There were many others who wanted to help, but got lost themselves.

For example, Hank Gosney had worked for George Youst above the falls before the war. He had just got out of the Army and he thought he could do some good. He walked into the Lake Creek area but after being lost without food for two days, he and his partner finally stumbled onto Cle Wilkinson's place, cold and hungry. No one was home. They went inside the house and cooked all of Cle's bacon, left a little money, cleaned up their mess, and departed.

Cle's place was used as a kind of headquarters for the rescue operation. Radio contact from Coos Bay could not be made beyond the ranch, and so it was considered to be at the very

Soldiers from Portland Air Base and Camp Adair, in the rain at the ferry.

240

edge of the known world. From the beginning, Cle was in the woods, advising the leaders of the search. The masses of people who later came up to be part of that search ended up taking over Cle's house.

On the third day a contingent of thirty-five personnel from Camp Adair and Portland Air Force Base arrived. The Army bought them each a new pair of caulk boots. The spikes on a new pair of caulks are razor sharp and are only worn in the woods, normally. The young Army men, however, were

Cle Wilkinson ranch with cars from searchers. House, left; barn right. Ambulance in front of barn.

oblivious to custom and boldly walked all over Cle's house with their caulk shoes as though it were a barn. They did this over a period of at least four days. When Cle returned, his floors were ruined. The wood floors were punctured with thousands of holes and splintered beyond repair. The linoleum was cut to ribbons. His daughter Alice remembers that the Army paid him $150 in compensation for the use of his property.

On Thursday, November 29, Kennett, Bailey and Clark headed down Lake Creek. They assumed, correctly, that a stream had to come out someplace. They didn't know, however, that with Lake Creek at flood it would not be possible to follow it. The Lake Creek valley was an impenetrable jungle of matted brush. They went perhaps two miles the first day, then decided to return to the cabin and build a raft. They didn't know, but a raft trip would probably have ended in disaster at the forty-foot Lake Creek falls.

On Friday, about 9 a. m. while they were building the raft, they heard an airplane overhead. It was a Coast Guard PBY. The parachute was already laid out on logs so it could be seen from the air. The crew of the PBY spotted it, dropped walkie talkies and K-rations, and reported the position to the command post. The PBY then returned to North Bend and picked up sleeping bags, food, clothing, and heavy shoes.

The Army officers in charge insisted that what was really needed was toilet paper and water. Cle pointed out that there was no shortage of ferns and brush to wipe on, and it had rained eighteen inches since the beginning of the search. In Cle's judgement, if there was anything they did *not* need, it was toilet paper and water!

There had been notices on the radio saying that experienced woodsmen were still needed. As usual in these kinds of situations, there was a notable lack of communications. Dow Beckham and his crew of about eight men were coming home from work at Irwin and Lyons logging camp on the South

Searchers passing the Allegany Store.

241

Fork. Dow stopped at the Enegren Ferry and asked an Army officer if they still needed any help. The officer replied, "Gosh no. We don't need any more characters running around up there!"

Two more characters did show up, however. It's a good thing they did because they are the ones who found Pfc Smoyer and saved his life. Early Friday morning Elvin Hess and Archie Clawson, loggers from Allegany, went up to the Wilkinson ranch to see if they could help. They knew the country quite well. Elvin had fallen timber for George Youst at the Wilkinson place before and during the war, and Archie was raised on the East Fork. Both had packed into Lake Creek many times on fishing trips.

Wheeled vehicles couldn't make it over the Weyerhaeuser fire access road up Woodruff Creek anymore. It was a rutted river of mud from the Army jeeps and other four-wheel drive vehicles that had already attempted it. Elvin and Archie walked the eight miles to the "dynamite" trailer, which had become something of an advanced command post. Army Lt. DeMers was in charge. Harold Noah and a few other loggers were there.

Jeeps on the Weyerhaeuser fire trail to Lake Creek.

About the time Hess and Clawson arrived, word came over the two-way radio that the Coast Guard PBY had located three survivors. They were said to be about "three miles away, on Pheasant Creek." The whole group headed out — no food, no bedding — expecting to be back in a few hours. After awhile the PBY radioed that it was not Pheasant Creek, but Lake Creek that the survivors were on. It also turned out that it wasn't three miles, but more like six miles, through the brush.

At that time, Hess and Clawson left Harold Noah with the rest of the group and went on ahead. They crawled on their hands and knees through the tangled brush of Lake Creek until, about a mile north of Bear Creek, they saw the footprint of a man, along with a gum wrapper. They continued on, Hess firing his rifle every few minutes until about six miles north of Bear Creek he found a track not more than twenty-four hours old. He yelled, fired his rifle, and heard a faint response. After searching in circles for a time, they came upon Smoyer, still sitting in the position he had assumed early that morning when he had crawled out from under the log. He couldn't move. This was at 4 p.m. Friday afternoon and ninety-six hours after the men had bailed out of the plane.

Hess and Clawson built a fire to warm Smoyer, but they had no food or warm clothing for him. Clawson stayed with him while Hess headed back upstream to the point at which the PBY was circling. He crossed Lake Creek on a fallen tree and came to Cle's old trapping cabin. Kennett, Bailey, and Clark were still there and, by coincidence, had now been joined by the trapper, Gard Sawyer.

Cle Wilkinson hadn't been trapping Lake Creek for several years now. He had pulled up his traps and moved them to Matson Creek in about 1936. Later, he moved over into the West Fork of the Millicoma after Frank Bremer died while running his trapline there in 1938. It is amazing, but it took almost fifty square miles of wilderness

242

to keep a trapper going. One trapper for each major drainage was about right. A few years after Cle pulled out of Lake Creek, Gard Sawyer, a descendant of an early settler on the Umqua, moved in. He came in and out by a trail from Elkton and as chance would have it, arrived at his cabin with a packsack of provisions just before Elvin Hess arrived.

Gard Sawyers cooked up a feed for the famished flyers, a feed they raved about later when interviewed by the press. The PBY had dropped sleeping bags, flying suits and K-rations at the cabin. Hess asked for a first aid kit, which the PBY dropped, but it landed in the top of a tree about two feet through. Hess chopped the tree down with the small ax at the cabin, but it hung up in another tree too large to chop down, and so the first aid kit could not be retrieved.

Kennett and Bailey stayed at the cabin with Gard Sawyers, the trapper. Lt. Clark headed back to Smoyer with Elvin Hess. The two of them carried the sleeping bag, a high altitude flying suit, an ax, a bottle of wine, and one half of the K-rations that the PBY had dropped. Lt. Clark, you will remember, had only one shoe. He wrapped his shoeless foot in a towel from the cabin, and went ahead anyhow. When I think of Lt. Clark, smoking his pipe in the top of the tree, climbing down on the pin knots, finding the can of carbide and knowing what to do with it — and now, heading six miles down Lake Creek with a load, in the rain, almost dark, and with only one shoe, I have a lot of respect for those Tennessee guys!

By now it was well after dark and Hess was exhausted. Fortunately, they met one of the Army searchers, Lt. Cummings, who was able to take part of Hess's load. When they finally got back to Smoyer, Harold Noah and Lt. DeMers along with two other soldiers were already there. One of the soldiers was a medic. According to the newspaper account later, he was identified as "a Negro named Stokes." He stayed with Smoyer for the next thirty-six hours, straight through, without sleep. It was probably through his efforts that Smoyer was able to pull through as well as he did.

When they got back to Smoyer they put a piece of malted chocolate from the K-rations into his mouth, put the high altitude flying suit on him, and placed him in the sleeping bag. None of the others had a sleeping bag. For them it was another miserable night.

Saturday dawned with a little less rain. It was a frustrating day. Elvin Hess got up early and went back to the cabin and about 10 a. m. the PBY returned. Elvin asked by walkie-talkie for blood plasma, sleeping bags, food and supplies. He also asked for loggers to cut a trail so that Smoyer could be carried out by stretcher. The material was dropped, but could not be retrieved.

"Advanced Command Post" near Lake Creek.

Frustrated, Elvin, along with Flight Officer Kennett and Corporal Bailey, headed back to Smoyer. Kennett limped along with his bad ankle, and they arrived about 2:30. At about 8 p.m. an Army doctor and twenty soldiers arrived. They cut wood and made camp, but for the second night there was no food.

Elvin Hess went hunting but had no luck. All of the activity must have scared the elk out of the country. While he was out it got dark and he heard a big racket which he took to be a herd of elk. It turned out to be twenty-five loggers crashing through the brush in the dark, with two flashlights among them.

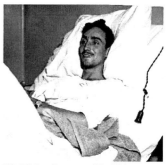

Hess led them off toward Smoyer and the camp, but two hours later they arrived back where they had started — they had gone in a circle. Hess then tried navigating with a compass, and finally got them through. There were a total of 10 K-rations to be divided among fifty men. Still, there was no bedding. Another horribly miserable night. Willis Peterson told me that he stood up all night on the lee side of a tree and was soaked.

Pfc Walter Smoyer of Bethlehem, PA.

Sunday morning at 6:30 they started back with Smoyer. This was the seventh day since he had pre-flighted the C-46D at Sedalia, Missouri. Afterward, he didn't remember much of the trip by stretcher.

The loggers broke trail and the soldiers carried the stretcher. Kennett's ankle was giving him a lot of trouble, and it was slow going. The soldiers managed the stretcher for about four and a half miles and gave up. The loggers took it the last mile and a half. Willis Peterson was one of the loggers. He told me that he wore all the hide off his hands on that stretcher. "That guy was in bad shape," he said. About a half mile from the advance camp they had to cross Lake Creek, with the stretcher, on a fallen log.

This was the most dangerous maneuver of all, but they made it across.

At 12:45 Sunday afternoon the fifty of them staggered with Smoyer into the advance camp. There was coffee and hot food there. Earlier in the morning the aircraft had been found. It was on Pheasant Creek, only a couple miles away. The pilot, Captain Hugh B. McMillan of Kansas City and the co-pilot, Harlow A. Marsh of Syracuse, New York, were dead. Jerry Baughman, who was there when they found it, told me, "They were just starting to get ripe." Jerry rode out with them in the ambulance.

The crash site looked as though the pilot had tried to crash land on the top of the trees. He didn't have much choice, of course, and might have made it but two of the trees uprooted, causing the plane to nose straight down the last 200 feet between some larger trees. The tail stood straight up, and the plane had to be pulled over with a cat to get at the bodies of the pilot and co-pilot. Jerry picked up a souvenir — a bent propellor blade. He gave it to me and I kept it in my bedroom for several years. Teen-age boys like things of that kind!

C-46D crash, nose down in the woods. Pilot and Co-pilot were dead, in their seats.

The rescuers and Smoyer were loaded onto some jeeps and weapons carriers, which were pushed with three bulldozers through the mud for most of the fourteen miles back to Cle Wilkinson's place. They arrived there at about 3:30 p.m. An ambulance took Smoyer to town and he arrived at the McAuley Hospital in Coos Bay at 6:45 p.m., 170 hours after he bailed out. It had been one hell of an experience. "I was very sick for about a week and I was starved," Smoyer told me in a letter. "They took very good care of me at McAuley Hospital and then I was transferred to Portland Army Hospital." He had gangrene in his feet, and remained in Army hospitals for about nine months before being discharged from the Air Force in August 1946. His feet were saved, but it was several years before he fully recovered He returned to his pre-war job at Bethlehem Steel where he remained until retirement.

The radio operator, Sergeant Robert T. Neal, was never found. I suspect that his chute may not have opened, and he landed in the raging waters of Lake Creek. Otherwise, one would think some trace would have been found. During the search, his fiancee's mother called the *Coos Bay Times* to say that she had no word from him since he called the night before they left Oakland, California.

Neal's parents came each summer for several years and hired guides to search the area for clues. His mother, who didn't have hiking boots, would borrow boots from Pat Wilkinson for those trips. Several years after the crash Neal's mother hired Elvin Hess to do a final search. Elvin didn't want to do it, but he was afraid that if someone else did it they wouldn't do it right. He spent about two weeks thoroughly searching the area. He didn't find anything and that was the last attempt to solve the mystery of what had happened to Neal.

I don't know what happened afterward to the other survivors. Each of their stories would be a chapter in the social history of post-war America, I'm sure. If the resourcefulness they showed in the woods above the falls is any indication of what they were able to do later, we can assume that they did all right. I sure hope they did.

Of the rescuers, most remained in the woods in Coos County for the rest of their working lives. This was certainly true for Archie Clawson, Harold Noah, Elvin Hess, Roy Spires, and many others. Harold Noah was involved in another spectacular rescue on the upper West Fork in 1949. A hunter had injured himself and was lost and given up for dead. Harold Noah didn't give up, and found him alive after a week in the woods.

Roy Spires, the high climber who rescued David Reid from his perch 150 feet in the old-growth tree, continued in the woods. I was told that when he was eighty years old he gave a high-climbing demonstration at the Coos County Fair. He was from an old pioneer family of Myrtle Point, and had started in the woods back in the steam donkey days before World War I. He was the stuff of legend.

During the 1960's many of the loggers from Coos County moved to Alaska. Elvin Hess was one of them. While there, he was cruising timber and ran across a Kodiak bear who grabbed him, shook him unconscious, and walked away. Elvin woke up just as the bear ambled out of sight. With his scalp ripped open and one eye hanging alongside his head, Elvin crawled out of the woods to a road where he was eventually picked up by a passing motorist. He was delivered to an airplane and flown to Juneau, where he remained in critical condition at the hospital for several weeks. Within a year Elvin was back working in the woods, where he remained the rest of this life.

As for the land above the falls, it would never be the same again. The world knew about it now. There had been more men involved in the search and rescue of the

245

flyers than had ever been in those woods before, from the beginning. Newspaper and radio coverage emphasized that this was "one of the wildest, most thickly forested sections of the state." It caught the consciousness of a public only beginning to be aware that wilderness was becoming a thing of the past.

In 1948 Weyerhaeuser contracted with the Morrison-Knudson Corporation of Boise, Idaho, to build the major logging road from Allegany up the East Fork and over the Matson Creek Falls. This road ultimately connected into the upper Glenn Creek and upper Lake Creek areas.

In July 1950, Weyerhaeuser hauled the first load of logs out of this forest. The logging started on Tyberg (Conklin) Creek just above the Matson Creek Falls. Fifteen years later they were into Lake Creek, hauling logs out of the area where the C-46 had crashed. Remains of parachutes were found, but no sign of any remains of Sergeant Neal.

As far as I know, none of the rescuers received any compensation for their efforts. They hadn't expected any. No awards or medals were given for what, by any standards, were heroic actions. None were expected. The stories about the rescue were told and re-told in logging camp bunkhouses, taverns, and everywhere that loggers gathered, and the stories have remained current now for almost sixty years.

The wilderness is now a labyrinth of logging roads and the original timber is gone. Most of the participants are gone. The memories of a wilderness that was, and a breed of men no longer with us, are now second-hand memories at best.

246

Note on pictures and sources: Photos of the rescued flyers were taken at the McAuley Hospital in Coos Bay by the *Coos Bay Harbor* newspaper, of North Bend. The photos are now in the collection of the Coos County Historical Museum and are reproduced here with grateful appreciation. The other photos are from the albums of Alice Allen, Audrey Milton, and Jerry Baughman. I have talked casually and otherwise with the following persons, and have incorporated information from them in various parts of the story: Hank Gosney, Alice Allen, Gary Hess, Willis Peterson, Dow Beckham, and Jerry Baughman. The contemporary newspaper accounts in the *Coos Bay Times* by reporter Leroy Inman and Editor Walter J. Coover were excellent and form the basis of what I have assembled here. I am also grateful to Dow Beckham for allowing me to use the unpublished manuscript of an article he once wrote about the rescue. Following the original publication of *Above the Falls* in 1992, some new information has come to my attention. Coos Bay *World* reporter Elise Hamner did interviews with Walter Smoyer and with Archie Clawson in 1995, and her article appeared in the November 27, 1995 edition of the paper. I was able to exchange letters with rescued flyer Walter Smoyer of Bethlehem, Pennsylvania, and his wife Mildred, and with one of the soldiers on the rescue, John P. Anderson of Milford, Kansas. From their information I was able to correct certain errors in the original, and add a few more details.

Army C-46D, crashed Nov. 25, 1945.

A Letter from Walter A. Smoyer

Hellertown, Pa
December, 1995

Dear Lionel,

We took off from Sedalia, Mo. on Nov. 24, 1945. One of our planes was grounded in Oakland, California and we were going to pick up the four pilots and take them to Portland, Oregon. We stopped in Denver, Colorado for fuel and picked up four more passengers going west. From Denver we went to Ogden, Utah. We flew over seven hours and I was plenty tired. The next day (25th) we had a rough trip. Then we flew from Ogden to Fresno, California over the Rocky Mts. We flew at 16,000 ft. Since we had no oxygen I felt pretty sick after 2 hrs. of flying. We flew up to Oakland, California and stayed for the night. Sgt. Neal and I went to San Francisco across the Bay from Oakland and since Neal had been there before he showed me around. We had a great time riding the Cable Cars and then took a Ferry ride across the Bay. The whole evening cost me $1.05 and we had a great time.

The next morning (26th) we picked the other four passengers and left for Portland, Oregon. We had 12 men on board – four of the crew and 8 officers. We had flown about 4 hrs. when things began to happen. The weather grew bad and the plane began to collect ice. The storm grew worse and our radio went out. We were by this time near Portland but because of the storm we could not contact the ground. The Pilot decided that we had better turn back and try to make California. We started back but ended up lost and almost out of gas. We had no radio and we could not see the ground, so we did not know if we were over land or water. We had flown about 6 hours when the Pilot gave orders to put our chutes on and get ready to bail out as soon as we sighted land and by this time one of our engines cut out because we used up all the gas.

The cargo door was opened and we started to jump. The officers jumped first and after that it was Sgt. Neal's turn. He was very scared. He kept asking me if he should count to four before pulling the rip chord. I told him to pull it right away as we were very low. I went out last and my chute opened and I started to sail to the ground. My chute caught on the top of a Giant fir tree that must have been 250 ft. high. I looked at my watch and I landed in the tree at 4 p. m. I heard the plane crash and then everything was silent. I do not know why the Pilot and co-pilot did not bail out as they would have had enough time to get out.

There I was all alone just hanging in my chute and scared to death that my chute would blow off the tree. The wind blew me into the trunk of the tree. I tied myself to the trunk of the tree that night. I don't think I slept but I did doze off a little. The storm lasted all night and by Tuesday morning I was soaked thru and thru from the rain.

248

Tuesday it took me about 4 hours to get out of the tree. I climbed down about 100 ft. and then I had to jump the rest which must have been about 50 ft. The jump knocked me out for about an hour. When I came to I was very lucky as I did not break any bones and I could walk. I walked for 6 days in the wildest country I have ever seen or ever hope to see again. I had nothing to eat but I had some chewing gum and there was plenty of water to drink. I don't ever remember being hungry.

The search party found me on Saturday and I was just about gone by that time from exposure and hunger. They gave me 4 pts. of blood plasma and shots of morphine. I was kept in the woods until Sunday until they could get a stretcher in. The place was so wild that they had to cut a path to get me out. They took me to Coos Bay Hospital which was about 38 miles from where they found me and the nearest town. I don't remember too much after I was found.

I was very sick for about a week and I was starved. They took very good care of me at McAuley Hospital and then I was transferred to Portland Army Hospital. I was told I would be there until I was well enough to travel. I could not walk for about 5 months. I had no feeling in my feet and my legs were beat up from the knees down. I had no pain but my feet felt as though they were asleep. I just walked on them until they were numb. They were all black and blue and swollen and later I found out I had gangrene.

Sometime later I was transferred to an Army Hospital in Spokane, Washington for rehabilitation. My wife contacted her Congressman and asked to have me sent east and closer to home. So in April I was sent cross-country by train in a private car and a male nurse to attend to me. I was sent to Camp Upton, Long Island, N. Y. I was only there a short time and then transferred to Walter Reed Hospital in Washington D. C. I stayed there until I was discharged from the Air Force in Aug. 1946. I then went back to Bethlehem, Pa, where my wife and 3 yr. old son were living with her parents.

For many years after the crash I had psychological effects in the month of November. I would just shiver and actually feel sick.

I took this information from a letter I wrote to my wife on Dec. 8, 1945 as the crash was still very clear in my mind.

Thank you for taking such an interest in my story and I sure was a lucky fellow.

Sincerely,

Walter A. Smoyer

Extracts of letters from Mildred Smoyer

Nov. 16, 1995

Dear Mr. Youst,

After all these years a man by the name of John Anderson contacted my husband. Mr. Anderson was in the search party & helped to rescue my husband. He told us about a book which was written by you and that there is an Epilogue about the crash in the book.

The reason I am writing to you is to find out if this book is still available. We would love to purchase this book to pass down to our grand-children.

I also thought you might like a follow-up as to what happened to my husband after he was found. He spent nearly a year in Veteran's Hospitals after which he was discharged in 1946. He developed gangrene on both feet and for awhile the doctors thought he might lose them. God was good to us and his feet were saved. Walter went back to his job at the Steel Mills and spent 30 years there. He retired in 1982 and we have been married 52 yrs. We also have 3 children and 3 Grand-children.

We would appreciate hearing from you.

Sincerely,

Mildred Smoyer
Hellertown, Pa

Nov. 29, 1995

Dear Mr. Youst,

We received your most welcome letter and book. We read with great interest the account of the plane crash and all the men who survived the crash. Also all the brave and courageous people who were involved in the search. If it weren't for them my life would have been a different story. We shall always be indebted to all those people whom we never met and will never be able to thank.

Again may I thank you for writing and only wish I could convey my thanks to every one who was involved.

Sincerely,
Mildred Smoyer

Extracts of a letter from John R. Anderson

October 31, 1994

Dear Mr. Youst:

At the time I was in a Search and Rescue Unit as master of a 42' crash boat. We were stationed on the Columbia River at the end of the most used runway at Portland A F Base (between Hayden Island and Government Island). When the plane crash at Coos Bay occurred we were called there for the search. We came in on Wednesday.

I was with the group that was with Pfc Smoyer and helped on the long carry down. Only since I got your book did I learn that he made a fast recovery. Most of us, of course, were completely out of our usual environment. None of us had been in a wilderness mountain forest before, but we were young and tried to adapt the best we could and give a good account of ourselves. The "spiked" boots that we got were a great help. Without them I fear we would have had more injuries.

I was a bit disappointed in that no mention was made, in your book, of the Portland AF Base Unit at all. In fact, I am 99% certain that I see myself and my Lt. in the photo captioned "Soldiers from Camp Adair etc" on page 297. We all looked alike, however, wet and cold. No big deal.

Sincerely,

John R. Anderson

Chapter Twenty-seven

The *fin-de-siecle*

Weyerhaeuser began logging their "Millicoma Tree Farm" in July 1950, at the top of Matson Creek Falls, and it was about ten years before they were over the ridge and into the Glenn Creek drainage. At the beginning, they held fairly close to their original plan of a sustained yield based on a 100-year cycle. The times, however, "were a changing," and the timber industry was changing too. The change received a huge boost from nature on October 11, 12, and 13, 1962, when the standing timber above the falls, and all along the coasts of Oregon and Washington, was hit with the most devastating storm in recorded history. A typhoon had spun storms along the coast on those three successive days, with winds as high as 150 mph, and tens of billions of board feet of timber were blown down. The unprecedented volume of logs suddenly available after salvage operations got underway was far more than the domestic market could absorb, but the Japanese came obligingly forward with money to buy all that would meet their rather high grading standards. Probably most of the logs from above the falls met those standards, and the accelerated harvest that began as salvage, continued on until Weyerhaeuser's Coos and Douglas County timber — its Millicoma Tree Farm — had been logged off sixty years ahead of schedule. It is probably no coincidence that in 1963, the year following the Columbus Day Storm, Weyerhaeuser listed its stock on the New York and the Pacific stock exchanges. For the first time in its history its stock would be publicly traded. From that moment there were new company objectives, and maintaining stable local economies through the sustained yield of individual tree farms was not among them.

The top management of all the large timber companies, and the Forest Service, simultaneously developed an economic and ideological commitment to early liquidation of the old growth (a vaguely defined term), partly so that the large sawmills such as the one in North Bend could eventually be replaced by the fast, high-tech gang mills designed in Germany for very small timber and very small crews. And so, after 1963, logging in the

Long logs for export. 66 feet long, to be cut in two for Japan. Load is from Lake Creek, more than 20,000 board feet. Driver: Roger Ott.

Millicoma Tree Farm stepped up with much more timber being cut than the sawmill could handle, the surplus exported to Japan. Nobody complained about it because everybody was working and everybody had money to spend. It was great, in the short term. It was well into the 1980's before all of the Glenn Creek drainage had been logged, and on January 4, 1989, the last raft of logs from the Millicoma Tree Farm went down the river from Allegany. All of the logged off land had been replanted with Douglas fir seedlings, in accordance with the new Oregon forest practice laws and the principles of the newly developed "High Yield Forestry" being adopted throughout the timber industry. High Yield Forestry would hopefully produce a marketable crop of small, second-growth Douglas fir within forty or fifty years. Among its techniques was the aerial spraying of herbicides, intended to kill all species of plants that were deemed to be in competition with Douglas fir.

Spray

I was in the Air Force until 1975, at various locations around the world and missed out on the beginning of this. During the entire year of 1970 I found myself in Vietnam, but my job there was not very exciting nor dangerous, although it was interesting. I was at 7th Air Force Headquarters at Saigon and my job was collecting the previous day's aircraft sortie data from all the air bases in Southeast Asia, trying to make sense of it, and briefing the generals and their staffs in the morning, every day. If any messages came in during the night that I thought one of the colonels should know about, I would decide who and go wake him up.

One night about half way through my Vietnam tour, a long message came in from the Pentagon saying that as of that moment the Air Force was prohibited from using a chemical defoliant called Agent Orange, a 50-50 mixture of 24D and 245T, popular phenoxy herbicides used in agriculture. Over a period of several years hundreds of tons of that defoliant were sprayed onto parts of the jungle thought to shelter people who were designated as enemy. The message went on for pages, delineating the genetic and carcinogenic effects that the 245T had on laboratory animals, and the potential risk that it posed to human health. The Department of Defense was ordering the Air Force to cease and desist in its use. After reading the message, I felt relieved that the diabolical effects of those chemicals had been discovered and their use stopped before more damage was done. I woke up the appropriate colonel and promptly forgot about it.

After my one-year tour in Vietnam, I was home on leave in Coos Bay when I mentioned the Agent Orange incident to my brother-in-law and he told me, "They're using that stuff here to kill the alder." I couldn't believe it. To kill the alder? What the hell would they want to kill the alder for, I wondered? It was well known that alder was the only tree in these woods that fixed nitrogen and actually enriched the soil it grew in. Granted, at the time there was no good market for alder logs in Oregon, but such a market was already developing in southwestern Washington. With the depletion of hardwood timber for furniture in the eastern U.S., it would only be a matter of time before alder would probably become a quite valuable commercial tree. But the ideology of the forest industry included a belief that the highest and best use of forest land in this area would always be from pure stands of Douglas fir, and Douglas fir alone.

A couple years later I thought about the Agent Orange being used in the Coos River drainage when duty brought me briefly to Johnston Island, in the middle of the Pacific Ocean. The commander there gave me a tour of the place, showing me the extraordinarily wide variety of uses the Air Force had for that very limited piece of ocean real-estate. I was astonished to find that one of the uses was short-term storage of the thousands of barrels of Agent Orange that had been in stock at the time that it was banned for use in Vietnam. They hadn't yet decided how to get rid of it. Meanwhile, it sat in a large fenced-in storage area on Johnston Island, awaiting a decision.

In June 1975, I moved permanently back to the East Fork of the Millicoma, to a house I lived in when I was in the third and fourth grade at Allegany. One morning in early June 1976, I was walking along the quarter mile of river that fronts my property and in that distance I counted more than 100 dead and dying crawdads in the water. Some were still moving, slowly, and I watched them die before my eyes. I called the Oregon Fish and Wildlife Department and could find no one interested, and I was advised not to worry about it because it wasn't important. "Crawdads aren't a very big industry in Oregon," I was told. I'm sure that is true, but I thought that perhaps the crawdads dying in the river might be something like the canary in the mine, giving us an early warning about something. But absolutely no one was interested — not the state agencies and not the newspapers. No one.

I soon suspected that herbicidal spraying could be the culprit, because during the spring and summers of 1975, '76, and '77 there was hardly a day that didn't bring the overhead sound of spray helicopters, sounds which reminded me very much of Vietnam. Frequently there was the unmistakable odor of the oil that was used as a carrier for the herbicide, and that odor would blanket our house and remind me again of Vietnam. Then, one day I was dumping my garbage at the Weyerhaeuser dump (which the company at that time graciously allowed the Allegany community to use) when a large number of red and yellow cans caught my eye. I looked closely and found that they were thirty-five-gallon drums of Weedone, a herbicide consisting of a 50-50 mixture of 24D and 245T, manufactured by American Chemical Company. I was flabbergasted. This was the civilian version of Agent Orange, and here was the place where the empty containers were thrown. Among the warnings on the label, it cautioned that it not be allowed to go into streams or waterways. "Kills Fish," it warned.

By the time the spray season for 1978 began, there were virtually no crawdads in the East Fork of the Millicoma, nor were there any fresh-water mussels, nor newts. At least I couldn't find any, and they were plentiful enough in 1975 and before. In three years, and before my very eyes, aquatic life in that river had been utterly devastated. I thought that I had ought to be doing something about it, but I didn't know what. I tried to get the Department of Forestry and the Department of Fish and Wildlife interested, but they were in lock step with each other in terms of denying that there was a problem. The newspaper would not take the story. Then, early in the spray season of 1978 Rose Lee, who lived on the West Fork, brought me a copy of the lab report of a blood sample, ordered by her daughter's pediatrician, Dr. Joseph Morgan of North Bend. The girl had been diagnosed with a blood disorder called idiopathic thrombocytopenic purpura, or ITP, a condition in which the platelet count of the blood is dangerously reduced. The lab report listed a phenoxy herbicide among the chemicals in the girl's blood. Her spleen was removed, and she had a very hard time of it. Rose Lee asked me if I could help her by chairing a public meeting at the Allegany School, to which a number of Weyerhaeuser and state agency people were invited. My own blood was aroused, and I was stirred to become, for a time, an environmental activist!

The meeting was the evening of February 23, 1978, at the Allegany School cafeteria and there were more than 100 people there, including Weyerhaeuser scientist Jack Walstad, representatives from various state agencies, several newspaper reporters and a TV camera from the Medford station. There were also two or three people from an anti-pesticide group in Eugene who had probably heard about the meeting from Rose Lee. I didn't know them, nor did I know that this was a small part of the beginning of a story which, it appeared, had been chosen by the national media to be "news" at this time. News, I was to discover, is whatever the media decides is news. But the overwhelming majority of those in attendance were concerned residents of the East and West Forks of the Millicoma River.

I started the meeting by introducing the problem and asking Rose Lee to tell her story. She briefly described the spraying above her rented house on the West Fork — giving dates and times, and of her daughter's blood disorder and the lab report showing phenoxy herbicide. She said, "I don't know if the spray caused her problem or not, but it doesn't belong in her blood." I asked Jack Walstad to give us the industry view. Jack, a PhD in something or another, took a piece of chalk and drew a vertical line on the blackboard, telling us that it represented knowledge. Then, beginning at the bottom of the vertical line, he drew a horizontal line which, he told us, represented alarm. He said that knowledge and alarm were inversely proportional. He, for example, had lots of knowledge and there he indicated a spot high on the vertical line. By use of his diagram he demonstrated that the reason we were alarmed was because we lacked knowledge.

The people of Allegany quietly listened to Dr. Walstad's condescending description of themselves, and after a few minutes Warren Browning's brother John stood up to speak. John Browning was an internationally respected scientist, and he had retired a few years earlier to his boyhood home on the West Fork after devoting his working life to the Shell Oil Company research laboratory at La Jolla, California. He pointed out to Dr. Walstad that he appreciated the value of knowledge, and that he himself kept up with technical and scientific journals. "But," he said, then paused a second before continuing, "they are spraying awfully close to my water supply." And so in this case knowledge was not *inversely* proportional to alarm at all, but instead it was *directly* proportional. The more you knew about it, the more upset you got!

The industry had no good answer to John's concern, and the meeting then deteriorated into a sort of street theater. Someone asked the Fish and Wildlife representative if the spraying would hurt the fishing in the river. He said no. Then Henry Crump, who had been quietly sitting on one of the empty thirty-five-gallon herbicide drums, picked it up and said, "I'm sitting on a barrel of it here and it says right on it that it kills fish!" He brought the drum up to the table where I was officiating the meeting and I was able to confirm that indeed, the label warned that it must be kept out of streams and waterways and that it "kills fish." Dr. Walstad for Weyerhaeuser, and Jerry Phillips for the State Forestry, said that they would bring our concerns to their people and so the meeting ended. A few days later Jerry suggested to me that I might have some results if I attended the upcoming State Board of Forestry meeting, and bring my concerns directly to them.

I went to Salem and attended the Board of Forestry meeting on the morning of March 8, 1978. Dr. Carl Stoltenberg, dean of Oregon State University School of Forestry, was chairman, and as I entered, a discussion was in progress. One of the board members was asking incredulously, "Do you mean that we are to invite people in here who don't agree with us?" Dr. Stoltenberg indulgently acceded, "Yes. That's exactly what we will be doing." This was in compliance with a new policy in which boards and other state entities would be required to allow members of the public to participate more directly in controversial issues. Although there had been two public hearings on the proposed rules for herbicidal spraying, I was the first member of the public ever to appear before the full Oregon State Board of Forestry to present a position they "did not agree with"! It did not immediately revolutionize the way that forestry was done in Oregon, but I was able to convey directly to an influential group of people exactly what our concerns were in regard to the aerial spraying of herbicides around our homes and water supplies. After the meeting, one forestry official quietly informed me that there were quite a few people within the agency that agreed with me. That was gratifying to know.

Later that year there was a full public forum held by the Board of Forestry, regarding changes to the forest practices rules. I made another presentation, this time with specific recommendations as to notifying residents of impending spray operations that would impact them, of required buffer strips along streams, and a prohibition of spraying anywhere near domestic water supplies. One of the board members missed my point completely and asked, "Why are you all against logging?" I said, "We're not against logging. Logging only muddies up the creeks and we understand mud. But we don't understand these chemicals. If you stop them, everything will be all right." Of course, I didn't realize how many people were in fact against logging, but at least I made it clear that I was not one of them. When the new Forest Practices Rules came out later that year, it included virtually all the changes that I had requested. After that, for several years I was personally notified of any spraying to be done near private residences in the Allegany area and the alarm of the people here was noticeably reduced.

Someone had got hold of Portland Attorney Larry Sokol and he came down to Allegany for a couple days. I asked him if it might be possible to get an injunction against the spraying, until new rules could come out that gave us better protection. He said no, and told me that the only way to change corporate behavior is to slap a "10 million dollar lawsuit" against them. "It's the only language they understand," he told me. He was probably right, but I wasn't interested in litigation, and I don't think anyone else at Allegany was. On April 6, my neighbor Herb Bird, who had been for many years in charge of the roadside spraying at Weyerhaeuser, died from a blood cancer called multiple myeloma. While Larry Sokol was visiting the area I took him to the hospital to see Herb, who was on his death bed. His wife and a neighbor were there, and Larry left them a form, in case they should want him to represent them in any actions, but the family decided against it. Three of Herb's sons worked for Weyerhaeuser and it didn't seem smart to stir things up.

A few weeks after Herb died I got a phone call from Congressman Jim Weaver, who was interested in knowing whether it was true, as forest industry spokesmen were beginning to allege, that it was the marijuana growers who were behind the anti-herbicide movement. I told him that it was certainly not the case at Allegany, and I told him about Herb Bird and his multiple myeloma. "Multiple myeloma," Weaver exclaimed. "That's what the monkeys got!" "What monkeys?" I asked. It was the rhesus monkeys in the dioxin experiments the previous year at the Primate Research Center in Madison, Wisconsin. They were fed dioxin, a contaminant in all 245T, and they had contracted "anemia, thrombocytopenia, and leukopenia," which isn't multiple myeloma, but it was close enough for us. In fact, it was thrombocytopenia that Rose Lee's daughter had, along with the herbicide in her blood. The EPA had recently issued a rebuttable presumption against the use of 245T, and Weaver had read it on the way back to Washington D.C. that very week. It included summaries of all the relevant studies on the subject, including the one with the rhesus monkeys. So Herb Bird, working with the roadside spraying chemicals for who knows how long, contracted a blood cancer something like what "the monkeys got." Interesting, but nobody was sued for it.

It seemed that we had some pretty good reasons for concern. The Coos Bay office of the Bureau of Land Management (BLM) had monitored streams adjacent to their aerial spraying during fiscal year 1977, and determined that if they spray from the air, it was impossible to keep herbicides out of the water.[2] That was confirmed by the State Forestry monitoring of several small creeks on the West Fork following the spring spraying in 1978. All of them contained 245T in several parts per billion — and that included the stream that John Browning used as his water supply, a fact that validated the concern he voiced at the meeting with Jack Walstad. That fall, the Game Commission took organ samples of elk that were killed within the Millicoma Tree Farm during that hunting season.[3] All of them showed traces of 245T, one in the fifty parts-per-billion range.

As Congressman Weaver had intimated they would, Forest Industry organizations soon hired a man to speak at Chambers of Commerce and other civic organizations. His message was that the anti-herbicide movement was organized and financed by the "multi-million dollar Oregon marijuana industry." I attended his speech at the Chamber of Commerce luncheon at the Red Lion Motel in Coos Bay and was shocked by the blatant accusations that he made. At the end of his talk I stood and introduced myself as a retired Air Force Major. I saw friendly recognition in his face as I then introduced "Mrs. Peggy Hughes of Allegany, whose husband worked for Weyerhaeuser for over thirty years," and again I saw friendly recognition. I then pointed to a table in the corner and said, "Over there is Dr. Joseph Morgan, a well-known pediatrician." I detected a scowl on the speaker's face as I quickly pointed to the back

---

[2] John J. Cameron and John W. Anderson, "Results of the Stream Monitoring Program Conducted During FY 1977 Herbicide Spray Project, Coos Bay District Bureau of Land Management.
[3] Judith Kahle, "TCCD Found in Deer and Elk," *NCAP News* (Fall 1980).

of the room and said, "and there is Mrs. Margurite Watkins, president of the Coos Bay School Board and a member of the State Board of Forestry Rules Committee." I was abruptly interrupted by the speaker, who demanded angrily, "What are you driving at? What's your point?" I said, "None of us are a part of the multi-million dollar Oregon marijuana industry, and yet each of us have spoken publicly in opposition to current spraying practices in forestry. Who," I asked, "were you speaking to?" There was no reply, the luncheon was over, but the reporters who were present swarmed around me, not the speaker. I suggested that they interview Dr. Morgan, which they did.

We got a lot of publicity, because the media had decided that this was the local aspect of a national story that they wanted to exploit. Besides our local TV and newspaper coverage, Bill Curtis and a CBS television crew came out from Chicago. They stayed several days and interviewed quite a few people including seventy-year-old Henry Crump, who was living on Glenn Creek. Henry wanted them to televise him while he fell a forty-inch Douglas fir, and then he wanted to be interviewed while he was sitting on the stump. Bill Curtis went along with it, and did just as Henry suggested. Later, a PBS crew from Boston WGBS was here, doing a feature for NOVA on the subject of dioxin. It turned out to be the first two-hour special that NOVA ever did, and it was the first time they had ever approached a controversial subject while it was still controversial. The first hour was about Allegany and Alsea, Oregon, and the second hour was about Love Canal in New York.

But eventually the controversy cooled down. The EPA banned the use of 245T in forestry and we began receiving prior notification of time and place of any scheduled spraying that would affect us. New, presumably safer herbicides eventually came into use, and in the course of time it became a non-issue. This is not to say that the conflicts had been eliminated between the public and the new, global forest industry, however.

Endangered Species

There were groups and individuals who saw in liquidation of the old-growth, the "extinction" of a natural resource which was the common legacy of all Americans. Through a creative interpretation of the Endangered Species Act, they were able to get the courts to agree with them. The species that was most famously shown to be endangered by liquidation of the old growth Douglas fir was the northern spotted owl. Most of us had lived here through significant portions of our lives and had never seen one, and some of us had never even heard of the spotted owl before it was catapulted into public awareness by the media. Then, during the heat of our herbicide controversy what should appear floating in the waters of Glenn Creek, but a dead spotted owl, and then a few days later a dead spotted owl was found in the county road about a mile above my place. These discoveries were brought to my attention and I encouraged the finders to take them to the State Forestry office, which they did. One of the owls ended up mounted and on display at the Roseburg office, the other was checked for pesticide residue, with no traces found.

As it turned out, and unknown to anybody who lived here, the local woods were home to many spotted owls, now an endangered species. That put the logging of these woods into a perceived jeopardy, and there were loud voices from within the industry proclaiming that "environmentalists" would soon make it impossible for owners of timberland to ever be able to utilize the timber on their property. As a result, there was a mad speculative scramble to buy the timber owned by small timberland owners before all logging was prohibited. The price was bid up and up astronomically until everybody who owned even a few trees found it impossible to resist selling them. Timber that for the first forty years of the twentieth century held steady at a dollar or dollar and a half per thousand had jumped to $25 per thousand in the early 1950's. By the beginning of the spotted owl controversy, the price averaged perhaps $100 per thousand. At the peak of the controversy, in about 1992, Douglas fir timber was being sold for as high as $1,000 per thousand board feet. Nobody could resist selling at such artificially inflated prices, and even I sold a few acres of timber on my own property at that time. Who could resist?

The last old-growth

In the summer of 2000, I went up to the old homesteads just for the walk. I was stunned. It had all been recently logged, including the part now owned by Weyerhaeuser that my dad had logged for his sawmill during the 1940's. Dad had left three large old-growth Douglas fir that may have dated from after the time of the fire of 1440. They were a bit big for the mill and Warren Browning told me that they left them because Dad was afraid if they fell them, they might have gone into the slab chute and caused some extra work. And so those three trees stood another sixty years, but now even they were gone — the very last of the original old-growth trees in the valley.

John Muenchrath told me what happened. When Weyerhaeuser logged the hill above Joe Schapers place in 2000, they inadvertently went over the property line and cut about thirty of the second-growth trees that were on John's property. This was a major embarrassment for the Weyerhaeuser people, but John said that he would be willing to take those three old-growth, which were barely on the Weyerhaeuser side of the line, in exchange. Weyerhaeuser readily agreed, and John took the three trees — seven or eight thousand board feet in each one — had them milled, and built his new house with them. And so, the last old-growth trees in the Upper Glenn Creek Valley will have a good home — the home of John and Mary Muenchrath, probably one of the very last homes in Coos County that will be constructed of genuine old-growth Douglas fir!

The cycle above the falls was now complete. No one would ever live up there again, and I would expect the next crop of timber to be harvested in about forty-five years or so. Those future loggers probably won't know that the first time that any timber was removed from that land, it was removed by hand with no machinery, and the stumps burned so that crops could be grown and families raised there, and it took a lifetime to do it. They probably won't know that the hillside above the creek bottom was first logged during World War II, and that my dad employed a dozen men four years to log it and cut it into dimensioned lumber on the site. The most recent logging probably took a half dozen men a couple weeks. The next time, in about the year 2050 or so, the small-second growth will be removed by a half dozen men in just a few days. Future cycles above the falls will be much less interesting than in the past, because in the past there was a human history up there. By the year 2000, the land above the falls had experienced the end of history. No one will ever live up there again, and no one will even need to visit it except an occasional forester looking for insects. There will be no people above the falls.

Kenworth off-highway logging truck, from the Weyerhaeuser Timber Company fleet of about fifty. They used them during the forty years that it took to haul the logs from their 210,000 acre Millicoma Tree Farm to the heads of tidewater at Allegany and Dellwood. With ten-foot bunks and powered by a 400 hp Cummins diesel engine, those truck easily handled loads of up to 25,000 board feet. Driver Roger Ott, great-grandson of Elizabeth Shapers Ott Tyberg, is standing by the front wheel. He hauled his fair share of the logs.

260

Photo Credits

Bibliography

Oral Narratives and Interviews

Allen, Alice. Taperecorded narrative, Charleston, OR, December 1991.

Browning, Warren. Taperecorded narrative/interview, Sumner, OR, February 11, 1992.

Clarke, Belle Leaton. Taperecorded interview, Eugene, OR, January 12, 1992.

Henderson, Howard. Interview with Lionel Youst and Jerry Phillips, Coos County, May 23, 1992.

Wilkinson, Patricia Jacqueline. Taperecorded narrative, Hillsboro, OR, September 1991.

Youst, George. Taperecorded narrative/interview, Coos Bay, OR, August 1967.

Taperecorded interviews with Alice Allen, Warren Browning, Hattie Cotter, Helen Cummings, Wilma Hoelig, Al Lively, Charles Middleton, Bob Milton, Erma Ott, Harold Ott, and Pat Wilkinson. Allegany, OR: September 14, 1991.

County Courthouse Records
Coos County Circuit Court Records; County Clerk, Deeds; County Surveyor; Douglas County Clerk, Deeds.

Letters, Manuscripts, Newspapers, and Miscellaneous Unpublished Material

Anderson, Edmund A. "Trip to the Golden Falls." *Coos Bay News*, p. 3. August 11, 1880.

Anderson, John R. Letters to author, October 1994 through January 1996.

Beckham, Dow. Manuscript article on the Army plane crash of November 26, 1945. Undated.

Coover, Walter J. "Dramatic Rescue Effort Described by Searchers." *Coos Bay Times*, p. 1. December 3, 1945.

Edgehill, Lillian Austin. Letter to "Natives of Golden & Silver Falls." September 7, 1991.

Griffith, John. "Reunion Recalls Tales of Oregon Backwoods." *The Oregonian*, p. D2. September 27, 1991.

Hammer, Elise. "Crash Survivor, Rescuer Reminisce." Coos Bay *World*, Nov 27, 1995, p. 1.

Harrington, John Peabody. "Alsea/Siuslaw/Coos Field Notes." (Microfilm). John P. Harrington Papers, National Anthropological Archives, Smithsonian Institution.

Henderson, Howard. Interview conducted by R. W. McDuffie, June 22, 1976. Weyerhaeuser Company Historical Archives, Tacoma, WA.

Inman, Leroy. *Coos Bay Times*, articles pertaining to an Army aircraft crash, page 1, November 27 through December 6, 1945.

Larson, Adelien. Memorandum to author. November 1991.

Leaton, Clifford. Letters to author, August – October 1991.

Middleton, Charles. Letters to author, November 11, 1991; January 3, 1992.

National Archives and Research Service (GSA). Roseburg, Oregon Final Homestead Certificate File 4375 for Joseph Schapers; File 4374 for Elizabeth Ott; File 5483 for Joseph Larson. Washington, D. C. 20409.

Ott, Erma. Memoranda to author, September 1991.

Ott, Harold. Collection of clippings of articles about consolidation of Glenn Junction School District 76 with Allegany School District 45. From *Coos Bay News*, May 8, 23, 26, June 2, and 5, 1925.

Phillips, Jerry. "The Upper Glenn Creek Valley as Remembered by a 'Pot Bellied Plutocrat.'" (Manuscript) November 1991.

Saling, Elwin. "The History of Allegany." (English project) Marshfield High School, Marshfield, OR, (Manuscript) October 14, 1931.

Smith, Franklyn. "A Stranger in the Night at Golden Falls School." (Manuscript) August, 1991.

——— Letters to author, 1991.

Smoyer, Walter A. and Mildred. Letters November & December 1995.

U. S. Census Office. Twelfth and Thirteenth Census of the United States, 1900 and 1910. North Coos River Precinct, Coos County, Oregon (Microfilm). Coos Bay Public Library, Coos Bay, OR.

"Weyerhaeuser Coos Holdings Now 100,000 acres." *Coos Bay Times*, May 25, 1944, p. 1.

"Weyerhaeuser Plans for 100 Year Operation." *Coos Bay Times*, Nov. 26, 1947.

Maps

Aerial Photography. T 24S R 10 W, flown August, 1949 for Weyerhaeuser Company. Copy in possession of State Forestry Department, Coos Bay Division.

Metsker Maps. Coos and Douglas Counties, Ore., Townships 24, 25, and 26S, Range 9 W.W.M.; Townships 23, 24, 25S, Range 10 W.W.M.; Townships 24 and 25S, Range 11 W.W.M. Seattle, WA.

Phillips, Jerry. Boundaries of Forest Fires in the Glenn Creek Area, 1440 to 1868. (Map drawn at request of and in possession of the author) 1990.

———Pioneer trails and cabins in the Elliott State Forest. (In possession of Coos Bay District, Oregon State Department of Forestry) 1972.

Tyledyne Geotronics. Orthophoto map, N ½ T 24S R 10 W. Prepared for Oregon State Forestry Department, 1972.

U. S. Department of the Interior. Geologic Survey, Oregon, 15 Minute Series, Quadrangles of Tyee, Ivers Peak, Scottsburg; 7 ½ Minute Series, Quadrangle of Allegany.

Weyerhaeuser Timber Company. Hunting Map 1989–90, Millicoma Tree Farm.

Published Books and Articles
(* indicates essential reading)

Amato, Joseph A. *Rethinking Home: A Case for Writing Local History.* Berkeley: University of California Press, 2002.

Automobile Association. *The Pacific Coast Automobile Blue Book, California, Washington, Oregon, British Columbia.* Kimball Upson Co., Sacramento, AC, 1915.

Bailey, Ronald T. *Frozen in Silver: The Life and Frontier Photography of P. E. Larson.* Ohio University Press: Athens, 1998.

Baldwin, Ewart M., et al. *Geology and Mineral Resources of Coos County, Oregon.* (Bulletin 80) State of Oregon Department of Geology and Mineral Industries, 1973.

Beckham, Dow. *Swift Flows the River.* Coos Bay: Arago Books, 1990.

Beckham, Stephen Dow. *Land of the Umpqua: A History of Douglas County, Oregon.* Roseburg: Douglas County Commissioners, 1986.

Dodge, Orvil. *Pioneer History of Coos and Curry Counties, OR.* 1898; rpt. Bandon: Coos-Curry Pioneer and Historical Association, 1969.

Douthit, Nathan. *The Coos Bay Region, 1890–1944: Life on a Coastal Frontier.* Coos Bay: River West Books, 1981.

Gaston, Joseph. *The Centennial History of Oregon*, 4 vols. Chicago: S. J. Clarke Publishing Co., 1912.

Gorst, Wilbur H. *Vern C. Gorst, Pioneer and Grandad of United Air Lines.* Coos Bay: Gorst Publications, 1979.

Keeland, Ellen. *The Lusty Life of Loon Lake Lloyd: World War II Marine, Logger and Resort Owner, his true life stories.* Binford and Mort: Portland, 2000.

Lower Umpqua Historical Society. *Pictorial History of the Lower Umpqua.* 1976; rpt. Reedsport, 1981.

*Mahaffy, Charlotte L. *Coos River Echoes.* Portland: Interstate Press, 1965.

*Nevin, Hattie. *Reflections of a Logging Camp Cook.* North Bend: Wegferd Publications, 1980.

*Ott, Harold. "A History of Allegany," in *Glancing Back*, Vol. 1, No. 2. Mimeographed. North Bend: Coos-Curry Museum, June, 1972.

Peterson, Emil R. and Alfred Powers. *A Century of Coos and Curry.* Portland: Binfords & Mort, 1952.

*Phillips, Jerry. *Caulked Boots and Cheese Sandwiches: A Forester's History of Oregon's First State Forest "The Elliott" (1912–1996).* Author: Coos Bay, Oregon, 1997.

Putter, S. A. D. and Horace Stevens. *Looters of the Public Domain.* Portland: Portland Printing House, 1908. Rpt. New York: Arno Press, 1972.

*Rickard, Aileen Barker. *The Goulds of Elkhorn.* Xerographic. Eugene: Kinko's Copies, 1982, 1983.

Robbins, William G. *Hard Times in Paradise.* Seattle: University of Washington Press, 1988.

Rogers, Madelyn. "Allegany Cemetery." in *Glancing Back*, Vol. 1 No. 2. Mimeographed. North Bend: Coos-Curry Museum, June 1972.

Schlesser, Norman Dennis. *Fort Umpqua, Bastion of Empire.* Oakland, OR: Oakland Printing Co., 1973.

Secord, Ronald Lee. *A Genealogy of the Clifton, Leaton, Rourke, and Secord Families.* Glendale, AZ: September 30, 1988.

Sims, Ray O. *Loon Lake and Ash Valley Revisited: A History of Ash Valley and Loon Lake, in Douglas County, Oregon.* Author: Roseburg, Oregon, 1998.

Smith, Carol Ott. "Their School 'Bus' Floated!" In *School Days: Priceless Memories of those Dear Old Golden Rule Days.* Greendale, Wisconsin: Reiman Publications, 2000.

*Smyth, Arthur V. *Millicoma: Biography of a Pacific Northwestern Forest.* Forest History Society: Durham, North Carolina, 2000.

Ward, Harriet. *Gold Saga of the Umpqua.* Portland: Metropolitan Press, 1966.

Wooldridge, Alice H. *Pioneers and Incidents of the Upper Coquille Valley 1890–1940.* Myrtle Creek: The Mail Printers, 1971.

Index

(Photographs are in italics)